THE PROCESS OF COUNSELING AND THERAPY

THIRD EDITION

JANET MOURSUND
University of Oregon
and Center for Integrative Therapy
Eugene, Oregon

Pearson Education
PRENTICE HALL
Englewood Cliffs, New Jersey 07632

Library of Congress Cataloging-in-Publication Data

Moursund, Janet.
    The process of counseling and therapy / by Janet Moursund.–3rd
  ed.
      p. cm.
    Includes bibliographical references and index.
    ISBN 0-13-720657-7
    1. Psychotherapy. 2. Counseling. I. Title.
    [DNLM: 1. Counsling. 2. Psychotherapy. WM 420 M931p]
  RC480.M677 1993
  616.89'14--dc20
  DNLM/DLC   92-12024
  for Library of Congress   CIP

*For Val, who has discovered the excitement and challenge of being a therapist.
I love you, sis!*

Production Editor: KERRY REARDON
Acquisitions Editor: SUSAN FINNEMORE BRENNAN
Copy Editor: SUSAN KORB
Cover Designer: CAROL CERALDI
Prepress Buyer: KELLY BEHR
Manufacturing Buyer: MARY ANN GLORIANDE
Editorial Assistant: JENNIE KATSAROS
Production Assistant: JEFF GROSSMAN

Pearson
Education

© 1993, 1990, 1985 by Prentice-Hall, Inc.
A Simon & Schuster Company
Englewood Cliffs, New Jersey 07632

Printed in the United States of America

10 9

ISBN 0-13-720657-7

PRENTICE-HALL INTERNATIONAL (UK) LIMITED, *London*
PRENTICE-HALL OF AUSTRALIA PTY. LIMITED, *Sydney*
PRENTICE-HALL CANADA INC., *Toronto*
PRENTICE-HALL HISPANOAMERICANA, S.A., *Mexico*
PRENTICE-HALL OF INDIA PRIVATE LIMITED, *New Delhi*
PRENTICE-HALL OF JAPAN, INC., *Tokyo*
SIMON & SCHUSTER ASIA PTE. LTD., *Singapore*
EDITORA PRENTICE-HALL DO BRASIL, LTDA., *Rio de Janeiro*

CONTENTS

PREFACE

It seems rather odd, somehow, to be sitting down to write the first part of a book after all the rest has been finished. But that's how prefaces are done—and for very good reason. Most authors, you see, begin to write a book with a pretty clear idea of what the book will be like. But books have a way of changing in midstream, of taking on a life of their own, of growing into something different from what was originally intended or expected. The preface, which serves to introduce the book to the reader, to explain what it's about and why someone should bother to read it, has to be written last, after the author discovers what that book has become.

When I began this book, I thought it would be a quite scholarly volume, heavy on theory, the sort of book I myself have used in teaching graduate courses in counseling and psychotherapy. But the book had other ideas. It wanted to be a practitioner's book, a book about being a clinician. It wanted to talk about the kinds of problems and solutions that people deal with day after day and week after week as they work with real live clients. And who am I, a mere author, to argue with a book-in-the-making? You have to give a book its head, I've learned, or you're likely to break its spirit.

So now I'm writing a preface, to introduce you to *The Process of Counseling and Therapy*, a book which grew out of my typewriter and tells, as honestly as I can, how to be a psychotherapist. It also tells a lot about me, about the kinds of things that are important to me as a therapist, and the kinds of things that are difficult for me, and the kinds of things that work for me. I hope some of them will work for you too. And I also hope that some of them *won't* be right for you, because every therapist needs to build a unique style, taking and rejecting bits and pieces from all sorts of teachers and models. What you decide not to use from these pages will be as important for you as what you decide to keep, for in the very process of deciding you will be shaping your own personal way of doing therapy, your own way of being in the work.

There are a few things that may be helpful for you to understand before we actually get started. One has to do with pronouns—the bane of every modern American writer, forced to deal with a language that has no unisex words for her or him, he or she, hers or his. My solution has been to refer to the therapist consistently as "she" or "her" and to the client as "he" or "him" (except in cases where a client is obviously and necessarily female). I have two reasons for this choice. First, switching back and forth between masculine and feminine pronouns, in order to balance everything out, is something that I as a reader find distracting. Second, I have frequently been surprised at my own inertial sexist bias, my own unconscious tendency to assume that the "authority" in an ambiguous situation is probably male. If I, a professional woman, well aware of the issues of sexism in our society, still fall victim to this kind of thinking, then it seems likely that many others do too; referring to the therapist (who is usually regarded as a high-status person) as "she" helps to jolt both myself and you, the reader, into a different level of awareness.

Another shortcut I have taken the liberty of using is to omit the words *counselor* and *counseling* from most of the book, in favor of *therapist, therapy,* or *psychotherapy.* Using both ("Counselors and psychotherapists..."; "in the counseling or therapy session...") is cumbersome and unwieldy; switching back and forth seems confusing. While a very good case can be made for differences between counseling and psychotherapy, the exact nature of the differences depends on who happens to be arguing about it. Moreover, it is increasingly true that many psychotherapists do a lot of counseling, and that many counselors do a lot of therapy, and that the dividing line between the two is pretty blurred. This is a book about what I would call "therapy"; it's also a book about what occupies much of the professional life of competent counselors.

The first half of the book is concerned with the general practice of therapy with the individual, "garden variety" client. Chapter 1 begins with a short review of the history of therapy, the variety of therapies being practiced today, and the values and assumptions underlying therapeutic work.

Chapter 2 discusses the foundation skills of therapy; the basic tools which all therapists, regardless of orientation, must master in order to work with clients.

Chapters 3 through 6 move us through the overall course of therapy, from the initial interview to the early stage of therapy, into middle-stage work, and finally into the final or termination stage.

The first section of the book, then, is an overview, a general treatment plan, for working with a wide variety of clients. It also sets the stage for the special kinds of therapy situations which are discussed in the second half, when the book shifts from a how-do-we-move-through-therapy focus to a consideration of some of the special demands of various sorts of clients: crisis work, groups, couples, families. And, last but not least, the therapist: what she (!) needs in order to continue to do good work with her clients.

Many people have contributed to this book, with or without their knowledge. First on the list are Dr. Wesley Becker, who helped me take the leave of absence from teaching that started the whole thing. My colleagues in the Division of Counseling and Educational Psychology at the University of Oregon have been both helpful and supportive. My family too: poor dears, they've grown resigned to bagels and cold meat for dinner when a chapter wasn't going smoothly.

My most heartfelt thanks, though, go to those who have patiently walked with me on my road to becoming a competent therapist. Norma Ragsdale, Claudette Hastie, Carol Ormiston, and Mari Panzer were among my first mentors. Roberta Roth encouraged and taught me much about being a person as well as a therapist. All those with whom I have studied and laughed and wept: Helen, Joe, Karen, Marvin, Sally, George, Jerry, Mary, and many more. My partners, Sue and Lance. And, finally, all the clients who have so courageously worked through their own personal pain and problems and allowed me to share in that working-through. I owe all of these people more than I can say.

Writing the first edition of *The Process of Counseling and Therapy* was an exciting adventure. It was the first time I had allowed myself to write a book about what *I* believed, rather than collecting and integrating the ideas of others. It was wonderful to discover that people actually liked what I had to say, that they bought and read and used and taught from that book. When my publishers suggested that it was time for a second edition, that was another first—only one of my earlier books had survived through a second printing, much less a second edition! I added a chapter that my reviewers thought was needed, condensed a few others, brought the references up to date. And again, people read it and used it.

And now it's Christmas Eve, and I'm sitting down to write the preface to the third edition of *The Process of Counseling and Therapy*. And my thoughts, inevitably, go back to 1984, when I was writing that first edition. Of course, my thoughts have been there a lot over the last months, as I reread what I wrote back then. In a sense, it has been a very special Christmas gift to myself: what I discovered is that, for the most part, I still believe everything I said. So, again, hewing to the time-honored principle of "If it ain't broke, don't fix it," I have not made huge changes in the book. Since there was little that seemed to be "broke" in the second edition, there is little that has been "fixed" in the third. The chapter that was added has been taken out again (the reviewers were wrong); the references are updated; I have quoted people who have said things better than I could say them. There are some new ideas, to be sure, and I have tried to improve the clarity and readability of the writing, but the general tone and message of the book is unchanged.

There have been some changes since I wrote the words of appreciation for the first edition. There is a new associate dean of the Division of Counseling Psychology (no longer the Division of Counseling and Educational Psych): Dr. Jerry Kranzler is both mentor and dear friend and I cannot imagine a more supportive dean. Terry Fields has joined Sue McPherson and Lance McDonald and me in private practice and adds just the right blend of experience and enthusiasm. There are new reviewers—still wonderfully helpful: Roberta M. Driscoll, *University of Florida*, Anthony, C. DiCesare, *Towson State University*, and Clifford H. Swenson, *Purdue University*; and my fine editor, Susan Finnemore, has a new last name and is now Susan Brennan.

And as for me—well, I am older now, wiser (I hope), certainly more tired...and I still find the practice of psychotherapy to be exciting, demanding, frightening, and exhilarating. The first edition of this book invited you to join the company of therapists who share these feelings about their work. This third edition extends the same invitation. My thanks to you, who do me the honor of reading what I have written: may you find as much pleasure in the reading as I have had in the writing of it.

FIRST THINGS FIRST   1

Psychotherapy is such a common phenomenon nowadays—so many people have experienced it firsthand, or know others who have told them about it—that defining just what psychotherapy is should present no particular problem. Right? No, wrong. Psychotherapy means very different things to different people. For some, it is a scientific approach to problem solving; for others, an almost mystical experience. Some therapists describe what they do in terms of changing dysfunctional behavior patterns, while others talk about exploring the far recesses of unconscious feelings and beliefs. Some are idealistic, while others are cynical (or, they would say, realistic): "Therapists who write about the 'deeply meaningful' nature of the 'therapeutic relationship' tend to sentimentalize and obscure what is in fact a commercial transaction which has quite close parallels to that involved in prostitution" (Smail 1987).

It seems likely that the actual practice of psychotherapy is so varied that most attempts to define it meaningfully are doomed to failure. In fact, it may make more sense to talk about "them" rather than "it." Psychotherapies have in common that some person or persons, called "therapists," are hired by another person or persons, called "clients" or "patients," to help that client solve some sort of personal or social problem. Beyond that, the arguments start.

This is a book for people who are performing, or who intend to perform, psychotherapy. It is not a book just for one particular kind of therapist, working exclusively within a single framework. It is a book about out there, in-the-trenches working with real clients in real situations. I am a practicing psychotherapist, and I work with lots of people who have lots of different kinds of problems. To do so effectively, I borrow ideas, insights, and techniques from anywhere I can find them. Of course, I do have in my head a conceptual underpinning, a theory that helps me plan what I am doing and where I am going. What my specific theory of therapy is, though, does not matter here. I have not yet shaken hands with a theoretical orientation that is incompatible with most of the ideas in this book; if you know of one, I would very much appreciate an introduction.

Even though this is not a theoretically oriented book, however, and even though you (and I!) are eager to plunge into the real meat of how to work with clients, we do need to take a few pages here at the beginning to clarify what will happen in the book and to calibrate ourselves to each other, so that we will be able to communicate smoothly throughout our time together. That calibration is a major purpose of this first chapter. We will talk a bit of psychotherapy in general, what it is about, and where it has come from. We will discuss the bewildering variety of forms and shapes it is packaged in today. We will look briefly at the evidence for its effectiveness. Finally, we will lay out a few of the basic assumptions on which therapy depends. Then we will be ready to move on into the work itself.

So, first of all, what is psychotherapy really all about? Why do people need the kind of help that therapists offer? Surely people can manage to survive and grow and overcome problems on their own? Of course they can. Most of us do, most of the time. It is when that process breaks down, gets blocked, or is not moving along as quickly or as directly as we want it to that we call on a therapist. That's the first step in defining the therapist's job, then: she steps in to help when the natural growth process is not handling things well enough.

And *how* does she step in? What does a therapist *do* that makes her different from a friend or a pastor or a mother or a bartender or a hairdresser? Here is where variety rears its interesting head. Depending on what she believes about how people get and stay stuck, the therapist will do different things. But all therapists do what they do from a common perspective, and that is what makes us therapists: we create and work within a relationship in a way that focuses on the other person and his needs. We develop a form of being-with this person that is unique in that it involves genuine two-way contact at a deep level of knowing and caring, and yet has as its purpose the personal growth and enrichment of only one of the two participants.

I do not mean to imply that the therapist is not enriched through her relationships with clients. If she is doing her job well, she will and must grow as a result. But her growth and learning are incidental side benefits. The primary reason for being in a therapeutic relationship is the enrichment of the client, and the client only. Some other professionals, such as lawyers, doctors, and teachers, have a similar one-way focus. But only in psychotherapy is a personal relationship with another human being the primary vehicle through which changes in feeling, thinking, and behaving are expected to occur. It is the use of a relationship to effect positive change and growth that makes our work unique.

THERAPY THEN AND NOW

The history of psychotherapy, as with so many other aspects of Western culture, really begins with the ancient Greeks. Classical Greek culture recognized disease, both physical and mental, as a natural rather than a supernatural process and the Greeks identified different kinds of mental dysfunction. Their distinctions may have been crude by modern standards, but the classifications have a familiar flavor even today. While they did not recognize the healing potential of a relationship with a therapist, they began a tradition of treating mental illness through professional intervention.

This tradition spread through the developed nations of the Near East, and by the eighth century many large hospitals in cities such as Baghdad and Damascus had psychiatric sections for treatment of mental illness. The West lagged far behind, but in the thirteenth century hospitals in major cities in France, England, Germany, and Switzerland were providing psychiatric care for the mentally ill. The mental health movement in the West was held back, though, by the fear and superstition of the Middle Ages. Witchcraft and demonology competed quite successfully with more enlightened views; the mentally ill person was thought to be possessed or cursed, and treatment generally consisted of punishing him so that the evil spirits would leave his body in search of a more congenial home.

By the middle of the seventeenth century, superstitious views of mental illness were on the wane, at least among the better educated. But what replaced them was a confused mishmash of treatment ideas: bloodletting, temperature extremes, isolation. There was at least as much concern in those days with protecting the sane from the insane as there was in curing mental illness. Mentally ill people were considered dangerous and unpredictable and were usually locked up when their behavior became too bizarre to be ignored.

Gradually, these views changed. In 1680, Thomas Sydenham wrote on hysteria as a specific illness which could be cured by drugs, a diet of milk, and much horseback riding. Interestingly, the 1600s also saw one of the first attempts to use blood transfusion as a medical treatment. A Parisian doctor, Jean Denis, put arterial lambs' blood into the veins of mental patients. (The practice was discontinued when it was noticed that most of the patients so treated died shortly thereafter.)

By the eighteenth century, psychiatry had become a true science. The Age of Enlightenment was one that glorified logic and reason and saw logical thought as the birthright of all humans.

> As reason was their highest god, how they sympathized with those who had lost reason! Their optimism was boundless, as was their belief in attaining human perfection. Thus they overcame the fatalist belief in the incurability of insanity; they founded numerous institutions for the mentally sick, and improved the regime within those institutions until the day when, through the great symbolic gesture of taking off the chains of the "mad men," these were definitively reinstated as human beings. [Ackerman 1968, p. 34]

The movement continued: studies of hysteria, studies of neurosis, treatment through diet and drugs, and environmental manipulation. There is not the space here to trace the development of the great treatment centers in France and Germany, the use of hypnosis as a treatment method, the gradual realization that something could be done with and for patients by *talking* with them in one way or another. Of course, the great milepost along this developmental road was the work of Sigmund Freud, the young neurologist-turned-psychiatrist whose books shocked his own generation and have shaped the course of psychiatry and psychotherapy up to our own time. Freud's psychoanalysis, as it came to be called, spread throughout the Western world in the waning years of the nineteenth century and by the early 1900s had become the predominant, virtually the only, acceptable psychotherapeutic method. So it remained, right up to the cataclysmic years of World War II. Some of Freud's breakaway associates founded their own trends of psychotherapy, but these were (at the time) of minor influence and were, in any event, firmly grounded in traditional psychoanalytic principles. The only real rival to Freud's preeminence in the world of psychiatric treatment as the Big War wound down was a young American upstart named Carl Rogers—who ever heard of him, anyhow?

The Rogerian, client-centered approach was a harbinger of things to come. Other approaches began to appear: Taft and Allen's "relationship therapy," Frohman's "brief psychotherapy," Hertzberg's "active psychotherapy," and Thorne's "directive psychotherapy." By 1960, only about 40 percent of American psychiatrists surveyed still considered themselves to be doing psychoanalytic therapy (Garfield 1981). Even greater changes were occurring in two major areas. First, the community mental health movement was gaining momentum, bringing in its wake an emphasis on social and cultural factors in treatment, sanctioning the practice of nonanalytically trained therapists (many of them not even medical doctors!), and popularizing the notion of psychotherapy for the middle and lower classes. Second, the behavioral psychologists had begun to move beyond rats and pigeons and were applying their theories of learning to human beings with great and well-publicized success. The dam had broken, and the full flood of mental health enthusiasm was about to inundate the country.

And what a flood it has been! The late sixties and the seventies saw the flowering of the human-potential movement, through which everyone was to experience consciousness raising. Commercial ventures such as Lifespring and est sprang up to introduce suburbanites to self-awareness and the power of "getting It." Marriage encounter groups became available for couples, primarily through churches; children and parents were invited to family weekends; treatment centers for every sort of psychiatric ailment and nonailment emerged almost overnight. The variety of approaches, theories, and fads has grown in an equally bewildering way.

THE THERAPY SUPERMARKET

In 1920 there was one psychotherapeutic approach; in 1930 there were, perhaps, half a dozen, all but one of only minor influence. Then explosion—the world turned inside out. Psychotherapy, like nearly everything else, changed dramatically in the forties, and it will never be the same again. In 1947 Frederick Thorne wrote:

> Clinical psychology in America is still characterized by a primitive state of organization in which the leaders in the field operate more or less independently....Lacking any formally systematized viewpoint, the theoretical biases of [therapists] literally represent all the permutations and combinations of behaviorism, experimentalism, Gestalt psychology, Freudianism, Adlerian individual psychology, Jungian analytic psychology, and many other minor schools. [Ard 1975, p. 66]

Much has happened since then, and the net result seems to be that Thorne's list would have to be even longer today.

Therapies pile upon therapies in the nineties. There are more than 150 different psychotherapeutic systems guiding our professional practice today, and the number continues to grow. It is even possible to buy Consumer's Guides to therapies, road maps through the jungle of competing approaches and claims. It is this quality of competition that is perhaps the most disturbing aspect of the modern mental health scene. "Therapists are adept at making words mean what they want them to mean (a probably useful psychotherapeutic skill), yet when it comes to attempts at consensus, old words often stand as rigid barriers," says Beitman (1987, p. 84). All too often we therapists use our word skills to justify or promote ourselves, rather than to understand and learn from our colleagues.

Despite all this stridency, however, it is possible to discover some order among the confusion. The various approaches to therapy did develop out of and do borrow from one another, and those origins and borrowings can be traced. The value of the tracing lies not so much in the final product as in the process of developing an understanding of the relationships involved: we are forced to look for the similarities as well as the contrasts among the various approaches. We are used to shouting about differences, to championing theory A because it takes into account the trauma of birth or theory B because it assumes that all humans are capable of logic or theory C because it focuses on the here-and-now. We are less used to noticing similarities. And that is probably misleading. "In practice," says Aveline, "there is a gap between what therapists say they do and what they actually do; successful therapists are much more similar than different" (1987 p. 41). We all do more of what we hold in common than of what is unique to one or a few systems. Were it not so, this book could not be written, for this is a book about psychotherapy, singular, not about psychotherapies. It is a book about our common ground, a book based on the beliefs and skills and attitudes that undergird our diversity of specializations. Again quoting Thorne, in 1947: "With such a complex situation, it is inevitable that a wide armamentarium of therapeutic tools will be needed, each used as skillfully as possible based on a valid knowledge of what each tool can be expected to accomplish" (Ard 1975, p. 71). What was true then is true today: we do have many tools in the armamentarium, and we do need to know how to use them with clarity and skill. Perhaps a wiser generation of therapists will some day find a way to bring all of the different theories together, building on this common foundation. Perhaps we will some day discover that approach X is most useful in solving problems of type Y, and so on. Until then, we can only remember that we are more alike than different, and that because of this likeness each of us can teach and can learn from each of the others.

EVALUATING OUTCOMES

Just as the psychotherapeutic kettle was beginning to come to a boil, back in the early fifties, an Englishman named Hans Eysenck did his best to clamp a lid down on the whole scene. Having spent much effort in an investigation of therapeutic effectiveness, he concluded that "roughly two-thirds of a group of neurotic patients will recover or improve to a marked extent within about two years of the onset of their illness, whether they are treated by means of psychotherapy or not" (Eysenck 1952, p. 322). It is not difficult to imagine the reaction to that statement—the mental health community was up in arms! Forty years later, the dust has not yet settled. Therapists of all stripes and colors were quick to claim that although such an outrageous statement might possibly have relevance for other approaches, it certainly was not true of *their* brand of treatment. We are still making the same sorts of claims.

Rebuttal of Eysenck's findings has been difficult for a number of reasons. For one thing, improvement in mental health is hard to define in any specific, measurable way. The variables are elusive; the criteria are slippery. Does the client report that he feels better? That is probably because he wants to believe it; the same claims have been made for magical charms, leeching, Lydia Pinkham's Compound, and nearly every other imaginable curative plan. Give him some kind of tests, then, and see if his scores after therapy look different than they did when he started. But if they do look different, who is to say that the scores reflect real, meaningful changes? And if they do not look different, perhaps the test failed to measure what the real changes were. We could ask the therapist herself whether the treatment was effective, but she would obviously be biased in her reporting. What sorts of actual behavior could we look for that would indicate improvement? That depends on what was wrong in the first place, on the environmental constraints, on the number and kinds of options actually available for this or that client. Does it really make sense to look at psychotherapy as a single kind of treatment when there are so many different activities that fall into that category? Maybe one kind of therapy is effective with some clients but not with others; maybe some kinds of mental health problems are amenable to some psychotherapeutic treatments but not to others. Kramer, looking at attempts to determine which kind of therapy works best, says that the questions themselves are wrong: "We are comparing two 'drugs' without knowing their active ingredients (or how to purify them), or their mechanism of action, or their dose-response curves. A pharmacologist intent on testing such compounds would risk abbreviating his academic career" (1989, pp. 201–202).

The simpler question, "Does therapy work at all?" is even more difficult to answer definitively. In the early seventies, a number of researchers went back to

Eysenck's original data and concluded that there were significant errors in his research and statistical procedures. Two teams, in particular, were able to rebut the Eysenck report using Eysenck's own data; both concluded that psychotherapy does produce significant improvement in clients (Meltzoff & Kornreich 1970; Bergin 1978). Eysenck disagreed vigorously in print. So the argument raged on; the new studies did not succeed in dispelling the cloud of suspicion that Eysenck and others had raised. Is psychotherapy really just a big sham? Are these so-called therapists just taking people's money, making them believe they are getting something worthwhile? If some therapies (and some therapists) are good and some not so good, how can a prospective client know the difference?

More recent efforts to tackle the evaluation problem have tended to use sophisticated statistical methods to combine and reanalyze large numbers of smaller-scale studies. Luborsky, Singer, and Luborsky (1975) may have started this ball rolling when they examined comparisons of group versus individual therapy, time-limited versus unlimited, client-centered versus other traditional approaches, and behavior therapy versus psychodynamic therapy. They were unable to find consistent differences in effectiveness—anywhere! In 1977, Smith, Glass, and Miller published the results of an even more massive project, which involved reanalysis of data from some 475 individual studies. They found that, overall, psychotherapy was clearly beneficial; on the average, the typical therapy client is better off after treatment than 80 percent of untreated individuals. However, the Smith team too failed to find consistent differences among different therapeutic approaches, or even between experienced and inexperienced therapists. "Despite volumes devoted to the theoretical differences among schools of psychotherapy, the results of research demonstrate negligible differences in the effects produced by different therapy types. Unconditional judgments of superiority of one type or another of psychotherapy, and all that these claims imply about treatment and training policy, are unjustified" (Smith & Glass 1977, p. 760) The American Psychiatric Association got in on the act in 1982, and after reviewing the evidence they concluded that psychotherapy was indeed effective (though they pointed out that about 5 percent of clients were actually made worse by therapy). However, they were again unable to point to any one approach as superior.

So the beat goes on. The most we can say for sure about psychotherapy effectiveness is that we can't be completely sure. Some, like Smail, are very dubious: "It is, I think, indisputable that so far nobody has been able to demonstrate to anybody's satisfaction but their own that any form of psychotherapy 'works'" (1987, p. 32). Others, including the APA, maintain that the research continues to show that something that therapists do is helpful. Usually. Most scholars take a middle course, saying that while important ideas about therapy are emerging, much remains to be understood (Beitman 1987).

Therapists out in practice do not know if they have been vindicated or betrayed by all this research. Most studies do seem to support the effectiveness of therapy, to be sure, but what is this about everybody's method working about as well as everybody else's? Or about inexperienced therapists being as helpful as experienced ones? That's not right; I *know* that what I do with clients works better than Brand X therapy…

There is, in all of this activity, one important aspect of psychotherapy that the outcome research people seem to have overlooked, and it is an important aspect indeed. Psychotherapy is intended not only to cure but also to help people to get through a troubled period in their lives with a minimum of pain and a maximum of growth and learning. Even if psychotherapy should not prove to cure mental illness (and the evidence at this point tends to be encouraging), it may still reduce the duration of the illness as well as making that ill period more bearable. After all, aspirin has not been shown to "cure" anything; yet it is still one of the major items used by Americans in the treatment of physical illness. We take aspirin not to make us well but to help us endure being sick. Similarly, a cast on an arm or leg does not heal the broken bone; it merely provides support and structure while the bone heals itself.

I believe that psychotherapy may, in some cases, truly cure clients. It allows them to grow and change in ways that would be impossible without therapy. I believe that in many other instances psychotherapy substantially shortens the duration of an illness (and we could spend a great deal of time, indeed, trying to define what is meant by that word). I believe that, even when it neither cures nor significantly hastens the self-curative process, psychotherapy may significantly decrease the pain, anxiety, and other debilitating emotional symptoms that accompany illness. Finally, although research seems to have overlooked this possibility, psychotherapy has enormous potential as a preventive measure. Engaging in therapy at the point where things are just beginning to go wrong may allow a person to avoid a full-fledged illness (either emotional or physical) later on. Further, therapy may prevent illness in the next generation: the client who deals with his own experience of abuse, incest, emotional deprivation, or addiction is far less likely to put his children through the same torment. In sparing them an abused childhood, he may also be sparing them his own disorder.

All of these statements are beliefs, matters of faith and hope, rather than facts. I have no data to support them, no research to prove their validity. Yet it is just such beliefs, borne out in session after session with client after client, that keep me working at being a psychotherapist. Research has a long way to go before it will be able to test hypotheses such as these. In fact, it may be time for practitioners to turn the tables on researchers and to ask seriously if traditional *research* does work. Ryder puts it well: "A laudable determination to be scientific and to accomplish great things has had some effects opposite to those intended. The apparent weaknesses in research, as I see them, have been greater than those in therapy" (1987, p. 15). Research, as we now know it, may never be able to capture the subtleties of what goes on in that incredibly complex relationship called psychotherapy. It may be that the researchers will need to develop a new approach, less "scientific" perhaps, if they are ever to get a handle on what is really happening in psychotherapy. What an exciting challenge that could be! But that is a digression, although a fascinating one; it does not lead us where we need to go. Let us shift gears again, back to our major concern: the practice of psychotherapy.

THEORY, ASSUMPTIONS, VALUES

Having emphasized that there are many, many theories of therapy guiding modern psychotherapeutic practice, and that nobody has been able to demonstrate the superiority or correctness of any one over the others, I am now going to insist that every therapist needs also to be a theorist. A contraction? I don't think so. In the company of a number of contemporary psychologists (Combs 1989; Morrison 1987), I am convinced that without an underlying structure to support and organize her work, the therapist cannot ever know what she has accomplished—much less plan coherently what she intends to do next.

Actually, everyone really does have a theory of personality and, if they think about it at all, a theory of therapy. One's theory can be found embedded in one's answers to questions like, "How did George get to be the way he is?" and "Why does the Swenson kid do those nasty things over and over again?" and "How could it possibly help Aunt Minnie to go and talk to that minister about her problems?" The danger in naive, unconceptualized theory, though, is that it is so often full of contradictions, inconsistencies, superstitions, and outdated information. It is only through bringing our assumptions out into the open, laying them out in an organized fashion, that we can decide what parts of them we want to keep and what parts we are better off without.

By learning about the theories of our older, possibly wiser, colleagues, we expand our own possibilities. As I read Freud, or Rogers, or Perls, I am introduced to ideas that I might never have thought of on my own. I can accept them or reject them; but even if I choose to reject them, I am the richer for having thought through my reasons for doing so. Each of us will find some theoretical stances more attractive and comfortable than others—and that's just fine. "I feel very strongly about the importance of a therapist finding a theoretical and practical approach which suits his or her personality," says Morrison (1987, p. 15). That with which I am comfortable will work best for me; I'll remember it more clearly and use it more appropriately. Theoretical frames that don't fit my personality will be awkward and uncongenial, and I will be awkward and unnatural using them, like someone trying to dance while wearing clothes that don't fit. It's the fact that each of us has developed a theory, has worked it through and honed it and refined it, and continues to do so, that counts—much more than what the content of the theory may be.

While we can relatively easily agree to disagree about our specific theories, we do need some consensus about the assumptions and values that the theories are built upon. These assumptions guide the way we think about problems, conceptualize them, set them up to be solved. Psychotherapy is, in the last analysis, doing something about problems. You and I will need to have some meeting of the minds here, if we are to think together about how this "doing something about problems" is to be accomplished.

I believe that there are two basic assumptions without which psychotherapy cannot be performed successfully. The first of these has to do with the worthiness of the therapeutic enterprise. "Simply by offering any form of therapy the therapist conveys his expectations that it will work, thus creating favorable expectations in the patient" (Frank et al. 1978, p. 30). If we do not believe it will work, we are no better than snake-oil salesmen, charlatans, and con artists. Frank goes even further with this basic assumption: he sees faith in the efficacy of treatment as the major reason, perhaps the only reason, why it works. Therapy, for him, is a powerful and effective placebo. Although most therapists believe that they offer more than just a good placebo, the usefulness of the placebo effect is undeniable. Again, our own belief in what we are doing makes such an effect possible.

The second assumption shared by all successful therapists is that our client is capable of change and of making choices about his changes. This is a belief about the nature of man; it is untestable because it is a philosophy rather than a fact. It is a faith in the human ability to be (or at least to become) free to learn what we need to know and to make responsible choices on the basis of that knowledge. All psychotherapists, from client-centered to behavioral to existential, must share this faith. It is one of the great paradoxes of orthodox behavioral therapy that, believing all behavior to be shaped by external stimuli, nevertheless the therapist first attempts to discover what behaviors the client wants to change. It is one of the great paradoxes of existential therapy that, knowing that humans can never be truly free from the "factitiousness" of such realities as death and isolation, the existentialist then works to help the client to transcend his fear of freedom and make his own choices.

Moving beyond these two fundamental and essential assumptions, we discover a host of questions about people and how they function. These are the questions upon which therapists may legitimately differ, the questions which each of us must consider and answer in terms of our own beliefs. Four of these questions, I believe are critical in determining the way we behave as therapists. They pose issues on which each of us must take a stand. They are (1) How/why do people get to be the way they are? (2) How/why do they maintain their thoughts and feelings and behaviors in a particular maladaptive or pain-producing pattern? (3) How can I facilitate their changing that pattern? and (4) What kinds and directions of change am I willing to support and assist? Your answers here may shift over time; you may not believe today what you will believe ten years from now. However, you must believe something, and you must know what that something is. The answers to these questions, and all the others that grow out of them, are the foundation upon which the whole structure of your therapeutic skill is built. Without a foundation, that skill collapses into an unrelated heap of tricks and nostrums, equally confusing to both you and your client.

With clear, consistent answers you are ready to become a therapist: acting spontaneously, genuinely, using your creativity with confidence as you construct your behavior from moment to moment, secure in the knowledge that you are operating out of a consistent frame of reference. You can do what "feels right," trusting that later, when you have time to analyze what happened in those fast-moving interactions, the feelings will fit the facts. You will be able to be calm in the face of the client's anxiety and agitation, grounded and optimistic in the face of the client's despair, able to accompany the client through his pain and rage while at the same time sensing the healing potential that he brings with him on that journey.

Not that all therapists operate at that level, or that any of us do so all the time. It's an ideal, something to aim for. Somehow, it's all right to not quite live up to it, not in every session. As long as I continue to learn, to grow, to improve my skills, always building on a firm and consistent set of beliefs about myself and my fellow humans, I can be pleased with my work and my competence.

This brings us to the end of the introduction, the end of the beginning, and the beginning of the main course. How do we continue to grow and to improve our skills? What are the skills that contribute to good psychotherapy? It is a long journey that we are embarking on, one that will probably last a lifetime. The door is open, and the road lies before us. Shall we explore it together?

FOUNDATION SKILLS

2

"I have become more convinced that the person-centered emphasis on the creation of a psychological climate conducive to growth is fundamental to all therapy, and that if this climate can be consistently and generously offered, past pain can be relieved and transformed no matter how far back it is lodged in the client's history" (Thorne 1987). Whatever theory we may adopt, whatever techniques we may find effective in our psychotherapeutic behavior, every therapist must be able to create this sort of "psychological climate." In order to do so, we must learn a number of basic skills. We must know how to listen, to attend to what a client is saying, and to let the client know that we are attending. We must know how to help the client deal with problems: to clarify what the problem is, consider various solutions, make and implement decisions. We must know how to encourage the expression of feelings, and we must have some guidelines about what to do when strong feelings are expressed.

It is often asserted that good therapists, no matter how widely their theoretical frameworks differ, seem to have about the same level of effectiveness. Much of current research, as was pointed out in Chapter 1, reaches this same conclusion. According to Irvin Yalom (1980), one reason for this similarity may be the "throw-ins"—the things that effective therapists do so intuitively or automatically that they are seldom talked about or included in writings about the various theories.

One such "throw-in" is surely the set of abilities I have called *foundation skills,* the therapist behaviors that encourage a client to talk about his problems/needs/concerns, to focus on areas where useful change may occur, to explore new facets of himself and his situation. These behaviors are similar to the sorts of things any good conversationalist does, but they differ from conversational skills in that they focus on only one-half of the conversation dyad. Moreover, therapeutic foundation skills are goal-directed; they are not used just to pass the time pleasantly but to accomplish a specific purpose. And they are used for the benefit of and in the service of the client. A conversationalist can monopolize the conversation with anecdotes about herself or can give up on an uninteresting partner and move on to someone else. She can use the interaction to make herself look important or clever, to manipulate the other person, to gain social advantage. The therapist, in contrast, is committed to the welfare of the client who happens to be in her office at this particular moment; the client's needs, not her own, are her primary concern. While the client, of course, shares in the responsibility for what will happen, it is the therapist's job to ensure that the exchange is as therapeutic as the client will allow it to be.

The therapy session is not a chance encounter between two people who just happen to be spending time together. Nor is it an interrogation, in which one person digs into another person's private life in order to paste a label on his case folder or to pin him neatly into some diagnostic category. At every point during psychotherapy, the therapist must create an atmosphere for learning, exploring, problem solving, and growth. Even if assessment and diagnosis are primary goals (and they should be, early in treatment), the therapist must not neglect her responsibility for nurturing this atmosphere. We tend it carefully, whatever else we may be attempting to accomplish. The therapeutic atmosphere is determined more by the way in which therapist and client talk to each other than by what they talk about. It grows out of the process of communicating, of expressing ideas and feelings. The client will, by and large, be responsible for the content of that communication; client and therapist together will negotiate the goals to be aimed for; but setting the tone, the rules and expectations for the process itself, is the therapist's job.

The process of communicating is the stuff of which therapy is built. It determines the quality of the interaction, the openness of the relationship, and the degree of trust that the client comes to feel in you and in your ability to help. More than anything else, your task is to attend to this process—which means attending to the client. The way in which you listen will color everything else that happens in therapy. Listening, and listening with skill, is the single most basic and essential therapeutic activity.

Good listening skills can be more than a foundation for psychotherapy; they can be the primary therapeutic intervention. Carl Rogers spearheaded the development of modern American therapy with his assertion that, given the proper conditions of genuine attending, clients will respond by growing and changing in positive ways. For Rogers and his followers, listening (and communicating that one is doing so accurately) *is* therapy. For many others, the art of listening empathically may not be the only necessary ingredient in successful therapy, but it is one upon which all other therapeutic activities depend. After all, whatever we do in therapy is accomplished by means of communication. That is what we do with clients. Communication is simply listening to and sending information, listening and responding.

We will begin this chapter with a consideration of some of the specifics of skillful attending behavior: how the good listener does a great deal more than simply listen quietly. Then we will discuss attending in the context of two major frameworks or focus areas of therapy, the cognitive (thinking) and the affective (feeling) focus.

Readers who have had experience working as therapists or counselors may be telling themselves that this is going to be old stuff, a rehash of the done-to-death materials on listening skills and I-statements. To some degree they are right. We will, in this chapter, be reviewing some very basic therapy ideas. I have frequently been surprised, however, to discover how much I can benefit from a review of foundation skills. Almost inevitably I am reminded of some guideline or techniques that I have used more effectively in the past than I do now. Reviewing is like cleaning a cupboard. It brings to light all sorts of useful items that have been obscured by more recent additions.

So as you read these pages, I invite you to try an experiment. Keep one or two of your clients in mind. If possible, review tapes or notes of their last session with you. As we discuss the foundation skills of therapy, pause now and again to ask yourself if you have utilized these skills fully in the sessions you reviewed, how you might have proceeded differently were you to have gone back to basics, and what the result might have been had you done so.

LISTENING

Listening is often thought of as a passive behavior: the other person is the active communicator, while the listener simply takes in what is being said. The therapist, whose stock in trade is listening, knows that good listeners are very active indeed. Her job is to make sure that she really hears and understands what the client is telling her. She makes sure that she receives and responds to the whole content of the communication, nonverbal as well as verbal. She knows that what is *not* said is often even more important than what is spoken aloud. The therapist helps the client to talk about all of the parts of his concern, not just what is superficial or immediately apparent or comfortable to deal with. The therapist is responsive in such a way that the client experiences being attended to and knows that he has been heard and that he is not being judged or condemned for what he is talking about. Therapeutic listening also helps the client to listen to himself, to slow down, attend to himself, and respect his own wisdom. Rogers says:

> By listening acceptantly to every aspect of the client's experience the therapist is modelling the notion of listening to oneself. And, by being accepting and non-judgmental of the feelings within the client, the therapist is modelling a non-judgmental self acceptance in the client. By being real and congruent and genuine, the therapist is modelling that kind of behavior for the client. In these ways, the therapist does serve as a useful model. [Baldwin 1987, p. 47]

In order to accomplish all this, the therapist may use a variety of specific listening skills and techniques.

PARAPHRASING

At the risk of sounding unscientific (a dangerous thing to be!), I want to begin this section by sharing with you a description of a segment of therapy that Carl Rogers did as a demonstration at the Conference on the Evolution of Psychotherapy in Phoenix, in 1988. Among the people present at that demonstration was Carlos Amantea, a hardheaded and often cynical reporter of the therapy scene. What he saw and heard that day forced cynicism into the back seat, at least for a while. Listen to his words: "A bit of clay, passed back and forth between the two of them, to be reshaped, molded, perhaps made into some sort of monument—one that is growing outside herself, one that she can externalize so that she will be able to look at it and understand, a little bit, what is going on in the mystery space called mind." (Amantea 1989, pp. 35–36) That is the art of paraphrasing, at its very best.

Paraphrasing consists of rephrasing what the client has just said. It sounds deceptively simple until we begin to realize that "what the client said" includes much more than just his words. The elegant paraphrase captures what the client *means* by what he has verbalized. The therapist expresses this meaning in her own words, perhaps using a concrete illustration, example, or metaphor to convey more vividly what she understands the client to be telling her. Paraphrases go beyond just parroting what the client has said, or even recasting that verbalization into a different shape. Typically, they summarize whole units of the client's behavior; they mirror the essence of what the client is thinking and feeling as he speaks. They recognize the immediate emotional perspective of the client, while at the same time they respect his separateness from the therapist (Shea 1988). Paraphrases allow the client to rehear a statement and thus verify that the therapist did, in fact, listen to him. They also allow the client to correct any misperceptions on the part of the therapist, to deal with misunderstandings before they have a chance to derail the train of thought. In other words, good paraphrasing is designed so as to provide ongoing feedback for both therapist and client, a constant retuning of the communication channel, a way for each to ensure that she is on track with the other.

For many clients, the therapy session may be a first experience of talking to a sympathetic and attentive listener. Being heard without being judged, tuned out, argued against, or shouted down can be quite therapeutic in and of itself. Experiencing a respected other's interest in what I am feeling, her concern about my expression and my voice tone and my posture and the things I leave out, as well as what I actually put into words, can help me to learn how to express myself even more fully. And all of this builds a foundation for future work.

A number of writers (Combs 1989; Cornier & Hackney 1987) have emphasized that paraphrases must do more than simply mirror what the client has said. They must invite the client to explore further or to understand better whatever he is dealing with. While the ostensible focus is often the cognitive aspect of a client's message, the best paraphrase will also acknowledge feelings and behaviors. A client may be talking, for instance, about how close he and his father have been. He describes a heated argument with his father over the father's refusal to lend him money to buy a new car, and as he talks of his rage his eyes fill with tears. The therapist might paraphrase: "Sounds like you're angry with your father for not giving you the loan, and at the same time you feel sad." This paraphrase takes into account the content (my father would not lend me money), the verbalized feelings (I am angry at him), and the nonverbal behavior (tears suggest sadness).

It is important to invite the client to confirm or reject paraphrases like this. If you get regular corrective feedback from your client, you don't have to worry so much about making a mistake, and this frees you from any need to be superinsightful, enormously wise and perceptive (Teyber 1988). You can be an ordinary person who is extraordinarily interested in this client's personal experiences. Asking for corrections of your paraphrases will also help you to decide what to do next. If you say something like, "Am I hearing you right?"to the client who was described above, he might respond, "Yeah, I hate to see our relationship fall apart like this." Or he might say, "No, I'm not sad—I just get so mad and frustrated that I don't know what to do, and I feel like I'm going to explode.' The former reaction is an invitation to pursue the sense of sadness and loss, the second corrects the therapist's perception and warns that (for now, at least) the client does not feel or does not care to discuss his sadness.

Paraphrases used appropriately are highly effective therapeutic responses. Used inappropriately, they can bog down the process and irritate the client. The therapist who only responds with paraphrases may appear to be ducking the client's requests for help, information, or feedback or to be hiding her real self behind a facade of phony professionalism. An undiluted paraphrase, no matter how accurate, is seldom appropriate as a response to a direct question The client who struggles to tell you of his problems with his son and then asks, "What do you think I should do?" is not likely to be helped much by a grave, "You'd really like me to tell you what to do." A more appropriate response might be to combine your paraphrase with some additional response. You could, for instance, summarize what the client has said, share your personal response to his situation, and add a question to help him move forward:

> Let me see if I understand all of what you've told me. You ve come up with a number of ideas about what to do about your son's difficulties, and you've gotten advice from several different people. But you're still not ready to make a decision; none of the things you've figured out for yourself or heard from others feels like a perfect solution. You feel a lot of pressure to do something, and the more pressured you feel, the harder it is to think clearly about what would be the best thing to do. I feel uncomfortable about trying to tell you what you should do; instead of giving you still more advice, what I'd like to do is help you sort out your thoughts and feelings, so you can come up with the decision that will fit best for you. What seems to be the biggest roadblock to your making a decision and acting on it?

Another problem with using paraphrases is that you may fall into a set way of introducing them, using the same words over and over again: "I hear you saying that…" "So you're telling me that…" "Sounds like you're feeling…" All of these are good introductions, but overusing them can annoy your client and lead him to think that you are using a formula rather than truly listening to him. Vary your way of leading into a response, and use a variety of examples and images to convey your understanding.

Finally, give yourself permission to share your best guess of what a client is trying to tell you, even if you are not sure that you are right Remember, the client really doesn't expect 100 percent accuracy, as long as you're open to his setting you straight. It is better to be mistaken—even way off—than to sit and nod and try to fake understanding. And it's better to be wrong and get set right by the client than to build a whole escalating series of misunderstandings, just because you didn't check it out. Misunderstandings are a natural part of communicating and do no harm if they can be clarified and corrected. The client will not lose respect for you if you check out an inaccurate perception with him. Your willingness to be fal· lible may help in establishing rapport.

PERCEPTION CHECKS

A perception check, like a paraphrase, is designed to clarify and underscore what the client has just said. It goes beyond the paraphrase in that it includes the therapist's inferences about what may be going on for the client, inferences derived from a whole range of the client's responses rather than from what the client has just con veyed in the last transaction. It also always includes a request for feedback as to the accuracy of those inferences. "I get the impression, as you have been telling me about your husband's problems at work, that you find yourself feeling angry and irritated with him pretty often. Is that true?" "You've given your friend lots and lots of advice, and she never seems to pay attention to it. Sounds like you may be wondering if she even listens to what you say to her. Is that what's happening?" Since perception checks go beyond what the client has actually told you, it is especially important to check out your accuracy before moving on. As the name suggests, the checking-out is an integral part of the perception check, and your focus should move immediately to the way in which the client gives (or doesn't give) feedback. Beware of the too-facile or grudging agreement: "Sure—and so I went ahead and..." "Well, maybe that could be true, sort of..." The client may be so engrossed in telling his story that he has not really listened to your comment, or he may dis agree but be unwilling to say so. In either case, the perception check was off target; it did not meet the client where he was or further the unfolding of his story. Your understanding may, indeed, have been correct, but your timing or your phrasing (or both) were off. Store for future reference the idea and the response the client gave to it and come back to focus on what the client is doing and saying now.

Combinations of paraphrases and perceptions checks can be used to comment on and ask about discrepancies or mismatches between different parts of a communication: "You've been telling me how you get very scared when you are with a group of strangers, but I notice that you've been smiling as you tell me that. What's the smile saying?" "Your voice sounds angry even when you tell me that you don't feel angry. Does it sound angry to you?" Remember, again, that the purpose of a perception check is not to persuade the client to accept your point of view or to catch him in some kind of error or omission. Under the guise of being empathic, it is all too easy to push clients into admitting that they feel the way we want them to feel: "because she's the doctor," reasons the client, "maybe I really am mad/sad/scared about that and just don't know it." Clients may need to be reminded that they, not we, are the experts on what it feels like inside their skin. Perception checks allow them to educate us about those inside-the-skin experiences; the discrepancies that we ask them about simply point out our own need for better understanding. Sometimes a perception check will result in greater self-awareness on the part of the client, sometimes in a clearer understanding on the therapist's part, sometimes both. Whatever the combination, the therapist's job is to accept whatever correction the client may offer (perhaps with mental reservations or with some intent to return to the idea later) and to go on from there.

One last word about technique: perception checks and paraphrases can occasionally be very effective if given in the form of a fantasy or a metaphor. "As you describe all the demands on your time and energy, I have an image of someone with ropes tied to all the parts of his body and people pulling those ropes in all directions at once. Is that how it feels to you?" "You'd like, just once, to have someone else do it and do it right—just like in the story of the elves and the shoemaker, when the shoemaker got up to find all of the shoes finished while he was asleep. Does that fit for you?" Using words from more than one sense modality will give your comments vividness; construct your similes and metaphors so that they invite the client's eyes, ears, tongue, and skin. Thorne says, "Empathy and its expression often leads into a world where language becomes ever more richly expressive and where the practice of therapy assumes the characteristics of an art form" (1987, p. 50). Learning to notice and trust the ways in which your own creativity reverberates with your client's story can add a dimension of richness and excitement to your therapy sessions.

SUMMARIES

A summary can serve a variety of purposes in therapy. You may use it to prompt the client in the early part of an interview or to close the discussion of a particular theme or issue. Summarizing what has been said can allow you to test your understanding of how the session is going, or it can encourage the client to explore an idea more completely and thus enhance his own understanding. It can reassure the client that the session is going well, or it can be used to focus thought and feelings when one or both of you feels stuck or confused.

However it is used, a summary has the same general form: it gathers together the main points which have been discussed and puts them out in a package that can be examined and then confirmed or corrected. The earlier response, in which the therapist summarizes what the client has told her about his son, is a good example. The client may have taken twenty or thirty minutes to describe how he has thought about his problem, talked to other people about it, struggled to come to a decision. The therapist's summary sorts it all out, clarifying the content and yet acknowledging the underlying affect. The client now has a choice either to pursue the decision-making process or to focus on the feelings he is experiencing.

Brammer and Shostrum provide a number of useful guidelines for summarizing in therapy. First, they advise, attend to the client's various themes and emotional overtones. Next, put together the key ideas and feelings into "broad statements of his basic meanings." Do not add new ideas to the summary, however good you think they might be; stay with the ideas the client has presented. In fact, it may be more useful to invite the client to do the summarizing rather than doing it for him. Finally, in choosing a way to implement a summary, be sure to take into account the purpose for which that summary is intended: opening, closing expanding, focusing, etc. (1973, p. 94).

I-STATEMENTS

Several of the examples given in this section have contained therapist I-statements. These are statements about the therapist's own feelings, thoughts, or behaviors, clearly labeled to differentiate them from what the therapist believes or understands about the client. Such differentiation and owning of your personal responses are essential. "I feel uncomfortable about telling you what to do" is a straightforward owning of your feelings. "Your question makes me uncomfortable" or "that statement is confusing" gives the client responsibility for your feelings and muddles the therapeutic waters.

I-statements are often most effective when combined with a paraphrase or perception check: "You wanted to talk to her about it, but you were afraid of what she'd say. As I listen to your description of that, I find myself getting very tense and tight. Is that what happened to you?" By describing your own response, you can suggest that such a reaction is not unusual; at the same time you are not telling the client that he does or ought to feel the same way.

We began this section with a comparison of therapist foundation skills and the skills of a good conversationalist. One of the major differences between the two, it was pointed out, is that the focus in therapy is on only one of the participants. Paraphrases, perception checks, and summaries all maintain the focus on the client. I-statements, in contrast, shift the focus back to the therapist. In doing so, they relieve the pressure on the client. Just as blinking one's eyes helps one to see more clearly, so this brief shift in attention gives the client a chance to come back to his own reactions with a better focus. The contrast of the therapist's response with that of the client allows the therapist to step out of the role of neutral, detached, uninvolved observer and to be a real person. This creates the possibility of relationship. True contact is only possible between two people; the therapist who will not allow herself to be a person, owning her honest thoughts and feelings, cannot be a genuine participant in the therapeutic relationship.

The therapist must take care, of course, not to overuse I-statements. After all, the purpose of a therapeutic interview is to facilitate the client's growth, increase his self-understanding, and help him achieve his personal goals. I-statements, like every other response, must be used for that purpose. They always carry the implicit message, "with regard to you." Thus the therapist may respond, "I am feeling confused right now" (with regard to what you are saying), or "In that situation I think I would be angry" (about the way your needs were ignored), or "I'm remembering what you said earlier about your brother" (and thinking about how that relates to what you are telling me now). Used with care, I-statements can form a bridge between client and therapist, moving the client into a deeper exploration of his own needs and goals while at the same time assuring him of the therapist's continuing interest and support.

PROBLEM SOLVING

The classic triad of client behaviors to be cons dered in therapy is *thinking, feeling,* and *doing.* "Doing" is the behavioral outcome of changes in thinking and feeling; it can also help create those changes by providing new experiences for the client to react to cognitively and emotionally. Since the advent of the behavioral approach to therapy, psychologists have been deeply divided as to the appropriate causal sequence for creating lasting change in a client. Do we help him to change how he thinks and feels, assuming that these changes will lead to new behavior (the traditional approach), or do we encourage and coach him in new behaviors, assuming that these will bring about changes in thinking and feeling (the behavioral approach)? In the remainder of this chapter, we will deal primarily with the tradi tional point of view, looking at ways to help clients to explore their issues from cognitive (problem solving) and from affective (feeling) perspectives. We will begin with problem solving.

Problems are the raw material of therapy. The task of solving problems— defining, clarifying, and generating alternative solutions—has become so central to the therapy process that a significant number of practitioners would agree with Rabkin's dictum: "Patients attempt to master their problems with a strategy which, because it is unsuccessful, the therapist changes. All the rest is commentary" (quoted in Confer 1987, p. 61). From this point of view, therapy *is* problem solving, and the more effective and efficiently we can help the client to solve his problems, the more effective we will be as therapists.

There are many models of problem solving (Gibson & Mitchell 1986; Dixon & Glover 1984; Stewart et al. 1978; Egan 1975). Most involve a series of steps to be followed in order. Stewart et al., for example, suggest the following seven steps:

1. Identify the problem.
2. Identify one's values and goals which relate to the problem.
3. Identify the available alternatives.
4. Examine the alternatives.
5. Make a tentative decision.

6. Take action on the decision.
7. Evaluate the results; cycle back through the steps if necessary.

Although this sounds straightforward and logical enough, most clients need help with one or more of the steps. Moreover, the help needs to be given in a way that is empowering to the client. As Teyber (1988) reminds us, the goal is not just to solve the client's problem but to enhance his sense of competence and mastery as well. We succeed as therapists to the degree that we become unnecessary to our clients; solving their problems for them moves us, ultimately, in the wrong direction. As we examine some of the major problem-solving techniques in more detail, we need to remember that a truly successful outcome is one in which the client, not the therapist, can take credit for what has been accomplished.

GOAL SETTING

It is a truism that clients often do not know at the outset what problem has really brought them to therapy. The client who begins by talking of troubles with his chil dren may come to recognize a deeper problem in his marriage relationship; the client who initially complains of panic attacks may discover a need to become more assertive. Many clients are confused and bewildered by multiple problems; so many things are going wrong in their lives that they do not know where to begin.

A major therapeutic task is to help the client find a starting point. It need not be the most important aspect of the problem, the basic, underlying root from which all of the other troubles develop; it must simply be something that therapist and client agree is causing trouble for the client. Just as the knitter trying to untangle a snarl of yarn must first find a loose end and work from there, so the therapist and client work their way into the tangle of problems from this first, agreed-upon starting point.

Agreement is a key issue here. If you have one goal, one problem-that-needs-to-be-solved in mind for your client while he is concerned about something else, you are likely to be working at cross-purposes. A young college student, for example, may have sought treatment because he is failing in school. As he talks, you begin to see a pattern of procrastination, of overuse of alcohol, of too many parties and not enough studying. You are convinced that he needs to develop better work habits, an ability to delay gratification, a less egocentric view of the world. He, on the other hand, wants to figure out why his professors are being so unfair to him. Treatment is likely to go nowhere until you can establish some goal that both of you can agree is desirable and possible, toward which you can work together.

A different kind of goal-setting challenge is presented by the confused and overwhelmed client. For him, everything is going wrong; he has no preconceived notion about what needs to change. Things are falling apart at work, at home, socially, physically. No matter what he starts to talk about, he soon switches to something else. Troubles with his boss remind him of the fight he had with his wife; he could not ask his friend's advice because his friend recently moved to California and now he has nobody to talk to; he got so upset about that that he wrecked his car, and he does not know what to do because he let his insurance lapse and cannot afford the repair bill; he cannot fix it himself because he gets these terrible back pains; sometimes the pain is so bad he cannot sleep, and then he lies awake and feels anxious and wonders if he is going crazy....This kind of client needs to be helped to focus on one part of the problem, one single thing that he can, in fact, do something about. You may ask him to go back and list the major points he has covered (writing these points on a chalkboard as he talks can further aid the focusing process), or you may summarize for him. When the summary is complete, invite him to choose one item that he wants to concentrate on now. And it's often quite helpful to encourage him to choose the *least* important thing to start with, so that he has a better chance of chopping off a doable chunk. This will allow him to begin his therapy process with a success, which can do wonders for morale and motivation.

Having chosen a focus, further work may be necessary to frame it as a solvable problem. "I want my wife to stop nagging me" cannot be dealt with directly in therapy. "I want to learn to respond differently to my wife's nagging" can. A solvable problem is one in which the desired change can be made by the client. A successful solution does not depend on someone else's behavior. The wise therapist will not accept as a therapeutic goal some change on the part of family, friends, co-workers, etc., no matter how desirable such a change might be. Therapy can help the client change only those things he is in charge of—his own thoughts, feelings, and behaviors. Others may change as a result of his changes and often those changes in others are quite desirable, but they are not the major goal of therapy.

It is often extraordinarily difficult for a client to accept this kind of problem framing. "The only thing I want is to get my husband back; I'll never be happy without him." "If only I had a different boss at work, everything would be fine." The therapist must call upon reserves of patience and empathy, understanding the feelings of frustration and despair that the client experiences while continuing to search for some goal, however small, that the client can experience as desirable, reachable, under his control. Such a goal is often introduced as a first step in resolving the total problem; neither client nor therapist need know at the beginning exactly where it will lead. For example, both may agree to sort out the sequence of events that leads up to a spouse's nagging. Understanding what happens is an achievable goal and, once achieved, can be a jumping-off place for further problem identification and solution.

As the client explores his situation, as you work together to find a point at which further steps in problem solving can begin, he will often wander off the track. He may become confused, change the subject, forget the point he was trying to make. Going back to the original focus can bring a sense of order and solvability to the jumble of ideas he is struggling with. Try a "delayed paraphrase": restate whatever it was he was saying just before he got sidetracked. This allows the side issues to be relevant background for the originally agreed-upon goal; he can recapture his train of thought, knowing that you are attending to all that he has to say and will help him keep it all available when needed.

Helping the client to focus on identifying a solvable problem requires that you, the therapist, maintain your own sense of direction. You cannot afford to get lost in the client's confusion or to become overwhelmed by the difficulty of his situation. Two guidelines will help you here. First, remember that *there is always something that can be done*. No matter how desperate the client's plight or how helpless his circumstance, he is not condemned to stay depressed, miserable, guilty, or crazy. Ultimately, each of us is in charge of how we respond to our lives; there are always alternatives among which we can choose. The client may indeed feel trapped and helpless; the therapist must remain grounded in the knowledge that the client can, in fact, change. Second, *you are not responsible for solving the problem*. Your task is to make yourself and your skills available to the client, not to do the work for him. You can help. That is what you are paid to do. Ultimately, however, it is the client who must set the goals, make the decisions, and implement the changes.

USING QUESTIONS

Therapists need to know what their client is saying, why he is saying it, why right now, why in this context, why he is not telling you about something else, what other things are going on for him, etc. Actually, it would be more accurate to say that the *client* needs to know these things; but it is often the process of the therapist's finding them out that most helps the client to learn the same answers. Ideally, the client moves logically from one point to the next, with each answer that he discovers unveiling and highlighting the next question. But therapy is often far from ideal. When the client doesn't ask himself important questions, or confuses himself (and you) by leaping about from one unanswered question to the next, you may have to invite him to look in the direction you think will be most helpful.

In general, your questions will be so designed as to move the client from generalizations to specifics, from past into present, from "out there" to "in here." They will help him put his data in order, separate the essential facts and feelings from the side issues. "This gentle urging in the direction of being more specific and more personal is one of the most basic moves of the therapist," says Rowan (1983, p. 131). No matter what sort of specific information your question may deal with, its overall direction should always nudge the client's attention back to "how, specifically, is this relevant to *me?*"

Many experienced therapists avoid asking direct questions because of the way in which questioning can interrupt or distort the flow of an interview. There are dangers in using questions; knowing some of the possible pitfalls will help you to avoid them. Among the most common dangers is that the therapist inadvertently may take control of the session. By directing the client's attention to what she thinks is important, she decides what will and what will not be discussed. After a series of question-answer transactions, the client may settle back and wait for the therapist to indicate what should come next, rather than volunteering information on his own. The therapist is in charge, and the client follows directions. Once this pattern has been established, it will be difficult to change; the client will have learned that the therapist is supposed to figure out what to talk about. Not only does this kind of expectation practically guarantee that you will miss hearing about things which are, in fact, important to the client, but it also gets in the way of the client's learning to take responsibility for his own behavior. It leads to an attitude in which the client passively waits for the therapist to produce a magical idea or suggestion that will solve the problem, make the bad feelings go away, or change the world for him.

Another danger in using questions with clients is that of coercion: asking questions in such a way that the client is maneuvered or pushed into saying or accepting something he does not want to say or accept. "Don't you really think...?" "Isn't it true that...?" "Do you agree that...?" are lead-ins to such coercive questions. More subtle coercion includes techniques such as coming back to the same question again and again (until the client finally gives up and tells you what he thinks you want to hear) or setting a verbal trap and triumphantly snapping it shut ("You told me that you..., and later you admitted that...; how can both those things possibly be true?"). Good questions help the client tell his story, clarify that story, fill in gaps when something is missing, distinguish the main road from the side avenues. They don't bludgeon him into accepting your point of view or revealing more about himself than he is ready to trust you with.

Beware of the question that is really a disguised interpretation. Interpretations are slippery things, especially early in therapy, and should always be labeled as the therapist's own idea or opinion or hypothesis. "Does your wife remind you of your mother at times like that?" or "Do you find yourself reacting to your boss just the way you react to your husband when he gets angry?" are interpretations pretending to be questions. It's better to take responsibility for your own perception: "It strikes me that you may react to your boss just like you react to your husband when he gets mad." Then follow up with an equally clear request for feedback: "Does that fit for you?" "Does that match your sense of it?"

From all of this, we can extract some specific guidelines for using questions in problem solving: (1) Use questions sparingly. The client will feel more responsible and in control when he is not following your structure but is rather building his own. (2) Ask for clarification when you do not understand what the client is saying. Make it clear that the question arises out of your own confusion rather than from something the client has done wrong. (3) Avoid yes-no questions or questions that can be answered in a single word. Questions like, "Do you work days or nights?" or "What time did you get home the night you had the fight with your wife?" shift responsibility for solving the problem from the client to the therapist. (4) If there are major gaps in the client's story, ask for information to fill them; do so with open-ended questions. Say, "What did you do next?" rather than, "Did you talk to her about it?" (5) If the client avoids answering, do not insist on an answer at that time; you can always come back to the question if you need to. (6) Ask questions which circle *in*, toward the client, rather than *out*, away from the client. If you need to ask about something outside the client, do so in terms of the client's perception of or ideas about that something: "What did you think she wanted?" or "What do you now believe she wanted" are better questions than, "What did she want?" (7) Use questions which direct the client toward constructing new alternatives and finding his own solutions. Do not ask, "Did you ever think of...?" but rather, "What are some of the things you have thought of?"

FEEDBACK

At some point in the problem-solving process, most clients will find themselves stuck. If they were not stuck, they would not need your help to solve their problems. Sometimes a paraphrase or a carefully constructed question will help them find their own way out of the stuck place. At other times, though, they may need additional input. Feedback from the therapist—a statement about her own reaction to what is happening in the therapeutic interchange or about her own perception of some dimension of the problem—is another technique which can help a client get unstuck.

Therapist feedback, like therapist questions, can be misused. It is all too easy to impose one's own perception or solution on a client, to move in too quickly to do the work for him rather than to help him do it for himself. We therapists, like anyone else, want to be seen as wise, perceptive, clever folk; it is hard to refrain from giving answers or sharing some (to us) crucial insight with a client who seems to be floundering. We need to remind ourselves that this moment, right now, is not the last chance we will have to pass on our great idea; if it is truly relevant, the opportunity will come again. The most important rule in using feedback is: wait! The client will let you know when he is ready to hear what you have to say. In many cases, he will ask you directly; he will at least give you some nonverbal indication that he wants your input. The second rule is: be honest. If he asks you about something that you don't want to share with him, tell him that, along with your reason for holding back. Schofield reminds us that "the therapist who seeks to avoid the sharing of an opinion by claiming that he or she does not have any (a psychological improbability) is deliberately lying; all but the most naive of clients will probably detect the falsity, with subsequent erosion of the trust that is crucial to effective therapy" (1988, p. 131). Responses such as, "I'm not sure that talking about what I think is going to be useful to you" or "How will knowing that about me help you right now?" are honest answers; they can also open the door to exploration of the relationship/process between you and the client.

If you decide that your feedback would be helpful, and that the time is right to share it, give it in small amounts. Too much all at once creates overload; the client will not be able to take it all in and may end up confused or even resentful of you. You will probably notice many things in the client's behavior with you, as well as in the things he relates as he describes his problem, that he does not seem to be aware of. You don't need to tell him about all of these; pick just one and let him react to and work with that piece before going on to the next. You may never get around to "the next"; the part you have shared may be just enough to change his focus and let him begin, on his own, to consider other new-to-him aspects of the situation.

When you are talking about your own reactions to the client, be specific about what behavior you are reacting to: "I notice that your voice is getting softer and softer, so that I have to strain to understand you. And what's happening for me

is, I find my thoughts drifting, so I'm not hearing all of what you have to say."
"You told me that when she finally did get home, you sat with your paper up in
front of your face and wouldn't talk to her. If you did that to me, I might feel angry
and sulky toward you." Describing the behavior first and then giving your response
helps to keep clear boundaries between what you are thinking and feeling and what
the client is doing. The client is not pushed to take responsibility for your response
but is merely invited to be aware of it. He can choose to explore that line of thinking further or to move on to something else.

Usually, the client will share his reaction to your feedback without being
asked: "I never thought of it that way." "You mean when I talk softly people kinda
stop paying attention?" If he ignores your feedback and goes on to another topic, it
may mean that your timing was off, that he was not ready to deal with what you
had to say. If he does this several times in succession and if you are reasonably
sure that your feedback really was relevant to what he was discussing, you may
want to talk about *that*: "I've noticed something interesting that happens when I
share an observation with you. I'd like to tell you about what I see." Another common response to therapist feedback is silence. The client may be thinking through
what you have said or may be feeling confused or may be annoyed by your comment. It is important for you to find out what is happening behind the silence. Give
him time to think it through, and then ask him about it.

In general, then, feedback should be used sparingly and only when the client
is ready to hear it. It should contain only one idea at a time and should be phrased
simply and in the client's own language so that he can easily understand it. It
should clearly differentiate between what the client is doing or saying and what the
therapist is thinking or feeling. And, finally, the therapist should invite the client to
share his reactions to the feedback, including whether or not he found it on target
and whether it helped him to move in the direction he wanted to go.

ADVICE

Giving advice is a great temptation to therapists. We may think we know just
what a client should do; a bit of advice giving can seem so much easier than
watching the client struggle to find his own way. Giving advice is, unfortunately,
often more for the benefit of the therapist than for the client. In fact, the urge to
give advice may be a signal that you need to attend more carefully to your own
involvement in the client's issues. "If you are not able to articulate which feelings
or issues cause you to lose your composure, pay particular attention to those times
that you offer information and advice. Such a maneuver directs discussion to
[your] ideas and opinions—a far step from the client's emotions and struggles"
(Brenner 1982, p. 4).

Advice giving may be appropriate in crisis situations where some action
must be taken and the client is unable to think clearly enough to make responsible
choices. It is inappropriate for decision making when there is time for the client to
work things out for himself. "I think you should take action right now to have your

husband hospitalized" may be a caring and responsible therapist intervention. "I think you should go to graduate school" is neither responsible nor respectful of the client's own decision-making ability.

Be careful, though, not to confuse advice with information. When the client makes a clear request for information, and you have the information he wants, it makes sense to share it with him. "Do you think I could handle the academic demands of graduate school?" is a different kind of question than, "Should I go to graduate school?" In answer to the former question the therapist might appropriately respond: "Based on your test scores and on your college records, I think you would have to work pretty hard in graduate school, but I think you could handle it." An appropriate response to the latter question might involve commenting on the difficulty of making a decision, on the client's apparent desire that someone tell him what to do, or on the therapist's own conflict around wanting to give advice and yet knowing how important it is for the client to make his own choices.

Even when the request clearly has to do with information rather than advice, it is still important to note whether the underlying affect is one of dependency and helplessness. Asking for information can be an indirect way of asking to be taken care of or a means of putting off making a decision. If you suspect that this is happening, try reflecting the feeling of helplessness or neediness first and deal with the content of the request later; the problem-solving process may need to wait until the related affect has been worked through.

All of these techniques—focusing on a problem, questioning, feedback, and information giving—may be used at any stage of the problem-solving process. They can help the client identify options, explore consequences, choose a plan of action, or evaluate his success. They can also be useful in dealing with the affect associated with any stage of the problem-solving process. Working with affect, though, requires some additional considerations. We will talk about them next.

DEALING WITH FEELINGS

Emotions are an integral and inevitable component of every difficult problem. The cognitive aspect of a problem may be the most apparent—we need to make a decision about this, figure out how to manage that—but our figuring out is laced through with feelings about what is happening. Clarifying the feelings that surround the problem area is a major, perhaps *the* major, part of therapy; helping people to understand and come to terms with their emotions is the therapist's forte (Plutchik 1990).

The therapist, then, must strike a balance between the cognitive and the affective demands of the work. She must not focus on either to the exclusion of the other. In actual practice, cognitive and emotional work are intertwined: clients need to feel, to process information, to experience the emotions that accompany their decision-making dilemmas, to think clearly about those emotions as well as the decisions themselves. For the purpose of this discussion, though, we have separated feeling work from cognitive work. We now turn to a consideration of some of the issues involved in working with client affect.

The first step in helping a client work through his emotional problems is to recognize what the feelings are. Many people spend years repressing painful feelings, learning to push them out of awareness, to think about something else. Others are confused about the emotions they experience: they cover sadness with anger, fear with guilt, or hurt with resentment. They feel very intensely, but they do not identify those feelings. Both kinds of clients, those who repress feelings and those who misidentify them, need to bring the feelings out in the therapy hour, experience them, know them for what they are. And it is the client, not the therapist, who must be the final authority about his feelings. Even though he may be confused, numbed, or overwhelmed at the outset, he is ultimately the best judge, the only one who can observe his feelings first hand. Often, he must be reminded of this and helped to relearn how to notice his inner experience.

> Clients often come into therapy unable to discriminate what they are feeling. Not only lacking a data base against which to check what they are feeling but also being out of touch, they are vulnerable to being led by a more knowing therapist into believing anything that might explain their problem. Incorrect labeling of emotion by the therapist then simply compounds their own confusion. The therapist must therefore be careful not to impose a label on the client's emotional experience. [Greenberg 1990, p. 65]

If we are not to use labels, how shall we help clients talk about feelings? Many clients have a very small vocabulary of feeling words. Even if they recognize a familiar or recurring emotional response, they don't know how to describe it, to compare it to other sorts of feelings, to find out if other people ever feel that way too. Hutchins and Cole (1986) have put together a useful chart of feeling words (Table 2-1); clients who have difficulty talking about feelings can be encouraged to find the word or words on the list that best describe what they have experienced or are experiencing now. As he searches through the list for the word that is closest to his own feeling, the client will go through a natural process of observing, questioning, and comparing; and he will do so without being biased by the therapist's assessment of him.

Feelings are important and omnipresent. They are also doors to the most private and protected parts of ourselves. An honest exploration of feelings inevitably leads to exploration of self at its most meaningful, most tender, most vulnerable. The therapist must be careful not to move a client too quickly or too deeply into expression of feelings lest he feel seduced or betrayed into revealing more than he is ready for. Feelings can be frightening: many clients worry about looking foolish or losing control or being overwhelmed by a painful emotional response. Others experience intense guilt about their feelings. In our culture girls often learn that they are not supposed to be angry; boys are often brought up to believe that fear and sadness are not manly. The expression of forbidden or very intense feelings may need to be a gradual process, one for which the therapist has prepared the

TABLE 2-1 WORD LIST FOR DESCRIBING FEELINGS

RELATIVE INTENSITY OF WORDS	FEELING CATEGORY				
	ANGER	CONFLICT	FEAR	HAPPINESS	SADNESS
Mild Feeling	Annoyed Bothered Bugged Irked Irritated Peeved Ticked	Blocked Bound Caught Caught in a bind Pulled	Apprehensive Concerned Tense Tight Uneasy	Amused Anticipating Comfortable Confident Contented Glad Pleased Relieved	Apathetic Bored Confused Disappointed Discontented Mixed up Resigned Unsure
Moderate Feeling	Disgusted Hacked Harassed Mad Provoked Put upon Resentful Set up Spiteful Used	Locked Pressured Torn	Afraid Alarmed Anxious Fearful Frightened Shook Threatened Worried	Delighted Eager Happy Hopeful Joyful Surprised Up	Abandoned Burdened Discouraged Distressed Down Drained Empty Hurt Lonely Lost Sad Unhappy Weighted
Intense Feeling	Angry Boiled Burned Contemptful Enraged Fuming Furious Hateful Hot Infuriated Pissed Smoldering Steamed	Ripped Wrenched	Desperate Overwhelmed Panicky Petrified Scared Terrified Terrorstricken Tortured	Bursting Ecstatic Elated Enthusiastic Enthralled Excited Free Fulfilled Moved Proud Terrific Thrilled Turned on	Anguished Crushed Deadened Depressed Despairing Helpless Hopeless Humiliated Miserable Overwhelmed Smothered Tortured

client by providing permissions ("It's okay to feel what you feel." "Your emotions are neither wrong nor crazy") and protection ("You don't need to go into that feeling any more deeply than you want to." "It's important that you know how to take care of yourself as you let yourself feel that fear/rage/grief").

Trying too hard to move a client into exploring his feelings may have the opposite result, moving him back into a more strongly defended place. Experiencing strong emotions for which he is not ready can lead to denial or distortion, and one facet of the denial or distortion is usually some loss of trust in the therapist. And once this trust is lost, it is much more difficult for the client to use the therapeutic protections and permissions that he needs in order to help him through his painful places. It's a delicate choice, when to encourage a client to plunge deeper and when to support his choice to hold back.

Brammer (1973) suggests that therapists be particularly careful in encouraging emotional expression if (1) the client is known to have a severe emotional disorder; (2) he is under so much internal or external pressure that he is liable to respond with more intensity than he can handle; (3) he has a history of badly handled emotional crises; (4) he is strongly and explicitly resistant to exploring feelings; or (5) the therapist has doubts about her own adequacy in helping people deal with feelings. In these situations, the best guidelines come from the client himself. If you are sensitive to everything he tells you, and to your own feelings about what is happening, you will know when it is time to invite him into the next layer of genuine experiencing.

TIMING

The key idea here is, of course, the issue of timing. Our responses—paraphrases, interpretations, confrontations, questions—need to be accurate, and they also need to be precisely timed. Too soon, and the client either does not understand or feels pushed or trapped. Too late, and the affect has changed, the moment has passed, the client has moved on to something else. Make use of the natural pauses in the client's speech to insert your responses; do not interrupt the flow of his thought. Where possible, respond to the most recent part of what he has told you. If you have to go back to some earlier comment, acknowledge what you are doing: "You said a minute ago that..., and I noticed that your face tightened up. What were you feeling just then?" "I'm very interested in what you just said, but I'd also like to go back to what you were telling me about....Would you say more about what that means for you?"

It is usually more productive to deal with feelings experienced by the client during the therapy session than with those that are simply talked about. You may comment about inconsistencies between what the client says he felt and what he appears to be feeling now. (Again, such a response must be timed to catch the feeling as it is experienced.) You may encourage him to allow himself to reexperience the situation he describes. Sometimes just asking the client about his present feelings opens the door to such reexperiencing: "Are you feeling some of the same feelings now that you felt back then?" At other times, a more direct invitation is useful: "Let yourself feel right now the way you felt when that happened."

Remember that the more directive your intervention the more certain you must be of both accuracy and timing. When in doubt, don't! It is better to miss an opportunity to explore something that looks promising than to push the client where he is not ready to go. Tuck your observation away for future reference. (After all, if it really was that important the client will surely circle around eventually and give himself another chance.) Then refocus on what is happening between the two of you right now.

THERAPIST FEELINGS

Therapy is an interaction between therapist and client, and the client's emotional responses occur in the context of that interaction. The client is not the only one who experiences an emotional response; therapists have feelings too. One of the differences between more and less effective therapists is that the former use their own feelings to further the therapeutic exploration while the latter tend to ignore or discount the value of such feelings. Experienced therapists expect themselves to be emotionally responsive; they know where their emotional "hot spots" are and can use this heightened sensitivity as a diagnostic tool, a kind of affective Geiger counter.

The first thing we need, then, in using our own feelings productively, is to be aware of and on good terms with them. I can't provide an emotionally safe environment for my client if I'm afraid of my own feelings. Brenner cautions:

> To the extent that you are uncomfortable with or frightened by a feeling or situation that is described to you, your effectiveness is limited. Conversely, many will find your composure reassuring. Often, people will mention reluctantly a thought, feeling, or incident that they have not shared with anyone previously. If you react calmly, further exploration will follow; if you react with even the slightest detectable discomfort or apprehension, further examination of the issue will be unlikely. [1982, p. 3]

Nevertheless, any therapist may occasionally be taken off-guard by an unexpected emotional response to a client. When this happens, make use of it: What just happened to me? What am I responding to? What's going on that my conscious, logical mind may be missing?

But how can we focus on our own sensations and feelings and, at the same time, be aware of all that is going on for the client? For many therapists the answer lies in a kind of shuttling, a back-and-forth movement of attention from self to other and back again. I hear the client's words, see his facial expression and posture and gestures, notice his voice tone; I shift to an awareness of my own internal and external response. I notice my reaction to him and his reaction to what I do. His state, his communication, blend with my own state and my own reaction, and that reaction leads me back to him again. I follow the flow, now with myself and now with my client. Gradually, as my comfort with this sort of shifting movement increases, I am aware not so much of conscious shifting from one to the other as of a kind of blending, a process that occurs between the two of us. Carkhuff and Berenson describe it well: "The helper's ability to communicate at high levels of empathic understanding appears to involve the helper's ability to allow himself to experience or merge with the experience of the helpee, reflect upon this experience while suspending his own judgment, tolerating his own anxiety and communicating this understanding to the helpee" (1977, p. 8). As I "tolerate" my anxiety, I do not push it out of my awareness. Rather, my anxiety, or my confusion, or annoyance, or whatever is going on in me becomes an integral part of my understanding of that other person's communication. My own emotional response both is called forth by his behavior and helps to trigger that behavior. We are two people interacting, with all the richness of meaning and response that true two-person contact implies. I am able to respond to my client's feelings and experiences more deeply and accurately as I am able to respect and respond to my own feelings and experiences. I am, in a very real sense, a sounding board: what he communicates is expanded and elaborated upon in my reactions to him.

There are a number of specific signals or red flags to which the therapist should pay particular attention as she works to enhance her skill in this self-to-other shuttling process. One such signal is discrepancy, a mismatch between different parts of my total response. My voice tone may not fit the words I am saying, or my gestures or body posture will be at odds with my facial expression. Whether or not the client responds to this mismatch, I need to notice it; it is a signal that I have been neglecting something important in myself. Another useful personal alert is one's own postural shifts. Ask yourself at intervals, "What is my body saying?" Are you leaning forward or sitting back in your chair? Did you just cross your legs or your arms? Do you find yourself cupping your chin in your hand, scratching your head, or rubbing the back of the neck? Are you mirroring your client's body posture? Any of these can put you on notice that something important may be happening, something you need to attend to.

Speaking of attention, notice when you stop attending to the client! We all have those moments when we realize that we have been thinking about something else while the client was talking and have not really been present in the interchange. Such lapses are not accidental, random occurrences. They are warnings that something has been triggered in us, something we need to take care of. More often than not, the trigger was some part of the client's communication. Go back to what the client was saying or doing just before you tuned out and use that as a bridge to your own internal state at that time. If you discover something relevant to the client, plug it into the ongoing process; if not, if you were dealing with some external-to-therapy issue of your own, you will be better able to put it aside after recognizing and acknowledging it to yourself as a concern.

SHARING YOUR FEELINGS

It is easy to begin to feel overwhelmed by all of the things that are happening, all at once, in a therapy session. How can I pay attention to all that the client is saying and doing and at the same time stand off and observe myself? And even if I manage this, how do I decide whether or not to share those observations? There's just too much to notice, too much to think about, and everything happens so fast! There is an unspoken assumption here, an assumption that the therapist must always keep up with the client, must never take a time out for herself. Not so—it may be very appropriate to ask the client to wait a moment while you sort out what has been happening and what you are thinking and feeling about it: "Wait—as you tell me about that, I find myself getting angry. I need to think about that a bit." "Can you hold that thought for a moment while I sort through my feelings about what you've been saying?" "Let me take a time out to just feel what that may be like for you." Obviously, responses like this can get in the client's way if they happen too often; but used judiciously and honestly, they serve a number of therapeutic purposes.

First, and most obviously, they do exactly what they purport to do: they give the therapist time to think. Taking a minute or two to put your own cognitive house in order allows you to come back to the client with a restored concentration and a clearer focus on the business at hand. It allows you to make a less hurried choice of responses, to consider options that might not have occurred to you otherwise. It gives the client access to the best that you can be.

Second, the response which openly and unapologetically admits that the therapist, too, has feelings and needs and imperfections serves as a model for communication. You are showing the client how to sort through and report on internal processes. After all, this is one of the things he must learn to do if he is to profit from therapy. Teachers have long known that demonstrating a technique or skill is one of the most effective ways to help someone else acquire that technique or skill. In therapy, modeling personal openness not only gives information but also provides permission. It tells the client that sharing here-and-now feelings and reactions is acceptable in the therapy setting and invites the client to do the same.

The therapist is a human being, responding to the client as another human being. It stands to reason that the therapist's responses may well be similar to the way others react to that client. If the therapist becomes annoyed or tense or tunes out when the client talks in a certain way, then maybe other people do the same thing. But few of those others are likely to share their responses in an honest, nonjudgmental, nonaccusing way; that's hard to do and not often considered socially acceptable. Getting feedback about the therapist's responses to his behavior may be the first step for the client in figuring out how he sets up unwanted reactions in his social relationships. This, in turn, may help him choose alternative behaviors that will lead to different and more enjoyable kinds of interactions.

Perhaps most important of all is the effect of your appropriate disclosure on the therapeutic relationship. As you share your own honest responses with your client, you are conveying to him a sense of respect and trust. You respect him enough to be honest about what you are feeling; you trust him to be able to handle your reactions. You welcome his doing the same with you. This kind of communication, rare in today's social climate, invites him into a relationship which can be healing in and of itself. It invites him to experience contact with another human being, contact that goes beyond social convention and polite avoidance, contact that affirms the tender and vulnerable parts that most of us work so hard to protect. And it is in the affirmation of this core of self, this essential inner Me, that the therapeutic process takes root.

THE INITIAL
INTERVIEW

3

Therapists are likely to feel a certain amount of anxiety before the first interview with a client. This may, especially for beginners, be an understatement. I was flat-out scared the first time I saw a client: scared that I would do something wrong, that the client would not like me, that I might look foolish. I conjured up a hundred things that might go wrong. Some of that anxiety is inevitable, and it can work to your advantage. You can use it to keep yourself present, alert to what is going on in the client and in yourself. But some of it is not helpful at all and is also down-right uncomfortable. Knowing what you are about and what you want to accomplish will help you to reduce your anxiety to a manageable level and to ensure that both you and your client get what you need during the first contact.

PREPARATION

Frank lists four ingredients in successful therapy: a good therapist-client relationship, a therapeutic setting within which the work takes place, a belief system to undergird and legitimize what happens in therapy, and a "healing ritual" (Flach 1989, p. xiii). As you prepare to meet with a new client, it is a good idea to check yourself out to make sure that all of these are in place, or ready to be put into place. The relationship, of course, must be constructed between the two of you. Are you ready to attend to it? Have you taken care of any personal business that might otherwise disturb your concentration? We will talk about this in more detail when we get to the topic of "centering." The ability to center yourself and be fully present with another person is an essential part of the therapist's professional tool kit.

The next of Frank's ingredients is the therapeutic setting. This is the physical space in which you will meet with your client. We shall have more to say about the nature of this space in the last chapter of this book, under the heading of "professionalism"; but whatever the nature of the space you have created, give it a final, leisurely check before your client arrives. Make sure that everything you or your client may need is available and that the space feels clean and comfortable. Your belief system, the third item on Frank's list, is your internal equivalent of the therapeutic setting; it is the working space within which you operate as a therapist. Just as your physical setting should be comfortable and organized to meet the demands of the therapeutic task, so should your internal structure. Take a moment to scan over it: what you intend to do, and why, and how those goals fit with what you believe about the therapeutic process in general and your way of doing therapy in particular. As you do so, you will also be readying yourself for the therapeutic ritual, reviewing the framework upon which will be constructed the intricate and unique pattern of this client's work with you.

But wait, we need to back up a bit. The first session with a client really begins, in most settings, even before therapist and client actually meet. Someone has scheduled that first session, gotten the client's name and some information about him, decided when you will meet. The client may have had a preliminary session with an intake worker and may have talked about his reasons for seeking help, what he expects out of therapy, etc. Getting a general idea about what is going on for this person and what sort of help he wants, prior to that first therapy session, is a good idea; it gives both therapist and client some sense of direction with which to begin.

I make it a point, during the first contact with a prospective client, to get the client's address and phone number as well as the name of the person who referred him to me. Then if for any reason the client does not show up at the time of the appointment, I have the option of following up to find out what happened. Scheduling mistakes and misunderstandings about time and date do occur, so one need not assume that the client has changed his mind about coming in. Some therapists maintain that calling after a missed initial session sets up an "I will be responsible for you" kind of framework which is antitherapeutic. I disagree. I am willing to make an extra effort at the beginning to ensure that at least one session actually takes place. After all, seeing a therapist is a pretty anxious business for most people, and I want to do whatever I can to get us both into the same room looking at and learning about each other.

And what about prior information about a client—the filled-out agency questionnaire, or the report from a referral source? You don't want to clutter up the relationship with biases or preconceived ideas about this person; he has the right to present himself to you as he wants to be seen. And yet he knows (or suspects) that you do know something about him. He may have put considerable energy into filling out that questionnaire or talking with that intake person; what was the point of all that if his therapist isn't going to use it? Worse, he may suspect that you aren't being honest with him, that you really have drawn some conclusions about him but aren't willing to share them. Obviously, these kinds of suspicions don't help build a good working relationship. On balance, it is better that you do familiarize yourself with all of the information that may be available about a new client and tell the client that you have done so. You may then say that you prefer to form your own opinions, and you'd like to proceed as if you knew nothing at all about him—hearing his story from his own lips will be much more meaningful to you than getting someone else's ideas. Indeed, such an introduction can be a useful icebreaker with a client who doesn't know where to begin or what is expected of him in this strange new situation.

GETTING STARTED

Imagine yourself as a client, about to sit down with a therapist for the first time. You are hurting about some part or parts of your life. Things are going badly for you, and you have not been able to figure out what to do about it. At some level you are feeling inadequate, incompetent, somehow less valuable or worthwhile than other people you know. You are simply not as good a person as others or you would be able to handle this thing on your own. The very act of seeking help is, in most people's minds, an admission of personal failure. So, already feeling bad about yourself, you are now going to sit down with a total stranger and tell her how incompetent and inadequate you are. Worse, this stranger is someone who is trained to see right through your defenses, to be immune to the strategies you use to keep others from knowing all those dark, shameful things inside you. And you're supposed to help her do it, help her to strip you naked, take you apart, make you look at the very things you've worked to cover up. No wonder you're anxious!

The first challenge to the therapist in an initial interview is to create a climate in which the client can begin to relax and can dare to hope that this may be a place where he can get what he wants and needs. Gathering data, setting ground rules, and establishing goals all take a back seat to this first essential task. Creating a therapeutic climate does not precede actual therapy: it *is* the beginning of therapy. As the client begins to understand that this is a different kind of place, a place that is safe, a place that is truly for him, the healing of therapy is happening. If he does not have this experience, then whatever else you do may not matter a great deal.

Within this context, your second task is to get enough information from the client to make some tentative decisions about what to do, whether to offer him therapy, on what terms, and toward what sorts of therapeutic goals. But remember—while you are sizing him up, he is doing the same to you. An essential part of the data you collect will have to do with his first impressions of this place, this person, this process, and how they fit with his expectations. He may have fears or wants that he should talk about: he's not sure he can work with a woman, or he needs to know that his religious convictions will be respected, or he's concerned about confidentiality, for instance. All of these concerns must be respected, discussed, dealt with; otherwise they will sit in the middle of the therapy room, an invisible barrier to the kind of intimacy that makes for good work.

As you talk with this person, then, you are striving to convince him of your therapeutic intent and competence and to begin a genuine relationship with him; you are also beginning to construct a cognitive map of who he is and what he needs and how you may be able to help him. It's a lot to do all at once; there's a lot to keep in mind. Three "rules of the road" may help you to manage it all: (1) keep yourself centered; (2) follow the client's lead; (3) be yourself.

CENTERING

Therapists, like clients, can find themselves off-balance. In order to help a client find his own balance again, you yourself need to be centered: you need to have put aside your personal concerns so that you can be fully available to work with your client. You need to be aware of your purpose, confident of your own skills, and ready to devote your attention to the task at hand. By staying centered in this way you can offer your client a model for his own functioning; in addition, you will give him a sense of protection and of permission to deal with his issues. This is particularly important in the initial interview, when he is forming his first impressions about what you are like, what you expect of him, what he can expect of you, and what this therapy stuff is all about. Shea warns that "for the most part, patients have determined by the end of the opening whether they basically like or dislike the interviewer. These patient opinions are not irrevocably etched in stone, but it would take a rather large chisel to change them" (1988, p. 62). Therapy certainly goes easier when the client likes the therapist, sees her as competent and benevolent, and he is most likely to do so to the degree that she has learned self-centering skills.

So ask yourself, before your client arrives, if you are ready to give him your entire focus. Are you fully attuned to the hour at hand, or is some fragment of your attention worrying about making some stupid mistake, or whether you're going to have time to get to that lecture this afternoon, or how in the world you're going to scrape together enough money to pay your bills? If you have nagging issues that you can't seem to let go of, make a list of them and then put it to one side, knowing that the list will be there to remind you of what to worry about when your time with this client is done. Silly as it sounds, you'll be surprised at how helpful this technique can be.

Then take stock of your breathing. If you are feeling awkward, anxious, or uncertain, your breathing is likely to be shallow or jerky. Before your client comes into the room, take the time to steady your breathing pattern: take several deep breaths, letting the air out slowly. Let yourself experience the tension draining out of your body as you exhale. Give yourself permission to focus on yourself for a few moments, on your own body and your own feelings. Let yourself know that there is plenty of time and that it is okay to be here in the present without hanging on to what happened earlier in the day or worrying about what may happen next. Your agenda can come later; for the next hour it is quite enough to be here, fully responding to and being with another human being. If you are not able to do this, to put your own personal issues aside temporarily in the interest of availability to your client, then you should probably seek out a colleague, supervisor, or therapist of your own to work through whatever unfinished business is intruding on your attention and awareness.

FOLLOW THE CLIENT'S LEAD

Once you have slowed down, focused, and centered yourself, you are ready for your client. Now it is time to invite him in, to open yourself to what he is telling you about his needs, his actions, his thoughts and feelings. If he waits for permission to plunge in, give that permission. If he is already beginning to talk, just listen. If he seems confused and needs some structure, go ahead and ask a question that will help him to get started with what he wants to tell you.

In order to get to know, and be known by, a client, the therapist must find a way to allow him to tell his story. There may be some parts of that story that are especially important, some set of facts that will need clarification. But don't worry about them right now; there is time enough for that later. At the beginning, the client should be encouraged to follow his own agenda, to talk about whatever is in the foreground at this moment. Shea advises the use of several empathic statements early in the session—specifically, within the first ten minutes or so (1988, p. 24). This can serve to put the client at ease, reassure him that you are not only listening to him but do in fact understand what he is saying.

Especially for beginning therapists there is a temptation to ease into an initial session by making some sort of social gesture. Offering coffee or tea, or commenting on the weather or the traffic or how messy your desk looks today, may seem like a way to make the client comfortable. In general, though, it is not a good idea, for several reasons: it doesn't set the proper tone for a working therapy session, it can mislead the client as to what kind of relationship you and he will have, and it can increase his anxiety and confusion as he tries to figure out what is expected of him as a client (Schofield 1988; Seligman 1986).

There are any number of opening questions or statements that will invite the client to begin to talk without conveying that there is a right or a wrong way to go about it: "I'd like to know something about you and how you decided to come for therapy at this time." "Where would you like to begin?" "Later on I will probably have some specific questions, but right now I'd like you to tell me about whatever is most on your mind." "How can I be of help to you?" At the beginning of this first interview it does not really matter where the client starts; what matters is that he simply starts somewhere and in so doing begins to experience the quality of the relationship that will characterize his treatment. "Being able to encounter the therapist with whatever is occurring at the moment and finding that the therapist responds in a therapeutic fashion provide an experience that confirms clients' sense of validity and allows them to feel entitled to their experience and view of the world" (Greenberg & Safran 1990, p. 73).

As the hour progresses, the therapist listens at many levels. The easiest and most obvious level is that of content. The client is talking about what is important to him; he is sharing facts. He wants someone to attend to this information; he has a right to expect that the therapist will remember it and understand his later remarks in the context of what he has already said. Another level is that of nonverbal communication: posture, voice tone, facial expression. The nonverbal communications of the client provide a constant commentary on the actual words; they often explain or elaborate on what the words really mean. Words and nonverbals are a kind of duet, in which each part is important and yet the real message is conveyed in their interaction.

Yet a third level of listening is that of style, or pattern: the rhythm of the dialogue, its coherence and logic, the client's active or passive stance, the general rapport (or lack thereof) that is developing. The first therapy hour is a preview of things to come as treatment progresses; it is also a microcosm of the client's whole world of social interactions. Much can be learned about his relationships, his sense of self, his strengths, and his weaknesses by attending to the overall ebb and flow of this introductory session.

BE YOURSELF

This last guideline warns against the dangers of pseudoprofessionalism. In our anxiety and uncertainty about how to present ourselves, in our fear that the client may see us as fumbling amateurs who do not really know what we are doing, we may bend over backward to appear knowledgeable. Says Wolberg: "The therapist should judiciously watch the personal need to impress the patient with complex words and high-sounding phrases. The use of language that is as unadorned and straightforward as possible will guarantee best results in interviewing" (1988, p. 460). Likewise, being brusque or stilted, or overly friendly and familiar, will poison the climate of warmth and genuineness before it has a chance to do its work. Your own self—spontaneous, human, real—is far more valuable than any kind of professional mask you may be tempted to wear. It is your most important therapeutic tool. Even if you are just beginning, do not hesitate to let your real self, warts and scars and all, show through. As a beginner, you may not be able to use that tool-of-self as effectively and efficiently as you will later on, when experience has sharpened and shaped it a bit; still, the sharpening and shaping come from getting out there, out from behind facade and pretense, into genuine encounter with your clients.

Be yourself is a simple rule, but it is not always easy to follow. You will find yourself slipping into insincerity at times, pretending to be what you are not or to know what you do not. You may be tempted to pretend to agree with the client, joining him in blaming friends or relatives for his plight or promising him more than you can deliver, even though you (in a more relaxed moment) know better. Do not despair; real people make mistakes and being genuine always carries with it the possibility—in fact, the inevitability—that you will sometimes stumble. That is all right; the relationship you are building as you risk genuine contact with your client can tolerate your errors. Admit them to yourself, and then move back into a genuine stance of concern, respect, and honesty. Your commitment to taking the client's concerns seriously, to working through any differences you and he may have, to creating a real human relationship with him is the most important element in the whole business of getting started.

GATHERING INFORMATION

Much of what I have said about the developing therapeutic relationship has to do with letting the client know the therapist as a genuine and trustworthy person. Part of that sense of trust develops as clients see their therapist coming to know them, accepting their concerns and their pain. Another part comes from experiencing the therapist as knowing what to do in the session, as being in charge, as getting the information that will be needed in order to begin the process of therapeutic change. In the first session, the client will be judging your competence largely on the basis of the quality of the questions you ask.

Therapists differ as to what kind of information to get, in what order, and in what detail; yet most agree that there is an optimum balance between an attitude of "give me the following facts" on the one hand and of "I have no idea what may be important" on the other. There are some things that you need to know in order to decide what kind of treatment—if any—will be best for this client; even though your first priority is to put the relationship on a firm footing, those need-to-knows must not be neglected. Indeed, as we have already pointed out, attending to them appropriately will significantly enhance the trust the client has in you, particularly if your questioning style is open-ended and sensitive. "With regard to this open-ended emphasis," warns Shea, "two frequent problems are encountered: (1) premature structuring of the interview before the patient has begun to relax and (2) the too frequent use of close-ended questions" (1988, p. 63). To avoid premature structuring, use what the client offers spontaneously as a bridge to the questions you need answered; allow him to elaborate and get off the subject if he wants, before bringing him gently back on task. And, whenever possible, avoid any question that can be answered in one or two words.

It is useful to know ahead of time what basic facts you will need about your client and to make sure that you do find out these things. Once you have your list firmly in mind, you can relax and be open to all of the additional information that will emerge as you go along. Many therapists try to get a fairly detailed picture of the client during the first interview. Their mental list includes demographic details such as occupation, marital status, number and ages of children, specifics about the onset and duration of the symptoms which led him to seek therapy, medical history, and so on. Here is the mental checklist that I've constructed over the years:

1. Statistical data (when not already available)—address, phone numbers, age, sex, occupation
2. Complaint—what's wrong, when did it start, has it ever happened before; what other things are going badly; how is all this affecting client's life right now

3. Physical health—overall physical condition, diet, exercise; current medications; substance use (including caffeine and nicotine); family history of illness, especially psychiatric illness
4. Current living situation—who lives in client's home; hours spent at home, at work/school, in other activities; general state of finances
5. History—family history; autobiographical information
6. Strengths—friends, interests, and hobbies; coping mechanisms (include things client has tried, in present difficulty, that haven't seemed to work)
7. Depression level–suicide potential

While not a formal outline to be pursued point by point in the interview, this list may be referred to occasionally as a reminder of what has been covered already and what may have been overlooked. Some of the points may be self-evident, some may deal with information already collected, and some may be inferred from the client's nonverbal behavior. Much will come naturally and spontaneously from the client. When the information does not emerge naturally, ask questions. A good rule of thumb is that the more confused or anxious the client, the more structure (in the form of direct questions) he will probably need.

A major drawback of systematic questioning is that it tends to set up an expectation on the part of the client that the therapist will take charge, will tell him what to do and when to do it. Such an expectation can be a serious hindrance for later therapeutic work. The client needs to know that ultimately he must do his own work; his must be an active rather than a passive participation—a very different sort of process than just sitting back and answering questions, no matter how searching or penetrating those questions may be. If you choose to use most of your initial sessions to gather information, you should let the client know that this first session is conducted in a different way (and serves a different purpose) than future ones. Cornier and Hackney give an example of how to open such a session: "Before counseling gets started, it is helpful if I have some preliminary background about you. So this time, I'd like to spend the hour getting to know you and asking questions about your school, work and family background, and so on. Then at the next session, you will be able to start discussing and working on the specific concerns that brought you" (1987, p. 66). This lead-in clearly distinguishes between what will be going on during this session and what will happen when the "real" therapy begins.

The amount and kind of information gathered in the initial interview will depend in part upon the therapist's theoretical orientation, the kind of therapy she intends to provide. A behavioral therapist will need to know the specific behaviors that are to be changed and the specific circumstances under which they occur. A more psychodynamically oriented therapist will be interested in the client's developmental history, his early relationships with parents and siblings. A client-centered therapist may deliberately choose to have no agenda at all but to encourage the client to talk about whatever is in his awareness at the moment.

Whatever the strategy that fits your theory of therapy, remember that the client can only tell you about his own perceptions and beliefs. His way of experiencing and understanding the world comes not just from the events of the present but from the interaction of the present situation with his whole history of being in the world. There will be things that he does not notice or does not consider important enough to mention; there will be other things that he distorts or only tells selected parts of. The omissions and distortions are significant bits of data, too. Part of the client's inability to solve his present problems has to do with his inability to step out of his frame of reference, to see new possibilities, different ways of reacting and responding to all-too-familiar stresses. The information you collect should help you to begin to identify the blind spots—the old, limiting habits of thought, feeling, and behavior—that the client, because of his personal history, literally is unable to see. Keeping this in mind will help you to be efficient and purposeful in your information gathering; it will also help you to know when to abandon a particular line of inquiry, with the mental note that something is awry here and will need to be returned to later.

Which brings us to one last word about information gathering: the client should not be pushed or bullied or tricked into giving information that he does not want to give. The first interview is not, for most clients, the time for confrontation and coercion. Demanding that a client reveal things that are sensitive, embarrassing, or painful casts the therapist in the role of inquisitor. It not only suggests to the client that the therapist's agenda is more important than his own and that the therapist (rather than the client) will be doing the work of therapy but also begins a power struggle that may set the tone of the sessions for weeks to come—if the client even comes back for another visit. Sometimes it is even a good idea to restrain a client who seems eager to tell you everything, no matter how painful. "A client can say 'too much' in an early meeting and feel exposed or embarrassed in a setting not yet known to be safe. You can help such people by suggesting that they 'slow down a bit,' knowing that this may help avert a feeling of panic after the meeting is over. Sometimes it is best to be 'therapeutic' from the very beginning at the expense of a prompt assessment" (Brenner 1982, p. 29). First trust and safety, then data, is a good guideline.

DIAGNOSIS AND ASSESSMENT

If I go to a medical doctor because my head aches or I have a persistent cough or my wrist is swollen and painful, I want that doctor to examine me and tell me what is wrong. I expect a diagnosis of my ailment. Many clients, seeking therapy for the first time, have that same expectation, and beginning therapists often expect themselves to be able to provide a quick diagnosis. The pressure to diagnose is increased by requests from agencies or from insurance companies who want a form filled out, complete with diagnostic category. Unfortunately, the medical model, in which diagnosis logically precedes treatment, is seldom appropriate for psychotherapy. Accurate psychological diagnosis may require a whole series of sessions and thus becomes inextricably interwoven with the therapy process. Diagnosis emerges from what occurs in therapy, just as therapy can occur in the process of gathering diagnostic information.

Not only is it often impossible to make an accurate assessment on the basis of one session with an anxious, defensive, or ambivalent client, but also the kind of working assessment you make will depend on the kind of treatment model you are using. The base-line data of the behaviorist, the script analysis of the transactional analyst, the lifestyle description of the Adlerian therapist—none of these fit the neat categories of the DSM III-R (the *Diagnostic and Statistical Manual of Mental Disorders*, 3rd ed. rev., published in 1987 by the American Psychiatric Association) standardly used in the United States for reporting diagnoses. The ethical therapist's first responsibility must be the welfare of the client, and this means gathering data and formulating hypotheses that will generate a treatment plan, a sense of what can be done therapeutically for this particular person. Assessment for other purposes must take second place to this concern.

Some sort of assessment and evaluation, however, is a necessity. "Without some skill in clinical assessment," comment Howard et al., "the therapist is like the lost traveler who has no map to tell him where he is and where he is going. To assess a client appropriately is to pinpoint where we are. To identify what needs to happen in treatment tells us where we need to go" (1987, p. 121). It is important to have such a map in mind as you work with a client. It is equally important to remember that the map is tentative, subject to change as your understanding of this particular client continues to develop week after week.

If you must submit a formal diagnosis because of the circumstances of your employment as a therapist, you will do well to keep two facts firmly in mind. First, the diagnostic system you are using (whether it is DSM III-R or any other) is an abstraction, a set of categories that may or may not provide a good fit for what your client is telling and showing you. You may be required to make a diagnosis of this sort; you are not required, once having made it, to believe that it is absolutely accurate. It is at best an approximation of what is true for any individual. Second, your diagnosis is subject to change as you learn more about the client—or as the client himself changes. Physicians are beginning to remind themselves of this latter possibility by using verbs rather than nouns in their descriptions of patients: he doesn't "have hypertension" but rather "hypertenses" (Kenny & Browne 1989). It seems easier for us to expect people to change what they do than to change a disease that they "have." Psychotherapists would do well to imitate this practice. As for your own changing impression, be grateful for it; nurture your ability to change your mind. New information may turn up that might drastically alter your initial impression, if you allow yourself to take it seriously. There is a great temptation, after having made a diagnosis, to use it to filter all subsequent information. This creates a self-fulfilling prophecy: no matter what the client does or says, the therapist can interpret that behavior so as to support her belief that the client is paranoid or has a major depression or an anxiety disorder. Initial diagnoses can take on a life of their own; like weeds in the garden, they tend to persist beyond the time when we think we have chopped them down and replaced them with something more useful.

For all of these reasons, it is generally not a good idea to share a formal diagnosis with your client. Telling someone that he "has" this or that "disorder" can be as frightening as it is misleading. The diagnosis sounds so formidable, so real. The client is not likely to understand it as tentative, as a hypothesis, as a shorthand way of summing up a host of partially formulated impressions. Instead, it becomes Truth; it becomes His Illness; it leaves him helpless and ignorant, waiting passively for treatment by someone who knows him better than he knows himself.

ANSWERS

The client, of course, does want answers from you. He wants to know what is wrong with him and whether you can help make him better. He wants to know how long it will take, how difficult it will be, how much it will cost. And there are other questions, too, questions that he is not asking out loud and may not even be consciously aware of: Who are you, really? What are you like? Will you really understand, care about him, be on his side? Are you trustworthy? Whatever else he may hear in your answers, he will surely be forming his opinions about all of these. Fong and Gresbach advise that "to address the client's concern, the counselor needs to respond to the underlying questions with an answer that reflects the counselor's ability and willingness to accept and empathize with the client" (1989, p. 29). Accepting and empathizing with him, you will want to give him all of the answers that will be helpful.

The most useful way I have found to give diagnostic feedback to a client is in two steps. First, summarize what you have heard the client say. In doing this, you let him know that you have been listening, that you do understand what he is telling you, and (by the fact that you are calm and matter-of-fact about it) that you do not think he is odd or crazy to be saying all this. Moreover, the summary that you give him *is* a kind of diagnosis in that it describes what is going on for him at this time; it is probably at least as accurate (and certainly more intelligible to the client) as a phrase filled with psychiatric jargon.

Having summarized how things are now, the second step is to consider what will happen next. Does it make sense for this client to be in therapy? If so, are you the best person for the client to work with? If you do work together, what will that work be like? These are all questions to be dealt with before the first session comes to an end.

WILL YOU CONTINUE?

While you may be tempted to offer your services to every new client who approaches you, there are a number of possible reasons for deciding not to do so. Foremost among these, of course, is whether the client is likely to benefit from treatment. Wolberg says, "If a patient is highly motivated for therapy, has functioned well in the past, has had at least one good relationship previously, is uncomfortable with the symptoms or life situation, seems to be able to relate well with the interviewer, has a curiosity about personal psychological forces (psychological mindedness), and is reasonably intelligent, he or she has a chance of doing well in therapy with a good therapist" (1988, p. 528). If one or more of these factors is absent, think twice about offering to work with him. I am not suggesting that you automatically refuse treatment, but rather that you consider seriously whether your particular type of therapy is likely to overcome the difficulties inherent in establishing an effective working relationship with someone who, for example, has never been able to sustain an interpersonal relationship in the past, or is quite comfortable with his life as it is now, or seems unmotivated for therapy. In my own practice, I generally do not work with clients who come to me in order to meet the demands of someone else—the alcoholic (perhaps) who comes because the court insists that he get some sort of treatment, or the spouse who comes in order to please his or her partner. Other therapists, with other styles, may do well with such clients; I have found that I do not. Each therapist must recognize what her own limits and inclinations are; your decision with a prospective client will be easier to the degree that you have thought out such policies ahead of time and set up guidelines for yourself.

Another reason for choosing not to work with a particular client may be that he can get better help from someone else. You may not be trained to deal with some kinds of problems. Treatment of substance abuse or sexual dysfunction, for example, calls for specialized skills. Part of the purpose of an initial interview is screening and referral, making sure that the client gets the treatment most appropriate for him. If you are not trained to work with the problems this client presents, say so and make a referral to a colleague. To do so is not only required by our ethical codes but also simply makes good, practical sense.

Another part of the process of deciding whether or not to work with someone is discovering whether therapist and client share the same general goals. "It is imperative," says Goldberg, "that the reasons for being in a therapeutic encounter be clearly understood and agreed upon by both agents, not merely inferred by one or the other" (1977, p. 3). One way to move toward this kind of agreement is for the therapist to summarize her understanding of what the client wants to get out of therapy and ask for feedback. Alternatively, she may state her own tentative goals for the client and ask if this fits with what the client wants. It is important to make such statements open-ended, to give the client ample opportunity to add, amplify, or correct. It is also helpful to expect that your first formulation will need some sort of editing by the client. "This is what I see us working toward. How would you change that description to make it fit better with what you want?" is a good invitation to this sort of editing.

It is not necessary that client and therapist agree on every detail of the therapeutic goals, but rather that they find some area of intersection that both believe important and worthwhile, and that neither be working toward some goal that the other finds objectionable. Goals can shift and change, and they often need to be renegotiated as treatment progresses. The initial menu is a starting place, a firm basis for beginning to work together rather than a final, carved-in-stone plan that must be followed throughout the course of therapy. We shall have more to say about goal setting in Chapter 4.

If you do decide to send a client elsewhere for treatment, do so matter-of-fact-ly: you believe that he can get better help in some other place, that someone else would work better with him than you would. Nobody is incompetent, or a bad client; you simply want this person to get whatever treatment will work best for him. Give the client this information as soon as you are reasonably sure of it yourself and allow some discussion of the recommendation. Don't string him along or let him commit himself to working with you, only to feel rejected at the end of the session.

Let him know, too, if you are interested in working with him. That's part of the information he needs in order to make his own decision about continuing. Only one part, though; there are other things he needs to know as well. You, the thera-pist, have an ethical responsibility to inform the client about the procedures you will use and any possible negative side effects of those procedures. He also needs to know your qualifications and your general policies—your fee scale, whether he will be charged for late cancellations or missed sessions, whether you make tape recordings or keep other sorts of detailed records, how you handle delinquent pay-ments. Many therapists use a standard form which describes these sorts of policies, and they ask prospective clients to read them before beginning the initial session; this allows time for the therapist to make sure that the client understands what he is getting into before he makes any commitment to continuing.

Now you have talked a bit with this client and have decided that it would be appropriate to work with him. He knows how you work, has read and signed your statement of policies. You have shared with him your understanding of what is going wrong and what you think needs to happen and let him know that you would like to be his therapist. The next step is to validate his attending to what *he* wants. Ask him directly; don't just assume that he will want to schedule another session: "Do you want to work with me on these problems?" Or tell him what makes sense to you: "I'd like to meet with you once a week, at least for a while. How does that sound to you?" You may want to encourage him to take some time to consider his decision carefully: "Sometimes people like to take a day or two to think about how things have gone in a first session before deciding whether or not to continue. Would it be helpful for you to have some time, and then let me know what you have decided?"

HOW WILL YOU WORK TOGETHER?

The client's decision about continuing in treatment may have been made before you get around to asking him about it, or it may emerge out of a discussion of what ther-apy might be like for him. By the end of the first session, each of you has begun to form some ideas about what the other is like and how therapy will be structured. The client, though, is at a serious disadvantage. He has experienced you only in the initial interview, and the structure of that initial session may be very different from later ones. Or his idea of therapy may have been shaped by experiences with other therapists or by movies or books or TV in which treatment procedures are quite dif-ferent from your personal style. Failing to spell out some of the basics may lead to awkwardness and confusion, with each of you wondering why the other is not doing the right thing. Not only is it an ethical requirement to tell the client in a straightforward way what you expect will happen during future sessions, it also makes good therapeutic sense. "Our hours together will be your time to use to talk about whatever you want" is a good frame for a nondirective approach. Other therapists may want the client to use a contracting method: "At the beginning of each of our sessions, I'll be asking you what specific behavior or problem you want to work on during that session." Still others will be most interested in emotional exploration: "Much of what you've been telling me has to do with painful feelings, feelings that are interfering with your ability to enjoy life. In our work together, we will explore those feelings and find out what can be done to change them."

Before sharing your own expectations, though, give the client a chance to tell you what he expects or hopes will happen in therapy: "Do you have any expectations about how we might work together?" "Assuming we do decide to work together, what's your fantasy of what that will be like?" If he has had previous therapy, ask what he found particularly helpful, and what was not helpful, in that experience. Questions such as these help the client to clarify for himself what he wants; his answers also give you some guidelines for how much and what kinds of structuring will be most helpful to him.

Remember that even though your own behavior makes perfect sense to you, it may seem strange or incomprehensible to the client. Tell him what you are doing and why. If you plan to take notes, explain how they will be used and whether you will continue to do so after the first few sessions. (In my opinion, taking notes during an interview, except possibly the initial one, is a poor strategy. Taking notes while the client is talking can derail his train of thought as well as distract your attention from what he is saying and doing right now. It is much better to allow yourself a few minutes after each session to jot down your notes while it is all fresh in your mind.)

Many therapists record their sessions, and some agencies regularly use videotape for training and supervision. Again, explain to your client why you are taping the sessions and what use will be made of the tapes and make sure that the client understands and accepts your explanation. It is particularly important to inform clients as to the confidentiality of the recordings, who will be allowed to hear or see them, and what provisions are made for protecting the client's identity. Are the tapes saved week after week, or are they reused so that no permanent record is kept of the sessions? How can the client be sure that some friend or acquaintance (a student in the agency's training program, a former colleague who works at the clinic, an acquaintance of his wife who works for another agency in town) will not hear one of the tapes? A simple explanation of how the records will be used and what will happen to them when the therapy is concluded is usually sufficient to allay client anxieties on this score.

HOW OFTEN, HOW LONG, HOW MUCH?

Obviously, before telling the client how often sessions will be scheduled and how long they will be, the therapist needs to decide for herself what sort of pattern

would be most helpful. In a structured situation in which all clients are seen weekly for the traditional fifty-minute hour, the decision has already been made. If not,
a particular client may be seen more frequently or less frequently. For most clients
and for most therapeutic styles, the once-a-week format works reasonably well; it
has the added advantage of simplifying the task of keeping track of appointments.
At the beginning of treatment, most clients need to be seen at least this often in
order to build up therapeutic momentum; with longer intervals rapport development is much slower, and the work tends to be choppy and disconnected rather
than cumulative. Some clients, especially those who are in acute crisis, may need
to be seen more than once a week. Occasionally a client will find it difficult to
schedule weekly appointments—his work commitments may make it hard to get
away, or he may be traveling from out of town—and less frequent sessions may be
arranged.

The fifty-minute hour, like the weekly session, facilitates schedule keeping.
It is almost certainly the therapist's convenience, rather than any theoretical consideration, which has made it so common. Yet it does seem to be a workable length
of time—long enough to explore in detail and with some leisure, yet not so long as
to fatigue either therapist or client unduly. In my practice, I deviate from the fifty-
minute hour only when I have some specific therapeutic reason for doing so. A
child or a severely disturbed adult may be unable to maintain concentration for a
full-length session, and for him a twice-weekly, half-hour session may work better.
For couples or families, or for certain sorts of therapeutic procedures, a single hour
may not be long enough to finish the business at hand, and ninety minutes may be
more appropriate.

How much is all of this going to cost? You can assume that every client
thinks of this question, whether he asks it aloud or not. The client should be
informed of the fee per session at the time scheduling is discussed; if some sort of
sliding fee scale is available, this is the time to settle the whole question of payment. Dealing with money issues is difficult for many therapists. (We will discuss
this issue further in Chapter 11.) Fee questions should be met head-on and matter-
of-factly, for no amount of hedging will make them go away. The client is paying
for his time with you, and he needs to know what that payment will be and how the
payment is to be made.

Ideally, clients also have the right to know how long their treatment can be
expected to last. Practically, it is often difficult or impossible to make such a pre-
diction, especially on the basis of a single interview. An estimate of the overall
length of treatment needed may be received by the client as a promise that you will
cure him in that length of time. (Notice who is active and who is passive here.)
You can certainly tell him about how long other people, with the same sorts of
problems, usually remain in treatment; and it is often useful to suggest that you and
he work together for some specific number of sessions, after which you can evaluate together what has happened and make a better judgment about how things are
going and how much longer you may need to continue.

ENDING THE SESSION

The first contact with a client establishes a whole set of precedents that will flavor future sessions for weeks to come. From relatively minor matters, like who sits down first and where, to more important patterns of talking and silence, choosing a focus for discussion, and how limits will be respected or not respected, the client is developing beliefs about what therapy with you will be like. It is particularly important, at the close of the first session, to set a pattern for ending the interview that will be as comfortable as possible for both of you. Many beginning therapists are tempted to stretch out the first hour, to allow more time if the client seems to want it. There is an awkwardness about ending, a social sense that we should not cut people off or leave a conversation before the other person is ready. After all, we have been taught all of our lives to be polite. Yet the end of the first session is often the first test of the therapist's limits, the first opportunity for both client and therapist to discover whether and how the therapist really will say no.

Although it is important to keep to an established time framework, it is unwise and unhelpful to cut the client off too abruptly. To say, "I'm sorry, our time is up," when the client is in the middle of a long explanation, especially if he is dealing with emotionally charged material, seems cold and unfeeling. Yet not interrupting can allow the session to stretch well beyond its allotted time. The best way I know to avoid this dilemma is to begin to wind up the interview at least ten minutes before it must really end: "We have only a few minutes left of our time together today, so some of what you are talking about may have to wait until we meet again. Let's see if I've got the main points, though." Or, "Our time is almost up, and there are a few things I need to clarify with you before you leave today." Having given notice in this way, it becomes easier for both therapist and client to accept the reality of the clock when the hour does end: "There's no more time left. I really want to hear more about what you've been telling me, so let's plan to pick up next time where we left off today."

Speaking of the clock, be sure to have one in your office, where you can glance at it easily without turning your head. Trying to glance surreptitiously at a wristwatch or to look over at a side wall when the client isn't paying attention seldom works—the client will know what you are doing and notice that you are trying to sneak it in. He may interpret your behavior as a hint that he should hurry up or think that he is boring you or doing something wrong. Also, having to wonder about how much time is left or whether you ought to be checking the clock will interfere with your ability to focus on the client and what he is telling you. You do need to keep track of time, in order to take care of necessary business and bring the session to a graceful conclusion; arrange your office so as to make this as natural as possible.

In closing the session, you may need to shift from the client's agenda to your own. This shift can be the lead-in to the whole discussion of continuation of treatment and must be done early enough to allow you to finish that discussion. If there's time left over, you may choose to go back to whatever the client was talking about before you shifted gears. Or you may end the session. There's no magic rule that the first session must last a certain length of time, and if everything feels comfortably closed, there may be no need to open it up again. With experience, you will learn to judge the amount of time needed to end things comfortably, as well as how to put a topic on hold until you can meet with the client again.

　　　The hour ends. A smile, perhaps a handshake, and your client is gone. If you and he have chosen to continue, you have set the stage for one of the most exciting and challenging relationships possible between two human beings. In fact, though you may not realize it, the relationship, with its challenge and excitement, has already begun.

THE EARLY PHASE   4

"Because the working relationship is so vital to success in therapy all tasks must be subordinated to the objective of its achievement" (Wolberg 1988, p. 493). Nearly everything that we shall say about the early phase of counseling is implied by these words. Establishing a healthy working relationship *is* the early phase; when this relationship is in place, the client moves into middle-phase work. This chapter, then, is about helping the client build trust, to experience both permissions and limits, to discover what the therapeutic process is and what kinds of learning and changing it can bring about.

At the beginning everything is new and strange. Neither client nor therapist knows quite what to expect of the other. The client wants relief from the pain that brought him to therapy in the first place, and he wants it now. The therapist, particularly if she is a beginner, may want to prove to the client (and to herself) that she can help, that therapy can make a difference. The danger is obvious: hurry up and fix it, hurry up and make something change. Everyone is eager for results, and it is all too easy to overlook the importance of creating a climate in which the client can begin to discover his own strength, his own rhythm of change and growth, his own self. And yet that internal process, uniquely his own, is much more important than some set of quick tricks from the therapist. "Fixing" himself can bring about lasting and meaningful change; "being fixed" by a therapist—no matter how wise or clever—brings at best temporary relief.

The best advice I know for the first phase of treatment is: slow down. Pouring a foundation is less dramatic than framing up walls and doors and windows, but it has to come first. The relationship between client and therapist must be established and experienced before it can be used in the service of growth. That relationship "is both the means of change and the substrate for the risky business of developing new strategies for personally difficult situations" (Aveline 1987, p.22).

Only the immediate physical safety of your client takes precedence over its development. And if you take this advice seriously and make the relationship your first priority with each new client, you will discover a bonus: as you do so, the client will nearly always experience some symptom relief, some renewal of hope.

Let's begin, then, to look at this business of establishing the working relationship. There are a number of rather technical tasks which are embedded in the process; when you attend to them and do them well, the client's initial changing and growing will usually take care of itself.

RAPPORT

We talked in Chapter 3 about the sense of defeat that is typical of the new client, the conviction that he has failed in managing his life and is not okay in some fundamental way. Depending on the kinds of defenses he has developed over the years, he may react to the therapy situation by appearing strong ("I've really got it mostly together; I just want to talk things over and get a little help on one or two minor points"), by freezing up and not knowing what he really wants, or by spilling into tears or rage or sullen hopelessness at the first possible opportunity. In referring to "defenses," I do not mean to imply that such responses are conscious efforts to conceal what he is really thinking and feeling—quite the contrary. They are the ways he has learned to protect himself, to cope with life; they are *him*, and he can hardly imagine that there could be any other way for him to be.

Whatever his reaction is, it is the most that he can show you right now. And he needs one basic thing from his therapist—acceptance. He needs the therapist to accept him as he is, to listen to and care about what he has to say. At the same time, he is likely to resist that acceptance, to distrust it. In fact, the better the relationship feels to him, the more accepted and comfortable and invested he becomes, the more fearful he may be of it. He dares not trust any relationship; so many of his past experiences with people have ended in pain and disappointment that he knows it is not safe to expect things to be any different.

So there in the other chair sits your new client: scared, belligerent, sad, strong, whatever. Underneath the mask that he uses to hide from the world is usually a very discouraged human being, one who is afraid you will not understand him well or like him very much because he really is not very likable or understandable. Your first job as therapist is to accept all of this person—the mask as well as the underlying feelings. It is too soon to start digging past the front he presents, and it is too late to pretend that the front is all there is. You are there for the whole person, for what he is able to show you and for what he must for now conceal. You value what he presents, and you respect his right and his need to reveal himself at his own pace. Later you may decide to push, to confront, to employ any of the techniques that you know how to use, but not now. Now your job is simply to listen and to be there with the client as fully and completely as you possibly can.

Rapport, that almost tangible sense of contact and trust between client and therapist, is created out of acceptance. And acceptance is conveyed by listening patiently, without judging or prompting. The therapist's genuine acceptance will show not only in the words she uses but also in her facial expression, her body position, her inflections, her gestures. Ideally, she will convey both her interest and her willingness to share further, and her equal willingness to be patient and adapt to the client's pace and style. As she does so, she invites the client into a new and different kind of being-with another person, a space that Havens has described as "being alone together" (1986, p. 84). Supported but not confined by the therapist's interest, the client can begin to feel safe. Interest without demand, the unforced willingness to know and to be known, is rare indeed in the currency of human relationships. The client may not know quite what to do in such a situation; he will be wary of trusting it at first; yet, out of his first hesitant tests (of the therapist and of himself), trust can begin to grow.

Listening, respecting, and being in contact with a client are relatively easy when the client is willing and able to talk freely about his problems. Often, though, clients do not know where or how to start. Everything is confused, complicated. They do not really know what the central problem is or how to describe it. Things just feel generally bad; if they knew what was wrong, and why, they would have taken care of it on their own. Many clients come to therapy with an expectation that they should be able to lay the whole problem out, step by logical step, but since their life does not seem to follow that kind of logical pattern, they do not know how to begin talking about it. Others come expecting the therapist to take over, to provide some kind of magical structure that will begin the healing process, and so they wait for direction, for questions, for someone to tell them what to do. With such clients, one can be supportive in providing some structure while at the same time giving them assurance that wherever their answers lead will be all right. "Tell me something about how you are feeling right now" or "What have things been like for you over the last few days?" are good lead-ins. You may invite your client to take a moment to reflect on what he is thinking and feeling and then report on what he discovered. Sheldon Kopp used to reassure his clients by saying, "Of course it's hard to begin, but you can start anywhere. It's all attached" (1977, p. 40).

It *is* all attached, and by reminding ourselves of that fact we can do much to calm our own anxious impatience to make something happen. All the verbal reassurance in the world will not make much difference if we are communicating nonverbally that we do not, in fact, want the client to be saying whatever he is saying. We define ourselves to the client by everything we do in these early sessions and by everything we do not do as well, and it is virtually impossible to hide our impatience or disapproval if that is what we really feel. Clients are amazingly sensitive to the tiny signals that we put out. Just as we may be unaware of what we are sending, the client may be unaware of what he is inferring about us. Out of awareness, though, he is performing a rather sophisticated data analysis. As Fong and Gresbach observe: "for trust to develop, the client must see observable instances of trustworthiness. How clients handle this need to assess trustworthiness over a period of time is to formulate conscious and unconscious 'tests'. In a sense, clients gather empirical data to determine whether their working hypothesis ('This counselor is trustworthy') is valid" (1989, p. 27). The most therapeutic thing I can do for a new client is to allow myself (and him) to do nothing, to wait and listen and take no responsibility for his future behavior. The paradox is that by not trying to make something happen, I do make the most important something of all happen. I begin to build a therapeutic relationship.

Waiting and listening, however, do not require that the therapist take a passive role. On the contrary, she is actively representing herself as concerned, involved, open, willing to accept seriously whatever the client wants to present. A good therapist will not discount herself, will not take on the role of critic or judge or trying-but-unable-to-help or frightened bystander (and any of these roles may be offered her by a new client). Good therapists value themselves and their skills just as they value their clients; one's respect for clients is conveyed, in part, by one's respect for oneself and what one is doing.

And how to summarize all this? It feels relevant, but somehow mushy, as though we are talking about an important thing but not really saying what it is. Wolberg comments that therapists and theorists don't generally specify the basic components involved in creating rapport; he goes on to give his own list: "gaining the patient's confidence, arousing expectations of help, accenting the conviction that the therapist wishes to work with the patient and is able to do so, motivating the patient to accept the conditions of therapy, and clarifying misconceptions" (1988, p. 75). Notice that "helping" or "solving" or "relieving" or words of that sort cannot be found in Wolberg's list. Lurking between the lines, though, is a great deal about *being*— being interested, acceptant, patient, confident, clear, honest. Your being, much more than your doing, will foster the rapport-building process.

THE THERAPIST AS TEACHER

Establishing rapport does not occur in a vacuum. It is built in the context of the activities of the therapy interview, and your competence and confidence—your *being*—will manifest themselves in the way in which you carry out those activities. One of the therapist's roles which is especially important in the early phase of therapy is that of teacher. Therapists do teach. They teach the client how to use therapy, and they may teach other skills as well. Clients usually expect this kind of teaching and are justifiably suspicious of a therapist who refuses to give it—they wonder why the therapist is withholding information that would help them do what they need to do. Looked at in another way, we always teach our clients; if we don't do it explicitly it will happen implicitly. Combs says: "Counselors, whether they recognize the role or not, teach by who they are, what they are, and by the ways they use themselves as instruments in the therapeutic process. These effects are inevitable" (1989, p. 75). Let us look, then, at some of the kinds of teaching that a therapist may choose to engage in early in the therapy process and how best to do them.

HOW TO TALK

Bernard Steinzor, in his book *The Healing Partnership,* quotes a new client's description of a previous therapy experience: "Most of the time I was hearing something like ' tell me about your parents,' which I found very abstract. It meant almost nothing at all to me. I think maybe you will have to help me somehow…to know how to talk about it" (1967, p. 68). Steinzor was fortunate in having a client who was articulate about his not knowing, able to communicate his difficulties in understanding how to use talking as a tool for growth. More often, clients think they know what they are supposed to talk about and are confused when we ask them questions that don't fit their expectations. Or they feel embarrassed or defensive about not understanding what is expected of them and try to cover up. They touch briefly on this and that or go into lengthy detail; they flounder; often they retreat into silence. They have not had the opportunity to learn what kind of talking is most likely to lead to change; they are locked into old patterns of accusing, complaining, or self-blame. They talk about others or describe incidents mechanically, as if they themselves were somehow not there. The therapist struggles to find the person behind the words, to make contact with the feelings and the needs that go with the content. It is tempting to get frustrated and angry with such clients, to label them defensive, resistant, or not really interested in changing. Rather than blaming them, though, it is well to find out if they simply need to be taught some other ways of talking about themselves.

One way to teach is to give direct instructions or ask direct questions: "What were you feeling right then?" Be aware, though, that some clients may not know how to respond even to such a direct question. "Why is my therapist asking this?" he wonders. "What kind of feeling does she mean? Didn't I just tell her? How can I give her what she wants when I don't even know what it is?" Inexperienced clients, unaccustomed to exploring their internal space, are likely to confuse thinking with feeling, and when asked what they are feeling, they will give you their thoughts: "How did you feel when that happened?" "I felt that they shouldn't have treated me that way." Don't suggest that your client has given you the wrong answer when he does this; just follow up with a more explicit question: "And, believing that they shouldn't have treated you like that, were you more mad, or sad, or what?" Later, when your relationship is on a firmer footing, you may want to point out that thinking and feeling are different and that the word *that* (as in "I feel/felt *that*") almost always introduces a thought.

A less directive method of teaching is that of selective attention. The therapist can attend to the personal response component of what a client is saying. She can respond by reflecting the feeling tone which appears to underlie the content of his story, and this conveys permission for and interest in further exploration of those feelings. Similarly, she can focus on and ask about the client's behavior or thoughts as he blames or sympathizes or worries about someone else. From a behaviorist point of view, she reinforces the client (by her interest and attention) for certain kinds of talking and withholds reinforcement for other kinds. Since people learn to continue doing those things for which they are reinforced, selective attention can be a very powerful teaching device. Beware, though: the principle operates whether you want it to or not. If you inadvertently get caught up in a long and fruitless digression, or if you overrespond to nonproductive client behavior out of some needs or fears of your own, you will inevitably be teaching that client to continue in the same way.

Modeling appropriate client behavior, if it is not overused, can also be a good teaching strategy: "If I had been in that situation, I think I would have felt..." "As I listen to you tell me about that, I feel sad." The danger is that such statements shift the focus from client to therapist and may also suggest to the client that the therapist's reaction is the proper one, the one a "normal" person ought to have. Be sure to use such self-disclosing statements sparingly and notice whether the client responds by exploring his own responses more deeply or by closing down (probably because he thinks there is something wrong with his own feelings) or becoming more interested in you than in himself.

Finally, just as with learning any other new skill, clients need to know that it's okay to be a beginner, not to know exactly how to do this, to make mistakes and go back and try again. Your quiet, patient, nonverbal support will be helpful here, as long as you are careful that your silence does not become patronizing or inquisitorial. You can also normalize the client's difficulties: "It's really hard when you don't know how to describe what's going on inside." "Lots of people have trouble getting started." "Sometimes when you first begin to talk about everything, you don't even know what you think or how you feel." And the permissions, too, can be explicit; you can suggest that the client take a minute to think about how he is feeling or what he wants and then tell you about what that was like, or that he go ahead and "say it wrong" and then go back and fix it if he wants to.

A COMMON VOCABULARY

Every therapist creates her own set of favorite verbal tools, words and phrases which she has found particularly useful to describe the concepts she uses in therapy. Some of these are based on her theoretical background. Behavior modifiers think about stimulus and response and base lines; neurolinguistic programmers may mention minimal cues or fuzzy functions; transactional analysts talk of ego states and script beliefs. Too much jargon, of course, hinders therapy. It insists that the client learn your language, rather than you learning his. Some teaching of terminology, on the other hand, can make things go more smoothly. Not only do the words provide a quick and easy reference to important ideas, but also the very teaching process can focus the client's attention on patterns and behaviors that he may not otherwise have noticed.

There may even be a special vocabulary that develops between therapist and client, unique to that relationship. Such vocabularies provide shortcuts in communication as well as reaffirming the specialness of the relationship. This is particularly likely to happen if metaphor and simile are frequently a part of the therapeutic process. My client whose depression is black, like a heavy black ball in her chest, can talk about her "black ball" in perfect confidence that we both know in intricate detail what that phrase means. David Grove has developed a detailed method for teaching clients to create metaphors of this sort and use them as healing devices (personal communication, 1990). As the metaphors are developed and referred to in later sessions, they evoke a rich recall of the original work and a sense of the continuity and directedness of the whole therapeutic relationship.

Early in treatment, you will need to check back many times with clients to find out if the words you and they are using mean the same things to both of you. To the degree that it is comfortable, learn to use your client's vocabulary; but do not use speech patterns and words that are alien and will sound awkward and phony coming from you. Respect his linguistic boundaries as well: avoid words that might be offensive to him or that he is unlikely to understand. Do, though, give the client a chance to learn and use those concepts of yours that may be useful for him. Introduce new vocabulary in a straightforward way, with clear definitions and examples (if possible, from the client's own experience), so that he can learn what they mean without feeling ignorant or foolish for not knowing already. You will both be the richer from learning from each other, and your common vocabulary serves as one more strand in the bond of rapport that is growing between you.

SKILL BUILDING

Skills to be learned in therapy come in at least two varieties. One is the set of skills to be used in the therapy hour itself; the other consists of new behaviors which will be used in the client's life, replacing old, dysfunctional ones. In reality, most skills turn out to be useful in both arenas. The outside-of-therapy changes may be practiced and used during the therapy session, and many of the activities of the therapy hour can turn out to be quite useful in everyday life.

One of the most fundamental skills that most clients need to learn is that of monitoring their own behavior. Surprisingly often, people simply do not notice what they are doing or thinking or feeling. Some will be alert and sensitive in one area and quite cut off in another. Others will confuse what is going on, will mistake thoughts for feelings (we've already mentioned this one) or will project their own internal behavior onto others or assume that other people's reactions are their own. And still others will become confused and inarticulate whenever they are asked to talk about themselves; they can describe or analyze others, can talk about what they see and hear outside themselves, but they don't know about looking inward.

Learning how to observe oneself is a significant, if not necessary, precursor to change. It is very hard to do things differently if you do not notice when and how you are doing them now. Even if changes do occur in such unobserved behaviors—accidentally, or as a spinoff of other more conscious changes—they are less likely to last if the client does not notice them. Clients need to learn to be sensitive to their internal and external responses, to separate their own reactions from those of others, and to differentiate among the different aspects of their own behavior in order to make and to keep the kinds of changes that they want.

Closely related to self-monitoring is the ability to relax. Many clients cannot relax because they have not learned to recognize when and how they are tense. For such clients, self-observation leads to awareness of the need for relaxation skills. Others know that they are tense but do not know what to do about it. Here the concern about tension may preclude other kinds of self-monitoring so that relaxation training would logically precede training in behavioral awareness. Teaching clients to slow down, attend to their breathing, focus awareness on body processes, and practice progressive muscle relaxation can facilitate other therapeutic work, and it can also provide a useful tool in coping with the bustle of everyday life. Teaching relaxation techniques is commonplace in behavior therapy; it is increasingly done in other therapeutic settings as well. It is appropriate to do such teaching during the early phase of therapy so that the client can use the skills he has learned as he moves into later phases of his work.

Another important set of skills has to do with communication. Many clients come to therapy sadly deficient in communication skills. They do not know how to express themselves clearly, nor do they know how to listen. Learning to say what one means has obvious benefits for therapy (and for life!); learning to listen well has equally obvious utility. Lack of skill in communication is so common that a whole network of classes, workshops, seminars, and the like have sprung up to meet the need for such training. It has even become a topic for humor. George Carlin once remarked that he was sick of hearing about people not being able to communicate: "If they can't communicate, I wish they'd shut up about it!" The inability to talk or to listen well, though, is a serious matter and should be attended to. You may teach the client yourself, or you may choose to refer him elsewhere for this kind of skill building. Your decision will be based on considerations of how else you would rather use your time (practice in communication may be a very helpful structure to use during an early rapport-building period) and what the client's level of readiness is (clients who are very disturbed or discouraged may simply not be open to a group training approach). However it is accomplished, communication training is a highly appropriate adjunct to the early phase of therapy.

HOW TO BE A CLIENT

As therapists, we come to recognize rather quickly that some kinds of client behaviors are likely to be therapeutically useful, while others generally lead to frustration and wheel spinning. Talking about what other people ought to do differently is the classic example of a nonprofitable therapeutic occupation. There are other behaviors which may be useful for some clients and not for others: the client who habitually hides his feelings behind a smoke screen of words may benefit from some silent, internal processing, for instance, while a shy and withdrawn client may need to learn to talk more freely.

You, the therapist, are likely to have a sense of what the client needs to do long before the client does. Part of your teaching job is to teach him how to use therapy or how to be a client. You do this in two ways: by attending and responding to the most therapeutically useful portion of every communication and by directing his attention to those topics and behaviors that he may be avoiding or overlooking. If he brings something up again and again, of course, you must attend to it—it is significant to him, whether you think it especially relevant or not. Here, you will help him to find new ways to look at that recurring theme: what he would be thinking about if he weren't preoccupied with this, for instance, or asking himself what it is that makes this so important to him.

Learning what to talk about in therapy, and how, is in essence learning to focus on change. After all, the purpose of therapy is change, growth, making things different than they have been. As you help a client to acquire this kind of focus, you are engaging in a kind of contracting process. Together, you and the client are building a contract to work toward new behaviors, new ways of being in the world. While contract building does involve teaching on the part of the therapist, it is important enough to deserve a section of this chapter all to itself.

CONTRACTING FOR CHANGE

Making a therapeutic contract is an integral part of some therapeutic approaches. For others it is an optional attachment. It is safe to say that, as the marketplace continues to demand briefer and briefer periods of time for therapy, the use of therapeutic contracts will become increasingly widespread. In the next few pages I shall be describing an approach to contracting which I have found useful in my own practice. As you read, be aware that this is only one way to deal with the topic; you will undoubtedly develop variations of your own which will fit your personal style just as mine fits for me.

WHAT IS A THERAPEUTIC CONTRACT?

"Psychotherapy," says Plutchik, "implicitly or explicitly deals with one or more of five fundamental questions. These are: 1. Who am I? 2. How did I get to be me? 3. What rewards do I get out of being me? 4. What do I want to become (or change to)? 5. How can I reach this goal?" (1990, p. 28). In its most basic sense, a therapeutic contract simply spells out which of these questions is/are to be dealt with, how it/they will be dealt with, and what end result is to be sought. The contract, then, is a statement of goals, together with how these goals are to be reached. Sounds pretty straightforward, right?

But problems begin to raise their nasty heads very quickly. Just specifying goals can be tricky: we've already talked about the fact that some clients don't know exactly what they want, others change their minds midstream, and some aren't willing to plunge into their major concern until they've had a chance to check things out. How do you specify goals with a client who can't or won't tell you what his real goals are? My solution to the dilemma is twofold. First, I assume that the contract-building process is an ongoing one. I expect goals to shift and change, and an early portion of each therapy session is devoted to updating our contracts and evaluating our progress. Second, I consider "getting a workable contract" to be a perfectly valid therapeutic goal early in treatment. Spending several hours sorting through the client's wants and needs, exploring where it hurts, and choosing the best place to dig in and get to work is time well spent. It is all too easy to assume that you know what a client wants or needs and begin to "help" him to achieve it, only to discover some weeks down the road that you have been working at cross-purposes and he isn't interested in that at all.

There are, of course, many instances in which a counselor may have a sense of some issue that her client will need to deal with, some change that the client can benefit from making, before the client himself understands or accepts that need. I may conclude that a codependent client will have to extricate himself from a toxic relationship, or that a hostile and antagonistic client will need to develop a different communication style, some time before the client himself reaches that conclusion. But these are means, paths, to a mutually agreed-upon end goal: a more satisfying home life, better social relationships, a more solid sense of self-esteem. Explicit agreement upon the end goal is the critical factor, and it is this end goal which is the focus of therapeutic contracting. Once the desired end state is specified, a diversity of paths to that end can be explored, along with the barriers that the client has encountered in the past as he has tried and failed to reach it. "How is it not working now?" or "What gets in your way?" are questions that can help the client begin to understand and move toward making necessary—and often initially quite difficult—changes in his ongoing behavior; these questions can only be asked in the context of a clearly formulated therapeutic goal.

PHASES OF THE CONTRACT

In order to understand how a therapeutic contract works, we can think of it as having several steps or phases. There is often overlap among the steps, and clients may double back to redo a previous step before moving on; but the therapist needs to have a clear sense of where she and the client are in the process. The first step is to identify the problem: What isn't right for you? Where does it hurt? Most people find it easier to talk about what they don't want than to say what they would like to have instead, so the "what's wrong" questions tend to be a good starting place.

The second phase of a therapeutic contract involves making a commitment to solve the problem. The client may not yet know what the solution will be, but he must decide that he is, in fact, willing to make a change in his thoughts, feelings, or behaviors in order to make things better for himself. This seems so obvious to us as therapists that we are tempted to take it for granted. We may even feel silly asking the client if he is willing to change something about himself in order to make his life better. Asking—and getting an answer—is important because it underlines the fact that the client will have to make changes. The other people in his life may change in response to his different behaviors, but he will have to make the first moves. It has been said that most clients begin therapy expecting to learn how to get somebody else to change. Even when this is not true, or only partially true, it is still very useful early in treatment to frame the therapy experience as one in which the client himself will be learning to do something different.

Having made the commitment to change, the client is ready to move to phase three: choosing a plan of action related to his goal. Here is where the greatest part of the actual therapeutic work often occurs. Different possibilities are explored, in a variety of ways. Ideas are suggested and discarded; experiments may succeed or fail. Exploring the feelings connected with this or that possible course of action can lead to new avenues, new hypotheses, new subgoals. Often the first two steps are revisited, and a different or additional goal is defined.

A final step, once problem and decision to change and plan are synchronized, is to decide upon a way to evaluate whether or not the contract has been met. The best contracts include an objective criterion for success, so that both therapist and client will know when the work of that particular contract is complete.

Contracting, then, is not just a "get it done and then begin therapy" endeavor. It is an integral part of the process itself, a kind of scaffolding upon which the whole process of therapy is built. A viable therapeutic contract is a developmental process; it is continually negotiated and reviewed throughout the entire course of treatment (Goldberg 1977).

THE *SAFE* CONTRACT

As you work with your clients to develop useful contracts, it may be helpful to remind yourself that the best contracts create a climate of safety. The client feels safer knowing ahead of time exactly what he is trying to achieve and knowing that his therapist has agreed to that goal. The therapist feels safer knowing that the client has been willing to be clear about what he expects to get out of therapy— that even though those goals may change, at least there is a common starting point. Moreover, just working together to get a treatment contract has given each participant a chance to find out how the other one works. It is no longer a matter of entering into a relationship with a stranger.

The idea of "safety" also provides us with an acronym for the qualities that we try to build into our therapy contracts: Specificity, Awareness, Fairness, and Efficacy. Let's take a look at each of these in turn.

The more *specific* a set of goals can be, the better the chances of achieving them. Help your client to use operational terms, to define therapeutic success in ways that can be observed by others. What will his friends and family see and hear that will be different, once he has successfully completed his work? If the desired changes are internal (I'll be happier, less fearful, more in touch with my feelings), what difference will that make in his life? It is entirely appropriate, by the way, for you to express some confusion if a client insists that he wants to make significant internal changes but that these changes will result in absolutely no observable differences in his behavior. If the changes are truly significant, how can they possibly not show—in any way—on the outside?

Awareness has to do with the client's full understanding of the implications of his entering treatment. As fully as is feasible, he should know what kind of methods the therapist will use and what belief structure underlies those methods. You may want to suggest a book or an article he can read if he wants to know more about your approach to therapy. He should know that there will be down times as well as up times, times when things seem to be getting worse instead of better; he should know that family members and friends may not always be supportive of the changes he will need to make. The more aware he is of what he is getting into, the more he will be able to commit himself to the contract and to the process of working it through. Says Morrison: "To get the client's full consent it is usually necessary to outline the methods used, the theory behind the techniques, and the possible side effects (positive and negative)....I know that I personally would not become a client...unless I knew an awful lot about this process" (1987, p. 15).

Being aware of all the "fine print" in the contract means that the contract— and the process used to get it—can be *fair*. The relationship can be balanced, in the sense that both parties have enough information to make sure that they are getting their money's worth, their energy's worth, their time's worth, their caring's worth.

And, finally, the best therapy contracts involve leaving the client with a sense of *efficacy*. No matter how sure the therapist may be of what a client needs, it is seldom good practice to simply tell him what to do. Putting aside the (horrid) truth that sometimes the client really does know himself better than we do, it is also important that he leave therapy with a sense that he no longer needs us, that he can go ahead on his own. The best way to achieve this is to keep it in mind from the beginning. The more he is in charge of the therapy and can experience successful choice and decision making all along, the more naturally that sense of efficacy will emerge.

So there you have it: specificity, awareness, fairness, and efficacy, the four ingredients of a good therapeutic contract.

BUILDING A CONTRACT

It is very well to describe a good contract and talk about the importance of letting the client help to build it—but how, exactly, do we go about it? Muriel James has developed a series of questions which form a handy outline or framework for the contract-building process (1977, pp. 106–107). First, she asks the client, "Is there anything you want that would enhance your life?" Few of us can resist the open-endedness of this question; it invites us to look at what we really want to have and to change. It also points in a positive direction, focusing on what we do want, how we would like things to be, rather than on how awful things are now.

Having described his ideal situation, the client is next asked, "What would you need to change in order to get what you want?" If the client says that someone else must change—wife must do thus and such, children or boss or friends must behave differently—the question is restated: "Well, unless they come in for treatment, we are not likely to change them. Are there any changes *you* could make in yourself that would enhance your life?" The client may then begin to look at things he could do for himself or at things he could do to get others to change. If he does the latter, it is important to focus the contract on his own changes. Do not make success contingent on someone else's behavior. "I could start asking my wife directly rather than hinting around for what I want" is a good beginning for a contract, provided that the contract is defined as successful whether or not the wife meets the request.

The next question is often an eye-opener, even though it seems on the surface to be very similar to the preceding one: "What would you be *willing to do* to effect the change?" Many clients are surprised by their own reluctance to make the first move or by their desire to be given a magical solution at this point. Others are excited by the idea that they can begin right now to bring about the changes they want. Still others begin to realize how they defeat themselves by deciding ahead of time that whatever they try will not work, how they set themselves up to stay stuck in their old, pain-producing patterns.

Once the client has decided what he is willing to do first, he is asked, "How will other people know when the change has been made?" This question not only helps to make the contract a safe one for him, as we discussed earlier, but it also makes it possible for him to pause and congratulate himself when he completes a forward step. It can also provide cues for reinforcements for his new behaviors from other important people in his life. "My wife will see that I'm not raiding the refrigerator every night" can be a springboard to a decision to ask the wife to reinforce the change by telling the client that she has noticed or by giving him a hug.

The last (and perhaps the most important) question is, "How might you sabotage yourself?" As the client describes the banana peels that he might throw in the way of carrying out his contract, he inoculates himself against such self-defeating behavior. He may recognize that the sabotage is a pattern, repeated many times in the past, and move to a contracting focus that will deal explicitly with a change in that pattern. He may also discover the emotional underlay, the fear or anger or grief that has helped to maintain his unproductive behaviors over the years.

Each of James's questions can precipitate useful therapeutic work, work that may well extend beyond a single session. Often getting a contract, or a series of contracts, constitutes the major part of the therapeutic treatment. At other times, dealing with the whys and hows of contracts that fail turns out to be the focal point of therapy. In either case, using James's model of contract building can be an excellent way of maintaining direction, of continuing to move the client toward getting what he came for and making the changes he wants in his life.

A FEW LAST WORDS

Under the best of circumstances, developing a therapeutic contract can run into snags. Some of the problems are truly insoluble, and we just have to make the best compromise we can. Take the whole area of awareness, for example—the "A" in the SAFE contract. Realistically, no naive client can possibly be aware ahead of time of what therapy will be like or of what demands will be made upon him or of precisely what will happen to him as a result of treatment. He is venturing into unexplored territory, and even the therapist cannot predict in detail what the journey or the journey's end will be like. And even that which the therapist *can* predict with some degree of certainty cannot all be explained or described to him; it would use up valuable time and might set up expectations which would interfere with the therapeutic process. Thompson, discussing the issue of informed consent, says that "one major problem with including everything in the contract that the client and therapist 'should' discuss and agree on before beginning counseling or therapy is that there is simply too much to communicate meaningfully, much less negotiate at that point" (1990, p. 22). So we compromise—we explain and describe as much as we can, until we reach a point of diminishing return. We are careful to deal with the issues that this particular client brings up, as well as those which we think may turn out to be particularly important to him. We avoid the use of technical terms and complex concepts that would get in the way of his understanding. In short, we do the best we can and stand ready to take responsibility for and to correct any misunderstandings that may come to light later.

And what about the client who is, either consciously or unconsciously, untruthful about what he wants to accomplish in therapy? The client who won't take the risk of revealing his real concern until he's had a chance to check this therapist out? The client who can't yet admit even to himself what he's most in pain about? The client who chooses to blame someone else for his behavior? How can we build a viable contract with a client who isn't being straight with us? Again, compromise. Build the best one you can, with the information you have. Build the best you can around the goals that the client is willing to accept right now.

Because neither therapist nor client can know for sure exactly what will emerge in the course of treatment, therapeutic contracts must be built flexibly; they must allow for adjusting to the unexpected. Crown (1989) warns that a lack of flexibility, a premature crystallization of therapeutic goals, is the most common mistake made in the contract-building phase of therapy. Here again we see the conflict, as the need to be specific, behavioral, and accountable collides with the need to be flexible, adaptive, and creative. This dilemma, though, does have a sort of "back door" solution: build in an expectation that the contract may be renegotiated throughout therapy. Therapeutic contracts are living things, not petrified things; like any other living thing they grow and evolve. As your client changes, he will outgrow some of his subcontracts and grow into the need for new ones.

LIMITS

In the early phase of therapy, client and therapist together are learning to use time in a curious way: they are learning how to be intensely involved in the Now, aware of what is happening within and between them; and to use that Now as a means to access both the past (in order to discover what has gone wrong and make it right) and the future (in order to predict and plan for what will happen next). It is in this latter context—predicting and planning what will happen next—that limit setting is important.

Many clients—most, perhaps, of those who become deeply involved in the therapeutic process—can be expected to test the therapist's limits at some time during the course of therapy. This is not necessarily a conscious testing; it is simply part of what needs to happen as one learns new ways of being and interacting with others. Being with a therapist is literally an experiment in living. It is with her that the client explores what is acceptable, permitted, needed in healthy social interactions. Creating a safe environment in which to do this testing is one of the major responsibilities of the therapist. And part of what makes it safe to test limits in therapy is *having* limits to test: clear, firm boundaries that one can explore and push and pull at without fear of being rejected or abandoned.

Each therapist needs to know for herself exactly what her limits are, what she can expect of herself, and where she will draw the lines of involvement with and service to her clients. Beginning therapists find it especially easy to get sucked into giving more and more to a needy or demanding client; knowing ahead of time what you will and will not do helps you to be clear about your degree of involvement without feeling guilty for saying no, or feeling resentful over having been conned into providing more than you had intended. Clients need to be told early in treatment what they can expect from the therapist, so that they have clear permission to use that therapist to the fullest and at the same time know what they will not be allowed to do or demand.

Among the most frequently tested limits are those of time. I make it clear to my clients that they are expected to be on time for their appointments and to let me know well in advance if they must cancel a session. Sessions end at the scheduled time, even if the client was late. I am not willing to punish myself for a client's tardiness. Appointments missed without advance notice are to be paid for. I impose the same limits on myself: I am on time for my appointments, and I give ample notice if I must reschedule a session. Occasionally I make a scheduling error; when that happens, I reimburse the client for his lost time and inconvenience.

Having set limits around time, it is important to respect them. Tacking an extra ten minutes on the end of an hour, to make up for the client being late by that much, tells the client that the therapist is willing for him to be late and will, in fact, penalize herself to help him continue that pattern. Similarly, providing extra time, extra sessions, or frequent phone check-ins (unless these have been clearly contracted for) is not helpful to a client who needs to deal with his own issues around living with limits. Therapists who find themselves frequently on overtime with clients would do well to question their own motivation, their own need to please or rescue or prove themselves.

As for behavior during the therapy hour, I have found it useful to begin by setting just two absolute limits: (l) the client may not hurt either himself or me; and

(2) anything that he breaks, he will be expected to pay for. Beyond this, we may need to negotiate if either of us engages in behaviors that get in the way of the work, and we will deal with these if and when they become a problem. Stating the rules in this way startles a lot of clients; it had never occurred to them that they might want to hurt someone or break something. The surprise effect can be beneficial in itself; it underscores the notion that this therapy stuff really is different from other kinds of relationships. If those are the only two things I cannot do in here, what in the world *will* I do?

Depending on your own personal style and your theoretical orientation, you may impose additional constraints on your or the client's behavior. Some therapists, for instance, will not physically touch a client or allow a client to touch them. Some have a particular chair they want to sit in, or a particular chair (or couch) for the client. Whatever your limits and ground rules are, the first and most important thing is to clarify them for yourself. The second is to share them with your client. And the third is to hold to them, unless you have a clear therapeutic reason for making a change.

Spelling out limits like this may feel awkward at first, but it is important that they be stated, and stated explicitly, from the start. You can soften the statements by prefacing them with some sort of introduction: "There are a few things I require of all my clients" or "There are only two rules for how you use your time here at the clinic." But spell them out one way or another. You may never need to bring them up again, but if you do need to, you will be very glad that you laid the groundwork earlier.

Of course, different clients may need different sorts of limits. What is hurtful to one may be helpful to another. Dryden comments that "counsellors who can appropriately vary their style of interaction and the power base in which such styles are rooted, are more likely to be more successful at initiating a therapeutic alliance than counsellors who use only one style of interaction and a single power base and expect their clients to adjust accordingly" (1989, p. 4). The "power base" again relates to how we define and maintain limits, and this will vary according to client needs. The rule of not hurting oneself in therapy may be extended and elaborated upon in many different ways. To a rebellious teenager, the therapist may say, "It's not good for you to come in and be angry week after week with no sense of how you want to change that behavior, and I'm not willing to support you in continuing to do that." The don't-hurt-yourself rule might be invoked in a different way with another client: "When you refuse to share your feelings with me, or even to let yourself know what those feelings are, you are following the same pattern that gets you into trouble with your wife and your friends. If you aren't willing to work toward changing that behavior, then I can't help you." In other words, the rule that the client may not hurt himself or the therapist goes beyond physical injury; it includes all sorts of behaviors which get in the way of positive change. Neither the client nor the therapist may know what these specific behaviors are when the initial rules are laid out; it is the therapist's responsibility to clarify, explain, and insist that protective limits be respected as the problem behaviors emerge.

As the therapist sets and maintains limits with her client, she demonstrates her respect for both his welfare and her own. She will not allow him to discount his own needs or values; nor will she herself be discounted. To do otherwise invites him, in the long run, to feel guilty, one-up, or cheated of the protection he needs— any of which will ultimately interfere with his treatment.

CONCLUSIONS

There is much more that could be said about the early phase of therapy. We could list typical presenting problems or describe the many ways that clients approach the idea of therapy. We could talk about how people get stuck and stay stuck, how they are frightened or hurt or angry and, because of their pain, fail to discover more comfortable ways of behaving. We could describe the frustrating moments and the triumphant ones, the times when the therapist feels she could cure the world and the times when she wonders why she did not go into some other line of work (like painting doorknobs, for instance).

These are the things that you will discover for yourself. You will learn what to expect in your early sessions with clients, and you will learn that you can never predict everything, that there are always surprises. Most important, you will learn that you can cope with the job, that you can handle the demands that therapy makes, and that you can even survive your own errors.

About the time you are beginning to believe all of this, you will discover that one of your clients has moved out of that now-familiar early stage and has entered (snuck in, really) a different phase of treatment. Middle-phase work is different from early-phase work, and so you will feel new and strange again for a while. When that happens, one way to take care of yourself is to review all that you do know about providing therapy; by now, that is quite a lot. And another thing you can do is learn more about the middle phase. That is what the next chapter of this book is about.

THE MIDDLE PHASE   5

Of all the chapters in this book, the one on middle-phase work has been the most difficult to write. Not because middle-phase work is so difficult (though it certainly can be), but because it varies so much from one client to another and from one therapeutic orientation to another. No matter what is said here, it will be an inaccurate representation of what some very good therapists do with some of their clients. Early-phase work with clients, like termination work, often falls into a fairly predictable pattern; middle-phase work is seldom patterned and seldom predictable. Because it grows out of a unique and intimate interaction between two individuals—client and therapist—it cannot be neatly wrapped or mapped.

The therapist has two primary responsibilities during middle-phase work, and at first glance they may seem contradictory. The first responsibility is to follow the client's lead and trust in his innate capacity to learn and to grow and to do the work he needs to do. We must be sensitive, flexible, tolerant of ambiguity. The client must be allowed to find his own way, to create his own growth; we can't do his growing for him. But our second responsibility is to keep the work focused and on target, to help the client avoid wandering off on tangents, spinning his wheels, or getting bogged down in irrelevancies. Now how can we manage both of these tasks?

The apparent contradiction is resolved when we realize that our clients operate at many levels and can move in many directions at once. For both client and therapist, one of the signals of middle-phase work may be a sense of confusion, of muddledness, of not really knowing what is going on. The therapist needs to be able to step back from the muddle far enough to sense the overall direction in which the work is proceeding and to invite the client to explore material which will further that overall direction.

Contributing to the confusion of middle-phase work is the frequent discovery that the problems which first brought the client to therapy are well on their way to being solved. Life isn't perfect—far from it—but things are better, and the client has a sense of how to keep himself on track. Many clients will terminate therapy at this point: they got what they came for; they are satisfied; they are done. Often with a sense of regret for possibilities not realized, and a nagging certainty that they will be back again in a few months or years, the therapist bids them farewell. Others, however, want more. Even though the immediate problems do not loom as large as before, these clients sense that there is more to be learned, more growing to be done. They are not content with chopping off the tops of their weed garden; they want to dig out the roots. A new contract is in order, one that includes a shift from external problem solving to internal growing and changing. Emotional issues begin to take precedence over cognitive ones, and the therapeutic relationship itself is often the arena in which these issues are worked through.

The shift from early- to middle-phase work, then, is marked by a shift from primarily cognitive concerns to an emphasis on emotional work, from focusing on external to focusing on internal events, from looking at relationships outside of therapy to experiencing relationships within the therapy session itself. Theoretically it makes sense, but often it is not nearly as clear-cut as I have made it seem. We cannot always tell just which phase a client is in. Even when he seems to have entered, worked through, and left a particular phase, he may do the same sorts of things again when he moves on to deal with a new problem. "Often the work proceeds in fits and starts (and often does not seem to be proceeding at all, but rather unraveling or working backward). The 'typical' case is in fact quite atypical" (Wachtel 1982, p. xiii).

When you stop to think about it, there is no particular reason why anyone should progress evenly from phase to phase. Your client has a number of external problems which might readily be dealt with in Phase 1. He has some internal issues which involve typical middle-phase work. As he deals with some of the early material, his sense of trust in the therapeutic relationship grows. He experiences a new kind of being-with-another, and he uses that experience and that trust to begin to work with some internal (Phase 2) issues. Later, he may go back to rework some of the earlier material from a different perspective, or he may return to a Phase 1-type stance with regard to a new set of problems. He may run into a particularly scary or painful spot in his middle-phase work and regress in the relationship as a way of staying safe or keeping control. Or he may choose to deal with less threatening material or to slow down and not open up new areas for a while. All of these are normal and appropriate shifts over the course of therapy.

We should not expect or demand that a client, once involved in middle-phase work, continue to work at that level. The permission to shift, to change, to draw back as well as to move forward, is an important factor in the client's growing and changing. It is hard to give that permission when you are feeling frustrated yourself, impatient, perhaps questioning whether some error of yours is getting in the way of the work. "One way the therapist may maintain control of personal feelings," says Wolberg, "is to anticipate setbacks in all patients. No patient will be able to acquire new patterns overnight. Each patient has a personal rate of learning which may not be accelerated by any technical tricks" (1988, p. 820). Reminding yourself of this, remembering that you don't have to "grow" the client but that your job is to foster his growing himself, at his own pace, will help you give genuine support to his need to move more slowly or to temporarily pull away from some facets of his work.

THE RELATIONSHIP AS A CHANGE AGENT

Nearly all clients who reach the middle phase of therapy are contact deprived in one way or another. Either they have few close relationships or those they do have are distorted or unhealthy. Because of this social deprivation, they have developed inaccurate and unhealthy ways of understanding others and understanding themselves. The relationship with you, the therapist, is a place where your client can begin to repair those distortions, to build a sense of confidence in himself and of trust in others. Simply by being an honest, open human being who values this client as another human worthy of your respect and concern, you lay the foundation for a kind of being-with-another that may be unique in his experience. "It is important to realize that, irrespective of the depth and the real worth of the healing measures that are being employed, improvement may be sustained in some instances for an indefinite period as a pure product of the relationship" (Wolberg 1988, p. 31).

It sounds so straightforward and simple. But it isn't. You see, at the same time as the client wants to be a part of this new kind of relationship—senses, perhaps, how healing it will be for him—he is also acutely aware that this is new and dangerous ground. He may have allowed himself to get close to people before and gotten badly hurt as a result. Or he may have been keeping his distance for years, for as long as he can remember, until wariness and defensiveness are second nature to him. It's a push-pull kind of thing: part of him wants to open up, to be known, to trust; but another part wants to pull back and protect himself. Combs sums up the client's conflict nicely:

> The goal of counseling [is] change in self-concept, and the basic need of the organism [is] maintenance and enhancement of the self. So, the need of the organism is to maintain its integrity at all costs while the goal of counseling is to facilitate its change. This creates a delicate dilemma for therapy. The self is the client's reality, her most precious possession, to be protected from threat when under attack and embellished whenever that seems feasible. Therapy must, therefore, find ways to circumvent the negative effects of threat. [1989, p. 59]

The boundary between the need to maintain and the desire to change is exactly the point at which the therapist must position herself in order to take full advantage of the tension inherent in this push-pull situation. The client is invited to use the here-and-now relationship as a laboratory, something that can be explored and experimented with. It's right here, right in the room with us; we don't have to depend on anyone else's description or analysis of it: "What is it like for you to hear me say that?" "How do you feel toward me right now?" "A minute ago I felt annoyed with you—did you notice?" The therapist models personal openness and invites the client to do the same. With each risk taken and survived comes courage to take the next one, and so the relationship—and the client—begin to grow.

Combs suggests that therapists systematically review their relationship-fostering behavior during or after each session, asking themselves what, specifically, may have gotten in the way of the client's moving more deeply into the therapy process. When the barriers have been identified, the therapist can move to deal with them. If they are barriers within the client, their identification may point toward important subgoals of the therapy. If they are in the therapeutic environment, or within the therapist, it is her responsibility to get whatever help she may need to eliminate them.

There is another factor that enters into this business of the therapeutic relationship, though, one that is as important as it is complex. As the client allows himself to become more and more engaged in the therapy process, and to become more and more vulnerable, he comes to experience the therapist in new and different ways. He begins to feel toward the therapist as he has felt toward other important people in his life and to expect—even demand—that the therapist deal with him as those other people did or should have done. This is the phenomenon of *transference*, and it is both a curse and a blessing in therapy. It is a curse because it gets in the way of genuine relationship: it's difficult to be real and contactful with someone who cannot experience you as you are but keeps pasting someone else's face on you instead. But it is a blessing because it allows the client to reexperience those old relationships in new ways. The therapist, standing in for mother or father or teacher or what-have-you, refuses to interact in the old maladaptive fashion. She refuses to meet the client's expectations. And, faced with this refusal, the client must learn new patterns to replace the old ones that don't fit any more.

As Tracey points out, working through the transference is anything but a smooth, cooperative venture. It is filled with conflict, as the client tries harder and harder to get the therapist to meet his expectations, while the therapist steadfastly refuses to do so. "It is this conflict stage that results in change in the client. The more the counselor does not act according to the client's definition, the more the client will increase his or her influence attempts to bring the relationship back to where it was" (1989, p. 65)—or, rather, to where he feels it ought to be. Only when these efforts have been soundly defeated will the client's expectations begin to shift.

Working through the transference, then, presents a constant challenge to the therapist. Clients are highly skilled in manipulating others so that history will repeat itself. It's not that they do it "on purpose"; rather, these self-defeating social maneuvers are literally the only way they know how to interact with people who stand in the role of significant others from the past. To behave any other way would feel dangerous, wrong, impossible!

From the therapist's point of view, the client's transference behavior often feels like a constant series of tests. The client asks for information that he can't have or asks for a favor that will be difficult or inconvenient to grant. He may tell the therapist a "secret" that the therapist will have difficulty handling. He puts himself down, or boasts about himself, or tells clumsy untruths that the counselor can't help seeing through. He may question the therapist's competence or motivation. Emotionally, his behavior may be like that of a child: he may sulk, rage, or sit helplessly. Through it all, the therapist must remember that she herself is not the true target; she is standing in for some important person(s) and in doing so is giving this client a chance to work through what could not be dealt with properly in the original relationship.

EMOTIONAL WORK

Problem solving—figuring things out—is useful. Together with relationship building, problem solving is one of the major activities of the early phase of therapy. As we move into the middle phase, however, we move into the period of personality change. Not only is the client figuring out how to deal with his world, he is learning and experiencing new ways to react, to feel, literally new ways to *be*. Understanding the old patterns is no longer the immediate goal. "Knowing the initiation of a pattern is not sufficient to produce therapeutic change—just as knowing what pushed a stone over a cliff is not sufficient to stop its fall" (Bugental 1987, p. 158). In order for change to occur at this level, he must experience the new patterns; most often, such experiencing takes place in the context of feelings. The client allows himself, because he trusts the relationship, to let go of his old defenses. He opens himself to emotions and sensations and memories which he had previously walled off or distorted. And he feels different! Sometimes the difference is pleasant, even exhilarating. Not infrequently it is quite frightening: the world is suddenly new, strange, unpredictable. He doesn't know the rules any more, doesn't know what to expect of himself or of others. Wessler and Hankin-Wessler (1990) postulate a kind of emotional set-point, a region of relative comfort and familiarity that each person stays within. When, through therapy or some other intensely emotional experience, we find ourselves outside of that range, we are unconsciously mobilized to go back, back to the old patterns, back where it is safe. Again, it is the therapy relationship which can overcome this tug toward the old and familiar: here, too, is a kind of safety, a freedom to experiment, support for growing and changing and coming alive in a new way.

Middle-phase work, then, involves more than simply examining what is happening now in the client's life and how it may relate to earlier events and behaviors. Talking about how things were with my mother can help me to find my way into this phase; but if I do not ever go beyond simply talking about it, I'll not make many lasting changes in myself. I must somehow reexperience that relationship emotionally and learn at an affective level that it is possible to respond differently. Only then will I be ready to take that learned possibility out into the world of my present-day relationships. As I do so, my new responses create new reactions to me, both from others and in myself. Clients often find that they have worked through one layer of difficulty only to find themselves floundering in a new one. Their changes provide them "relief from one level of dysphoria only to make them aware of other difficulties. Therefore a change may simply develop a new context, a new equilibrium from which future change may be addressed" (Beitman 1987, p. 176). One new experience invites another, which in turn makes a third change possible. Eventually the client may not even have to make an effort to sustain the changes: the world is literally a different place, in which the new responses seem natural and the old would be foreign and out of place. He still may have to work hard to change some old, habitual behaviors, but he will surely notice those behaviors in ways that he never would have been aware of before.

The therapist's first responsibility in the middle phase of therapy is to facilitate this kind of awareness. She must use the relationship she has established with the client to provide protection and permission for the client to relate to her, to himself, and to others in new ways. Consider Bugental's questions in the context of your work with your own clients:

> If our talk continues pretty much as it is now will the client become more deeply immersed or less so? Will he, of his own accord, move to a level at which we can deal more effectively with his issues, or must I intervene in the flow in some way to encourage that movement? In the way he's responding now is there a hint of his being threatened? Do I need to change the way I'm taking part to reduce the possibility that he may withdraw from our involvement? [1987, p. 62]

As therapist responds to client, and client to therapist, each becomes more attuned to the other. There are movements forward and back, changes in tempo, pauses to rest, and surges of growth and high adventure. Through it all the therapist must never lose sight of the client's overall goals. Our clients do not need us to entertain them, to dazzle them with our intuition or our deductive skills, or even to make them feel better. Our purpose is to help them change and grow. Now slowly, now quickly; sometimes sliding backward and sometimes striding forward; occasionally with clear purpose and direction but often with uncertainty and confusion, the client is shaping the way in which he wants to experience his world. When we further that process, we are doing our job.

EMOTION AND DISCOMFORT

Changing oneself—one's reactions, one's feelings, one's interactive style—is generally a very uncomfortable experience. Clients are being invited to move from a familiar, predictable state of affairs into a strange and unpredictable one. Even though that old familiar way of being is causing problems (otherwise, why would they be seeking therapy?), at least it's something they are used to dealing with. Maybe changing would only make things worse! Besides, most people have invested a great deal of effort in persuading themselves that their troubles aren't *really* their fault, that they've just had bad luck or gotten mixed up with people who have treated them badly. What they are looking for is a way to make the world change so that they can feel better and be happier while remaining pretty much the same as they have always been. At some level, of course, they know that this won't work; they know that the pain comes from inside. But how hard it is to acknowledge this, and how hard to summon the courage to do something about it! They want to change, but they're afraid to; they want to stay the same, but it hurts too much. The tension between these conflicting wants brings its own discomfort, its own need for relief. "Advancing into the jagged awkwardness of the tension is difficult but illuminating. It is in this moment that one potential for a corrective emotional experience and initiation of change lies" (Aveline 1987, p. 38). Without the discomfort, there is likely to be no emotional experience; without the emotional experience, change is likely to be superficial and short-lived.

In order to better understand the function of discomfort in therapy, consider how maladaptive responses get learned in the first place. As children (and throughout our lives, for that matter) we learn how to cope with life. We make thousands of choices, develop thousands of expectations. Because some of these learnings occur during times of stress, or when we are not well-informed about all the variables that are operating, they may not represent the best possible choices or decisions or beliefs. They may lead to behavior patterns or feeling reactions that will cause us pain later on. At the time, they are the best we can manage; given our resources, we make the choices and decisions that we believe will work. The point here is that these decisions and choices were often made so as to minimize pain. We learn how to avoid being terrified, how to escape punishment, how not to hope for that which we will not get. We hang on to those patterns because, at some level, we are still protecting ourselves from the same pain. To give up an old protective behavior, or to try a new behavior that we learned in the past might hurt us—why in the world should we do that? There is only one possible reason: we trust that the possible benefits of change may outweigh the possible losses. Notice, again, the sense of tension here: I hope it will be better, but I'm afraid it won't; I want to be different, but I'm scared to give up the protections I need. A major function of the therapeutic relationship is to provide a temporary "protected zone" in which the client can experiment with changes, can expose the parts of himself that are just too vulnerable and take the risks that seem just too dangerous out in the real world. That risk-taking, by definition, has to be an emotional experience; if it were not, it wouldn't be risky.

As we work to provide this protected environment and invite the client to use it therapeutically, we must be careful not to provide him with the same kinds of responses he is used to getting from others. These responses have been a familiar framework within which his old patterns have become stable, tried-and-true, there's-no-other-way-to-be kinds of habits. Instead, we ourselves must begin the process of doing something different. Often our own moment-to-moment emotional response to the client will be a useful guide to what this "something different" might be: our feelings about the client are probably pretty much like other people's feelings toward him and give us reliable information about what he elicits from those others. The experienced therapist will notice her feelings and her impulse to respond according to those feelings; she will then move to a deeper layer of empathy. "What in this client leads him to do or say this thing that I am having feelings about? How do I feel about the underlying, motivating part of him? How can I respond to that underlying part, in a way that will be different from my first reaction?" By reacting to the client in a new way, one which does not fit the old pattern, we shake the framework. We move, as in a game, so as to block the client off from the familiar, forcing him to try something new.

A part of the therapist's task is to help the client to hold anxiety and discomfort at an optimum level, enough to energize and motivate change, but not so much as to scare him irretrievably back into his old patterns or out of therapy altogether. It is almost always easier to talk about a painful experience than to experience the pain, and many clients will defend themselves from the experiencing by emotionally distancing themselves. At the opposite end of the scale, some clients will be so overwhelmed by their distress that they can hardly think at all, but can only feel, endure, wait for something else to happen. Neither of these two conditions allows for growth; optimally, the client is able to experience his pain *and* think about it, in order to discover what it is like to choose to react/believe/be something different. "It is not sufficient to appreciate abstractly that one is the creator of one's own affective experience," say Greenberg and Safran. Nor is it enough just to feel, to suffer passively. "People must actually experience the emotions or desires in question while they are taking responsibility for the experience; only then are they able to become aware of the process—or at least part of it—through which they are constructing that experience" (1990, p. 71). Becoming aware that he is constructing his experiences, learning through doing that he can do that constructing in a different way, gives the client a new set of possibilities. Trying out some of those possibilities in the therapy session, and living through it, paves the way for even greater change, greater risks.

PERMISSION AND PROTECTION

As clients begin to let go of old defenses and allow themselves to experience their feelings in a more immediate and genuine way, they often find themselves dealing with emotions at a level of intensity that is very new and strange for them. Many times, they experience these responses as forbidden, as if they are doing and feeling things that they should not be doing and feeling. The therapist must provide both permission and protection: permission to feel, and feel in new ways; and protection from the kinds of consequences that the client has learned to expect if he does let himself experience those feelings. Without believable permissions and protections from the therapist, the client is unlikely to break through his defensive prohibitions, and without such a breakthrough he will not have the opportunity to discover that it is all right, that he can survive breaking the old taboos and experiencing himself and his world in a new way.

"Therapy is an intimate experience. For people to grow and change they need to be able to allow themselves to become open, which makes them vulnerable. When they are vulnerable, they need protection. It is the therapist's responsibility to create a context in which people feel and are safe" (Satir 1987, p. 21). Simply accepting the client's expression of feelings without getting upset in response to them can go a long way toward providing such a context. If the therapist is not frightened or annoyed or plunged into sadness by what the client shows her, maybe it's okay to show her even more. The client may feel it is safe to peek into the *really* scary places, if there is someone who can be with him and approve of what he's doing and will make sure that he'll be all right doing it. Sometimes calmly and sympathetically reflecting the client's feelings is enough to convey your support and acceptance. At other times it may be useful to provide direct, explicit permission and reassurance: "It's okay to let yourself feel angry about that." "Of course you were scared, and it's natural for you to experience that same kind of scare right now as you talk about it." Some therapists go even further, acting as a sort of modified cheering section: "Stay with what you're feeling... you're doing fine!"

As the client allows himself to dig more and more deeply into his inner experience, he will encounter increasingly archaic material. He will find feelings that have been out of his awareness for years, feelings that have their origins much earlier in his life. Accompanying this archaic material there is usually a sense of neediness, a feeling of being unable to take care of oneself emotionally and of wanting someone to lean on or to be protected by. Dependent feelings are a predictable accompaniment to emotional exploration, and the therapist must accept them, too, as natural and appropriate to the situation. Giving the client permission to feel young or little, and protection while he is doing so, permits him to grow up again in a new way.

The client, of course, may not know that these sorts of feelings are likely to emerge and may feel frightened or guilty about showing them. Clients may castigate themselves for having revealed themselves too deeply to the therapist ("What will you think of me, now that I've shown you all those horrible parts of myself?") or for even having had those unacceptable feelings at all ("I hate to think of myself as being so selfish/cowardly/vicious/etc."). If a client shows signs that he may blame or punish himself in this way, it may be useful to contract with him not to do so: "Are you willing to decide not to beat on yourself for doing the piece of work you have just finished?" "I will help you find a way to express your anger/grief/fear, but first I want you to be very sure that, whatever feelings emerge, you won't use them as an excuse to put yourself down." Having decided at a conscious level to accept his feelings, the client is better prepared to deal with his unconscious resistances and prohibitions in a caring and self-nurturing way.

Clients often have trouble accepting their own wants. Most people believe that it's acceptable to meet their basic survival needs, but surprisingly often they regard themselves as bad or flawed somehow if they want more than that. They may have an unconscious rule that they must not want what they cannot have, or that they shouldn't want things that other people want (or don't want, or that they can't have). The point here is that these unconscious prohibitions also get in the way of the work, causing clients to wall themselves off from their wants or to punish themselves for experiencing frustration when the wants are not met. Again, the therapist's protection and permission oppose such obstructions and invite the client to explore and accept all of himself, even that which he will eventually change or outgrow.

Another situation that often requires explicit permission and protection is the return of previously worked materials. The client may discover anew some pain or discomfort which he thought had been dealt with earlier and experience a great deal of shame or discouragement or guilt that the issue has reemerged. Here the needed permission is to recycle, to deal with old feelings again from a new place. He needs to know that the work will not be the same as before, that he did deal with that issue appropriately for his needs at that time, and that it is natural and growthful to come back to it now. He also needs to know that the therapist's protections are still available, that just because he has been there before he is not now required to handle things on his own.

Perhaps most threatening to therapists, particularly beginning therapists, are those situations in which the client's expression of feeling turns upon the therapeutic relationship itself. The therapist may find herself the target of a client's anger, discover that the client is afraid of her, or that he is sad and disappointed about something she has done. He may become very demanding, determined that the therapist must provide him with the (magical) answers that he is sure she has. Or the intense feeling may be a positive one; clients frequently experience strong sexual feelings toward a therapist or want the therapist to be their best friend outside the therapy relationship. When a client expresses such strong feelings toward you, either positive or negative, it is important to recognize that this is probably a transference reaction, that your relationship with the client is a convenient (and appropriate) vehicle for him to use in exploring old and new responses. Knowing that it is not you personally who has done something to arouse all of this intense feeling helps you to remain calm and accepting and eventually to guide the client to an awareness of how his feelings toward you fit into his whole pattern of behavior.

TO TOUCH OR NOT TO TOUCH

One final issue needs to be mentioned in the context of emotional work, and that is the question of physical closeness between therapist and client. Let me say first that there is never any justification whatsoever for sexual intimacy between people who are in a therapist/client role. No competent or ethical therapist uses clients to meet his or her own sexual needs. It is easy for clients to mistake the emotional closeness and vulnerability that they feel toward a therapist for romantic love, and the therapist who is looking for sexual involvement with clients will have ample opportunity to gratify personal needs. Indeed, it is often difficult to find the most therapeutic way to avoid such involvement. It is also easy for therapists to make the same mistake, to become emotionally confused about the close and caring feelings that they experience toward clients. Because of this danger of confusion of feelings, and because we therapists (like most other people) have a great capacity for self-deception in the area of sexuality, I believe it to be a useful guideline not to touch or hold a client if I find myself sexually attracted to him or if I am feeling overly mothering or protective of him.

Some experts go even further, recommending that beyond a formal handshake, therapists never make physical contact with a client. Brenner, for instance, advises: "You will help clients gain control over troublesome emotions and learn to be comfortable in an intimate relationship with you, if you refrain from touching. Further, the client eventually will be able to bring this composure into other relationships" (1982, p. 6).

Many therapists, of course, do touch, hug, and hold clients, just as many clients at some point during the middle phase of therapy want to be physically close to their therapist. Hugging a client, for these therapists, can be a spontaneous way of expressing caring and joy over a shared breakthrough. It can be a potent nonverbal expression of support during a time of emotional turmoil and pain. Clients who have not experienced good parenting in their own lives may benefit from being held or rocked; reparenting is an integral aspect of some therapeutic orientations, and part of the reparenting process often involves physical closeness.

What is important here, I believe, is not so much whether you touch a client but when and why you do so. Touching as a way of meeting your own needs, or as a mechanical or awkward or distasteful technique, is not therapeutic. Hugging or holding can interrupt a client's process; at worst, it can be quite damaging. In order to promote growth, touching must be offered at the proper time, and it must never be phony nor exploitative. "Touching has powerful immediacy as an experience, and a profound primitive quality that bypasses verbal defenses," notes Kopp (1977, p. 90). Like any other powerful tool, it is easily misused. If you do use it, be sure that you do so with sensitivity and genuineness and that your timing is appropriate. It really does not matter how clear *you* are about the therapeutic usefulness of physical closeness if the client is not ready for or misunderstands it. In fact, the safest rule for beginning therapists (and probably for all therapists) is: when in doubt, don't. Clients can continue to grow and change in the absence of touching, but there are many circumstances under which its presence can seriously damage, if not actually destroy, the therapeutic relationship.

PLUNGING INTO THE PROCESS

If anything at all can be said to characterize middle-phase therapy, it is a sense of working at many levels and in many directions at once. There will be occasions when you literally will not know what the client is moving into, or when you will think you know only to discover later that you were mistaken. Ambiguity comes with the territory. Basch suggests that the times of greatest confusion may signal the most significant therapeutic moments, "when the vulnerable, problematic aspects of the patient's personality become directly involved in the therapeutic process. Usually, neither patient nor therapist understands what is happening. Often the patient experiences mounting anxiety at that point, and, though unable yet to identify its source, reacts by faulting the therapist and/or the therapeutic process" (1988, p. 20).

During middle-phase work, whatever we do is likely to be magnified in the eyes of the client. Because we are important to him, because we have been invested with power and authority by the role relationship of therapy, and because what is happening is often mysterious and hard to understand, anything we do or say can take on great significance. The client will tend to hold us responsible for both successes and setbacks. A general rule of thumb is that the client should be encouraged to take credit for any forward progress, while the therapist takes the blame for any negative events. We must be ready to backtrack, to clarify, to apologize, and to be intensely interested (but never defensive) about what our clients perceive us to be doing and how they react to those perceptions. By structuring the situation so that the client is always in the right, is always the author of his success yet never blamed for what goes badly, we create the safest possible environment for exploration and growth.

AGREEMENT AND DISAGREEMENT

The client is always in the right. At any given moment, he may be presumed to be dealing with reality as he understands it, in the best way he knows how. You must enter the frame of his reality, rather than trying to argue or coerce him into yours. This is not to suggest, of course, that the client can never change his ideas, or that you must never confront or interpret his self-destructive or pain-producing misperceptions. It does mean that your confrontation or interpretation must be tentative, subject to his corrections, and that it must be supportive rather than punitive. All too often, the interpretations we offer clients are really accusations in disguise. Wile contends that "an interpretation is an accusation *whether or not* it contains useful information when the implication is made that the person is doing, feeling, or thinking something that he or she should not be doing, feeling, or thinking" (1987, p. 89).

There are reasons why therapists make unhelpful psuedointerpretations, and they all have to do with our own insecurity. We may feel inadequate because we don't understand what is going on, or be annoyed with the client and ashamed of our annoyance, or tell ourselves that we are obliged to do something—anything—to help him get unstuck. Whatever our discomfort, it is tempting to relieve our frustration or self-blame by blaming the client instead. We are supposed to be patient, accepting, wise, so we stifle those negative feelings; but they pop out, in disguise, in the form of an accusatory interpretation. Wile goes on to say that "the only way therapists can interpret someone as being angry or dependent without it being an accusation is if they immediately talk about how it makes sense that [the client] would be feeling angry or dependent, that they may need to feel more free to have such feelings, and the problem may be that they are unable to enjoy these feelings" (1987, p. 90).

When you find that you have made an accusatory interpretation, back off! If the client is ready to hear you, tell him what was going on for you and apologize for dumping your personal business onto him. At the very least, find some time and some way to let him know that you were out of line in saying what you did. For that matter, you should be ready to back down from an interpretation or confrontation whenever the client demands that you do so. "Maybe I was mistaken about that" is always preferable to an argument about whether you were right in what you said. Whether or not the interpretation was accurate, the client was not ready to hear what you had to say. Let it be; if your comment had value, there will be another time for you (or the client) to rediscover it.

At the other end of the scale, learn to distrust an interpretation that is received with too much enthusiasm. Out of each client's awareness lurks a scared but very clever child, ready to use any available strategy to keep the therapist away from his real pain. This child will seize on a useless interpretation with delight. If I can decoy the therapist here, she may not discover what I really don't want to deal with! The client who tells you how wonderfully perceptive your comment was, how perfectly it fits for him even though he never thought of it before, and then launches into a glib stream of recollections or examples is not likely to be dealing with truly growth-producing material. Listen to what he is saying, but use the first opportunity you can to bring him back to what was going on just before you made your "great" intervention.

Errors of agreement and disagreement with the client usually occur because we allow ourselves to become too concerned with whether the client is pleased with our performance as a therapist. If you find yourself arguing with a client, trying to justify your behavior, or being too susceptible to his suggestions that you can work miracles, you are probably uncertain, deep down, about your effectiveness: "Did I really do the right thing?" "I hope he doesn't know how I really feel!" "How could he possibly think I said that—what *did* I say?" We tend to demand (illogically and often unconsciously) that clients must think well of us; we bolster our egos with their praise and tremble inwardly at their criticism. One way to deal with these self-doubts is to frame your success in any given session in terms of what *you* do rather than what the client does. The late Sheldon Kopp told his students: "Unattached to the *outcome* of the process for the patient, the therapist is free *not* to meddle. I mind my business by concentrating on doing the work I am paid to do" (1977, p. 116). A significant part of that work is to be the object of the client's misperceptions, to tolerate the state of not having all the answers, to assert the client's ability to find and correct his own course.

SILENCE

Silence, simply waiting and watching and listening and saying nothing, may be the most useful single intervention available to a therapist, especially during the middle phase. Although it is perhaps less useful in very brief therapy, or when the client is in crisis, silence means that you will not interrupt or distract the client who is groping his way through his own thoughts and feelings. Your silence is a powerful statement. It tells the client that you are there, respecting his process, open to his communication. It tells him that you will not jump in and solve problems for him, hurry him, or restructure what he has been saying. It gives him permission to think for himself, work things through, go where he wants to go at the pace that feels right for him.

It is also possible that a client will interpret your silence in a negative way. He may think you are withholding because you are angry or critical or uninterested. "A protracted period of counselor nonresponsiveness," says Watkins, "tends to heighten both the abandonment fears and anxiety of some clients" (1989, p. 92). Since the therapeutic session is a microcosm of the client's whole life space, such a reaction is invariably part of a general pattern of relating to people. As such, it is excellent therapeutic fuel, excellent material to be worked over in the session.

More potentially damaging than client misunderstanding is the possibility that the therapist herself may misuse or misunderstand her silence. The client's perception of your anger or disinterest may be accurate; if so, focus on yourself for a moment. What is going on in you, and what do you need to do about it? If there is something that you need to clear up with the client, do so; if that is not feasible, put it to one side until you have the opportunity to debrief with a colleague or supervisor. Then give yourself permission to use your silence appropriately. Some therapists criticize themselves for being silent; they believe that when they are silent they are doing nothing. They blame themselves for not knowing what to say—as if every space in the therapy session should somehow be filled with words. Fear of silence can lead us to speak unhelpfully; it can cause us to stop listening fully to the client, to miss what he is telling us nonverbally, to interrupt his process.

The reality of middle-phase therapy is that much of the time you will *not* have a fully adequate response. The sense of not knowing what to say is a quite dependable indicator that you should say nothing at all. What you must do, though, is recognize the difference between saying nothing and doing nothing. To say nothing is to do something: silence is a therapeutic behavior, and the competent therapist uses her silences with the same skill and selectivity that she uses any other intervention.

One further word about silence: we can talk ourselves out of being quiet with a client if we believe that we have to share everything that we discover about him. As the client tells his story, we see a pattern, a theme. Suddenly we are bursting to make this interpretation to the client. We want to check it out, to see if he will validate it. We want to impress him with our perceptiveness. We want to follow up on this delightful insight, to use it to march the client off down the road to health and happiness. So we talk, ignoring the client's own internal work, derailing his train of thought, stating, by implication, that what we are thinking is of course more important than what he is thinking. We need to remind ourselves frequently that we are not at our most effective when we simply tell the client everything we know; to do so may confuse him, raise his level of anxiety, activate his defenses. We should keep quiet until we have something to say that will invite *him* to go further, rather than teaching him to depend on us for ideas and direction.

THE IMPASSE

Early-phase therapy can be a time of extreme pain and despair on the part of the client. Often he has come to therapy in crisis, as a last resort after everything else he could think of has failed. It can also be an exciting and hopeful time, as he learns new skills and experiences changes in his life. Seldom, though, will he experience being stuck in the therapy itself during the early phase. In fact, the feeling of stuckness may be one of the defining features of middle-phase work, one of the clear indicators that you have moved into a new kind of process.

It is hard to be explicit in describing a therapeutic impasse. Therapists and clients can get stuck around any issue, any problem, any symptom, any relationship. The content does not matter; what makes it an impasse is that feeling of nowhere to go, nothing will work, no answers. It is a frustrating, itchy kind of feeling. And it is easy for therapists to respond to all of this by being either self-critical ("What's wrong with me that I'm not helping my client?") or critical of the client ("He obviously is resisting my efforts"). Neither of these therapist responses is particularly useful; they tend to pull the therapist right down into the stuck place with the client rather than providing a clear perspective about what is going on. In fact, the worst thing you can do with resistance is attack it head-on. Such an attack is too much for the client; he will be forced to defend himself by resisting even more strongly.

Resistance does happen. Clients do refuse to understand, refuse to let go of old patterns, refuse to change. While such behavior can be frustrating to the therapist, we need to recognize that it represents the best that the client can do at that moment. Resistance is a part—a natural, inevitable part—of the client's overall problem. Were there not resistance, he would not need treatment; he could solve the problem by himself or at worst would need some help with the kind of skill-building or information that is provided during the first phase of therapy.

> Resistance is the impulse to protect one's familiar identity and known world against perceived threat. In depth psychotherapy, resistance is those ways in which the client avoids being truly subjectively present—accessible and expressive—in the therapeutic world. The conscious or unconscious threat is that immersion will bring challenges to the client's being in her world. [Bugental 1987, p. 175]

Such a challenge is terribly threatening—"How could I survive as somebody who isn't me?"—and will be strongly defended against. Indeed, defending against it is a healthy response. People should not move too quickly beyond their familiar sense of self, even when that self-sense is painful (Mahoney 1991). Better that they force us to proceed slowly, to respect their natural pace and process; better that we appreciate and work with the resistance rather than try to break it down.

Unfortunately, from the outside, the resistant client may look as though he is doing nothing. We cannot actually see his fear, his sense of being overwhelmed, the terror of losing the only self he has ever known. What we do see is bluster and blaming, whining, ineffective trying of one tactic after another, the critical or passive or hopeless waiting to be transformed by some powerful bit of therapeutic sorcery. "To varying degrees, clients generally prefer to assume positions of confusion, helplessness, and inadequacy, or indifference" (Goldberg 1977, p. 55). Or the opposite: we may see frequent cheerful hours, minimizing of difficulties, great enthusiasm that lasts over several sessions; it does not quite fit and signals that some opposite sorts of feelings are being warded off. Something is happening here, something very important. The willingness to be at an impasse, to tolerate and even support all that stuff that does not work, may well be the critical factor in bringing about lasting change. Confronted with the client's stuckness, the therapist neither abandons nor rescues nor attacks. She continues to support the client's exploration, helping him to discover within the therapeutic relationship the permission (to change, to try new responses, to be different) and the protection (from all the catastrophic possibilities with which he threatens himself) that he needs. The more the therapist can convey her willingness to move with, rather than against, the client, the more likely it is that his resistance will be resolved; the more she attacks his behavior, the more firmly he will dig in to oppose her (Shea 1988).

RESISTING THE THERAPIST

It should be noted here that there are two major kinds of resistance, two ways in which clients get stuck. One of these is internal to the client: it is his old conflict pattern, his own push and pull around knowing and doing what he needs to know and do. That is the kind of impasse I have been talking about up to now. The other is an impasse between therapist and client, a stuck spot in the therapeutic relationship itself. While the two are often related, it is useful to distinguish between them. Therapist-client impasses are less likely to be an avenue for change and more likely a symptom of therapist error. Speaking of this kind of being stuck, Kopp says that "a therapeutic impasse is simply a time when the therapist is trying to make a patient do something that the patient is not ready to do" (1977, p. 13). If you are too intent on your own agenda, too concerned with hurrying up the process or with proving that you know what is wrong and what should be done about it, you are very likely to create such an impasse.

The therapist's greatest enemy in working with a stuck client is her own impatience. Impatient therapists can forget to use the skills they have, forget to be silent, and push both self and client harder and harder. Like struggling in quicksand, such pushing will only serve to further mire the process. Even more damaging is the angry therapist who uses her intervention to punish the client for his resistance. Criticism does not usually enhance growth; it stifles it. You cannot bludgeon a client into changing or moving on.

People do not come to therapy in order to change in ways that will please their therapists. Many do not really want to change at all, and those who do want the change to come about with little effort and no discomfort on their part. Yet, as we allow ourselves to appreciate their situation, to empathize with their experience of the world, we become aware of how truly courageous they are in their determination to survive and to improve their lot. How arrogant to quickly assume that we know what would be "good" for them, that we are better judges than they of what is dangerous or hurtful to their already damaged self-esteem! How unrealistic to object when they reject our suggestions, insisting on doing it in the way that seems better for them! And how incredibly validating, how healing, when they can experience our willingness to meet them on their own ground, to see the world through their eyes, to make ourselves available when wanted yet secondary to their own intuitive sense of what is right for them.

GETTING UNSTUCK

By this time, you are probably at least partly convinced that resistance is a necessary part of middle-phase therapy, and you have a fairly good idea of what you should *not* do with a resistant client. But the descriptions of what *to* do are somewhat vague and general. What, specifically, is the appropriate therapeutic strategy when your client seems hopelessly stuck, caught between his desire to change and his fear of being different?

First of all, it is important to recognize when you are dealing with a therapeutic impasse. Just having a label for what is going on, knowing that it is a normal and predictable part of therapy, is reassuring. Monitor your own emotional state and notice when you feel frustrated, confused, or defeated by the client's pushing you away; these feelings may be your first indicator that an impasse has been reached. If you feel excluded, discounted, treated as the enemy, step back and regroup. Notice what is happening to you and what you are responding to in the client. Take your time; be gentle with yourself and with him.

Sometimes your client, who is at least as aware of being stuck as you are, will ask you to take over and tell him what to do: "What should I talk about?" "I don't know what to say." "Do you want me to tell you about what happened at work yesterday?" It is seldom helpful to give the client specific instructions at such times: doing so only tends to reinforce his sense of helplessness or incompetence. Instead, help him to develop his own ability to discover what he needs, to know what is foreground for him at this moment. Bugental, for example, says:

> Typically, my answer to such questions is along these lines: "You have the only valid compass, so look into yourself and see what (or which) really matters to you right now." Sometimes link that up with a reflection, "You seem to feel that I know what's important to you better than you do. That's a startling idea. Do you really believe that?" [1987, p. 216]

Your client's resistance is a signal that he is dealing with very important issues. Used as a clue to the kinds of behaviors that he has learned to use in the past and that are no longer working for him, it has great value for both diagnosis and treatment planning. As you watch his patterns unfold and develop hypotheses about what may underlie them, help him to focus on his here-and-now experience—on the struggle itself, rather than on the problem with which he is struggling. Not only will this demonstrate to your client that you understand and respect his internal experience, but it will allow you to construct an appropriate intervention to be used when he is ready for it. "Process responses," says Shea, "provide clinicians with time to think and re-collect themselves. They are punts of a sort, which clearly put the ball back in the patient's hands. During the time in which the patient must come up with a response, the clinician can get a better idea of how to ultimately respond to the resistance in question" (1988, pp. 512–513).

If the client is resisting your inappropriate or ineffective attempts to be helpful, acknowledge your own role in the problem. Describe what you believe the client is thinking and feeling about you, and ask him if you are correct. Encourage him to talk about those thoughts and feelings, to explore the troubled parts of the relationship. If you become aware of a mistake you have made, acknowledge it; invite him to help you to figure out what would be more helpful for him. In doing so, you are not only (again) helping him to explore his process, but you are also modeling personal openness and willingness to take responsibility for your share of the impasse.

And always remember that silence, too, is a response. You may simply wait, supporting the client nonverbally, conveying by your quiet calm that you are neither impatient with or discouraged by what is happening. As you listen in silence, remember that the words and movements of the treatment hour are only the tip of the iceberg, that the client is working at many levels invisible to both you and himself. Much is happening, even when little can be seen or heard.

A client who is stuck is very likely to experience whatever you do as criticism, since he is already criticizing himself for being stuck. Help him deal with his critical attitude toward himself, rather than defending what you have done or said. As he learns that you honor his resistance, recognizing it as serving an important purpose in his overall self-organization, he will be increasingly willing to drop his defensive posture. Your compassion and genuine respect for his efforts will allow you to accept each other as partners, rather than as antagonists, in the process of growth.

TIMING

Although timing is an important aspect of therapy throughout the entire length of treatment, it is perhaps most critical during the middle phase. It is here that the therapist may use the widest variety of therapeutic techniques and must choose among possible approaches from session to session and from moment to moment within a session. It is here that we tune ourselves to notice and nurture what Keutzer calls the "pregnant moment," when "a person suddenly grasps the meaning of an important symbolic event. The pregnancy consists of the fact that it is never an intellectual act alone; the grasping of the new meaning always presents the possibility and necessity of some personal decision, some shift in gestalt, some new orientation of the person toward the world and the future" (1989, p. 162). Such moments are the very stuff of therapy, and the timing of our interventions will either encourage them to develop or snuff them out entirely. The complex and shifting interactions between the client's internal process, the therapist's own responses, and the relationship itself help us to anticipate pregnant moments and decide when to point ahead, when to look back, when to speak or be silent, when to support or confront.

There is no way (or, at least, I know of none) to spell out the specific rules governing the timing of interventions. Decisions about when to say what are based on the therapist's sensitivity to the client's process, her knowledge of what he is doing at any given moment. Much of this knowledge is based on nonverbal cues: facial expression, a shift in position, tone of voice. If these cues suggest that he is quietly working on an issue, pondering a new insight, searching through his awareness in order to push out the boundaries of what he has discovered about himself, let him be. When he does break the silence, respond to what you think was happening during his exploration. Says Watts:

> There is a kind of voice quality that seems to indicate an inner focus on something that is being seen or felt freshly. Sometimes in the midst of a long client discussion expressed in a highly externalizing voice quality one hears just a small blip of focused voice. The voice slows, softens without losing energy, pauses, and loses the "premonitored" quality of the externalizing voice. This should be an indicator to the therapist that this part might be heard and responded to. [1989, p. 118]

Some kinds of silences do need to be interrupted by the therapist. If your client is truly confused, honestly not knowing how to proceed, it may be useful to provide him with a suggestion, some structuring, or a question to help him find a useful starting place. If he is fearful or hesitant, he may need support, protection, encouragement. If he is angry or frustrated with your behavior, commenting on or asking about what is going on between you is generally a helpful strategy. The guiding principle is to do whatever you can to involve him, to get him moving, and then get out of the way and let him work.

Don't forget, too, that he will sometimes need to slow down, to review where he has been, to celebrate his successes. The therapeutic relationship is continually changing and unfolding. Like any other growing thing, it will not thrive if it is pushed to grow too quickly. We are often tempted to try to hurry things, to expect the client to trust us and take risks before he is ready. After all, we know him so well by now! We know (or think we know) what he needs to do, and we know we can help him to do it. But force-feeding in therapy can interfere with progress, just as too much fertilizer can damage a young plant. Errors in timing will occur, of course; better to err on the side of doing too little than of trying to do too much.

There is an ebb and flow, a kind of organic rhythm, in good therapy. New insights and new awarenesses on the part of the client strengthen his sense of trust in both himself and his therapist; thus the relationship grows stronger. This new level of relationship, in turn, provides a base for further exploration. The rhythm can be sensed, too, in a kind of alternation of movement and rest. Hard work is often followed by lightness and laughter. A highly emotional session may be succeeded by a very cognitive one in which the emotional awareness is integrated into the client's overall understanding. And we must never forget the importance of the impasse, the dormant time when nothing appears to move, or even the relapse, when the client seems to slide back into pain and problems that you thought had finally been overcome. The therapist who does not recognize and respect these patterns will criticize her client or herself, will become frustrated when the momentum of a fruitful interaction seems to dwindle away or reverse itself. In a word, her sense of timing may not mesh with that of her client.

When you are out-of-sync in this way—when you are all ready for another grand breakthrough and your client seems to set his heels and refuse to go anywhere—adjust your rhythm to his. Depending on your own style and orientation, you may choose to go along with some period of idle conversation, to remain silent, or to comment on what is happening and its importance: "You did some pretty heavy work just now, and it sounds like you may need a breathing spell before you plunge back in again." "I notice that you aren't talking about any of the things you worked on last week. Is there some particular reason for that?" The client may agree that he does want a breather, or he may choose to explore with you his feelings about wanting to postpone further digging. Whatever he does, you have shown him your willingness to respect his process and to support him in growing at his own speed.

CLOSING A SESSION

There is one exception to the general rule that the client be allowed to decide when he is ready to plunge ahead into the next piece of work. This has to do with managing the end of the session. It is not usually therapeutic for a client to involve himself in some highly emotional issue only to be told that his time is up and the session is over. Nor is it always possible (or even helpful) to tack extra time onto the session in order to take advantage of his eagerness to work. The therapist needs to be aware of the time and to invite the client to save the issue for the next session if it looks like there will not be time to deal with it adequately: "I think this is a very important/difficult/sensitive area for you, and I notice we only have five minutes left. I don't want you to get into it and then feel cut off. Would you be willing to bring it up at the beginning of our next hour, so that we'll have plenty of time to deal with it?" This kind of intervention is evidence of the therapist's interest in the topic and her respect for the client's judgment about what is important; it is also an explicit statement of her commitment to manage the therapy sessions in a way that is protective and growth-enhancing.

In spite of your best efforts, though, there will be occasions when a client gets into an issue and does not have time to work it through. Indeed, bringing up a critically important bit of information at the last minute is a typical game for some clients, a way of hanging on to the therapist or of maneuvering for extra time or attention. "By the way," says the client as he gets up to leave, "I've decided to quit my job." It takes a lot of self-control to avoid the hook in this kind of comment, not to get sucked back into another five or ten or thirty minutes of discussion. Insisting that time limits be observed in the face of "doorknob maneuvers" will probably guarantee that the client goes away unhappy, angry, or otherwise upset.

We want our clients to leave therapy sessions in a positive frame of mind. We want them to be pleased with what has happened, willing to work on their issues between sessions, eager to return for their next hour. We do not like to send them away miserable or angry, any more than we like to end the hour feeling uncomfortable ourselves. It does sometimes happen, though, and when it does we need not tell ourselves that we have done something wrong. In fact, discomfort during and at the end of a therapy session may lead to major changes. Dealing with some issues will invariably be uncomfortable, if not downright painful, for your client. Sometimes growing hurts, and some growing pains cannot be avoided. Moreover, some of the issues and their pain will have a carry-over from one session to the next. Emotional work cannot always be contained in neat fifty-minute packages. If you, as well as your client, are uncomfortable about the necessity for ending on time, you don't need to pretend otherwise; being honest about your feelings may make it easier for him to deal with his. France says of her therapy experience, "I found it helpful when the therapist made it clear that he or she too regretted ending the session, whether this was due to my distress or the fact that we were in the middle of something important" (1988, p. 56).

Sometimes the regret over ending will be more personal: sometimes you will manage things badly and not have time to repair the damage. You made an inappropriate intervention, for instance, pursued an issue better left until later, or failed to respond in a way that was helpful to your client. If the therapeutic relationship has been carefully nurtured, with openness and honesty and genuine caring, it will survive a few of these bad endings and may even emerge stronger for having survived them. On the other hand, if the therapist's management of time is frequently off, so that the client is left dangling at the end of each session, he may well decide that the benefit of therapy is outweighed by the discomfort he feels.

MIDDLE-PHASE RETROSPECTIVE

As I read what I have written in this chapter, I am painfully aware of how nonspecific much of it sounds. Some clients will do this; sometimes thus-and-such is useful, sometimes not. The beginning student would be quite justified in throwing up her hands and demanding a set of clear and unambiguous rules.

I wish that I could provide them. However, as I said at the outset, middle-phase work really defies being outlined or categorized. It usually does involve intense emotional work, but not always. Much of the time you will not know exactly where the work is going, and many times you will. Often it is true that silence is the best intervention, and occasionally silence can be harmful. Most clients will find themselves stuck at least once during the middle phase, but a few will not.

When I feel confused or discouraged about my middle-phase work (and none of us completely outgrows such feelings), I am most helped by reminding myself that every client knows, at some level, what he wants and needs. He knows where his treatment must go in order for him to grow and change. Sometimes the knowledge is part of his conscious awareness; more often it is at a deeper, more organic level. One part of him may be busily resisting what another part is urging him into, and he is conscious only of a sense of confusion and discomfort. But the knowledge is always there, somewhere. The art of the middle phase is largely that of listening to all of the levels he presents and of responding to what he tells you from all of these levels.

Often ambiguous, always unpredictable, middle-phase work can be painful and frustrating. It can also be a source of endless fascination. It is difficult and stressful to work in a situation where you do not know what will happen next. It can also be exciting! If you demand of yourself that you always do well, always make good interventions at the right time, you will almost surely begin to dread the middle phase and be relatively ineffective with it. If, on the other hand, you allow yourself occasional confusion, allow yourself not to know, you will learn how to really listen to your client. At that point you will have begun to be a therapist.

THE FINAL PHASE   6

The final phase of therapy is at once easy and difficult to describe. It is easy because its central issue is clear: termination. The ending of therapy, the ending of the therapist-client relationship, the client's moving out on his own are the major themes. There may be other themes, other issues, as well, and these are as variable as clients and therapists themselves. The end of therapy is not just the end, not simply the process of saying goodbye (although one would be quite foolish to call even that a simple process). It is a microcosm of the entire course of treatment.

Musical productions in the theater often end with something called the reprise, in which the major musical themes are repeated in a shortened and connected fashion. Perhaps the reprise is the best metaphor for therapeutic endings as well. The major themes, conflicts, and fantasies of the entire therapeutic process are reworked in the context of termination, of ending. Part of this reworking has to do with uncovering new issues that may bubble up as the client contemplates living his life without the now-familiar support of ongoing therapy; another part involves practicing, reporting on, and taking in reinforcement for the new behaviors and responses that he has acquired. Yet a third factor is the therapy relationship itself: the reality, for both client and therapist, of ending an interaction which has been a meaningful and important part of their lives.

In this chapter we shall discuss a number of issues relating to Phase 3, the final phase of treatment. We will talk about planning for termination, about recognizing the point at which clients begin to deal with termination-related issues. We will talk about the kinds of work that clients often need to do during the final phase and the predictable emotional components of that work. We will discuss some of the issues that the therapist may need to face in her own response to termination. Finally, we will introduce some special cases, some situations which differ in important ways from the traditional ending phase of long-term treatment. Even as we do this, however, it is important to recognize that we will not cover everything, will not deal with all the issues that may emerge for you and your clients. Termination is too varied, too individualized, to hope for that. What you can expect is an outline, a series of guideposts, that will help you to recognize and to plan for each of the varied termination processes which you will experience as a professional therapist.

PLANNING FOR TERMINATION

It is a hallmark of our culture that we are reluctant to talk openly about ending relationships or cutting off contact. We say "see you later" instead of "goodbye" and disguise the finality of long-term partings (graduation, moving away) with promises to keep in touch. Even death, that most final of endings, is referred to as passing on, and Western religion is replete with reassurances that important relationships need not end—that, in the words of the old hymn, "we shall meet in the sweet bye-and-bye." Ending a meaningful relationship is unpleasant if not downright painful; none of us likes to give up something we care about. It is easier to pretend that it will not happen, that it is not happening, that it did not happen, and then deal with the reality later, when we have found new friends and new interests and the pain of parting has had time to subside. It is a great temptation to clients and therapists (being, after all, people like everyone else) to treat their endings in the same way: to ignore the fact that termination is coming, to disguise its reality with pseudo-plans to meet again in one way or another, or to slide through the last sessions without knowing that they will, in fact, be the last.

That is a mistake for at least two reasons. First, it encourages the client to continue to exercise the very defensive maneuvers he has probably been struggling with throughout treatment. Whatever is maladaptive in his system is most likely to reemerge under stress, and termination of therapy is clearly stressful. By allowing him to go ahead and reactivate his old behaviors—or, worse, to actively collaborate with him—may undermine much of the progress he has made. Second, dealing explicitly with feelings around the termination issue may provide opportunities to explore new and important areas which have not been discussed before. These issues may relate directly to endings, partings, leaving and being left; or they may involve other concerns or problems that the client has been reluctant to talk about. Now, knowing that therapy will soon be over, he may be ready to deal with them.

While the issue of termination becomes a foreground concern in the final phase of therapy, it is really an appropriate subject for discussion throughout the treatment process. Says Kupers, "The client does not encounter the separation issue only once at the end of therapy any more than one ponders the experience of death only once at the end of life" (1988, p. 54). Knowing that therapy will end, planning for it to end, working through issues in the context of a relationship that will not continue indefinitely has implications for the whole course of therapy. The client is more aware of goals, more likely to evaluate and take responsibility for his own progress. Planning for termination becomes part of the contracting process: client and therapist together specify the goals of therapy and how each will know when the client has achieved those goals. It is appropriate to give a new client some idea of how long treatment will probably last, even though this is often an approximation subject to revision as the process unfolds, and to talk about any problem that either of you may anticipate with this tentative time line. Planning the therapy during this early stage will include provisions for pausing to evaluate progress and revise treatment goals at regular intervals; again, each of these steps is a logical and appropriate time to reintroduce the idea of termination.

The end of therapy, in other words, begins with the first interview. The whole process points toward its ending, and that fact is an integral aspect of the process. Talking about it, normalizing the client's discomfort with both the idea of terminating and of continuing indefinitely, will help him not only to make a good termination of therapy but to deal with the problems of endings in general. Teyber reminds us that "clients do not just talk with therapists about their problems in an abstract manner; rather they actually recreate and act out in their relationship with the therapist the same conflicts that have led them to seek treatment" (1988, p. 10). Nowhere is this more true than in the area of termination.

The issue of terminating therapy touches the heart of the great paradox of therapy: the dependency between client and therapist. The client needs permission to become sufficiently dependent on the therapist so that he can use the relationship to do his work. He must accept the protection and safety that the therapist provides if he is to explore and to change in ways that previously had seemed too dangerous or threatening. At the same time, he needs to know that he can grow past that dependent posture, once again becoming autonomous and confident. We tell him that right now he may feel that he needs us but that our work together will be to facilitate his moving through that need into a new way of relating to his environment. His needy feelings are real and may in fact be a positive factor in his treatment, helping him to use the therapist appropriately; and part of the way he will use us is to learn not to need us.

In order to establish an appropriate balance between dependence and autonomy, the client should be given some reassurances. He needs to be reminded that, no matter how important we may become in his life, some part of him is quite capable at any point of carrying on without us. He might not want to, and it might be quite uncomfortable to do so. But he could, if he had to. He also needs to know that we will treat his temporary dependency with respect, that we will be responsible and sensitive as he weans himself from us. Just as we expect that he will discuss any plans he might make to discontinue his therapy, we will discuss similar plans with him. Ultimately, each of us has the right to stop, without the permission or agreement of the other. In a well-managed therapeutic process, though, this will not happen. Therapist and client each respect and value the opinions, preferences, perceptions of the other, and neither will leave the relationship without a thorough discussion of what has been decided, and why. Thus the therapeutic relationship becomes the prototype of any healthy adult relationship in which commitment and freedom to change are two sides of the same coin.

WHEN TO TERMINATE

As in any relationship, therapy can be terminated by either of the parties involved. Should the client decide to end treatment, the therapist cannot force him to stay. Similarly, once the therapist chooses to stop working with a client, the client cannot force her to continue. Ideally, of course, neither of these situations will arise, and termination will be a joint decision on the part of both client and therapist.

As you find yourself moving through the middle phase of therapy with a client, you will need to consider the whole question of termination. Sometimes, of course, that decision is taken out of your hands from the outset: some agencies have firm limits on the number of sessions allowed a client, and a predetermined termination date is an integral part of some brief therapy models. More often, though, there is a good deal of latitude for the therapist to use her own judgment about the length of treatment. So, in such cases, how do you know when it is time to quit? How do you know when it is time to begin to talk with your client about quitting? The beginning of the end may be more difficult to recognize than the end of the end.

Part of the problem here lies in the fact that therapists are trained to recognize lots of reasons why treatment should not be terminated—defensive maneuvers, unfinished issues, transference not completely worked through, acting out, etc.—but we are not so well trained to recognize the signs that termination is appropriate. After all, who could fail to benefit from more therapy? Who has all their issues resolved, their life perfectly in order? Wolberg reminds us that "it may be impossible, due to other obstructions, to get some patients to progress beyond a certain point in therapy. To continue treatment may prove discouraging to the therapist and undermining to the patient. It is better here for the patient to retain some neurotic drives than to be exposed to interminable and frustrating therapy to which, in all probability, the patient will be unable to respond" (1988, p. 959). We can't always, or even often, do it all. But to many of us (particularly if we are relatively new and unsure of ourselves), suggesting that a client has gone as far as he can go seems arrogant and even dangerous. What if his inability to go further is our fault, rather than just the way it is for him? If we give up and quit, isn't that an admission of failure? So we plod ahead, keep trying, until the client tires of the whole thing and decides on his own to quit, leaving us feeling even more inadequate than we would have felt if we had met the issue head-on.

There is another reality, too, that is often overlooked in textbook considerations of termination. Although clinical concerns ought ideally to be of first (only?) concern in deciding how long to continue treatment, in reality such decisions usually have at least as much to do with money as with mental health (Kupers 1988). Clients who depend upon insurance to finance their therapy must discontinue therapy (unless you are willing to provide it at much reduced rates) if their insurance company decides that they are no longer in need of treatment; clients paying their own way will, consciously or unconsciously, weigh the benefits they get from therapy against the dollars removed from their bank account. As we talk about termination decisions, then, we need to remember that our discussion is somewhat idealized. The marketplace does significantly influence clinical practice, for better or worse. Just because finances sometimes force us to make termination decisions that we don't like, though, is no excuse for sloppy thinking about such decisions. We need to decide what we would like our clients to do, what we think is best for them clinically; armed with these conclusions, we can then help them work out the best possible compromise between what would be most beneficial on the one hand and what is feasible on the other.

If you have done a good job of contracting with your client, of setting out clear and explicit treatment goals, recognizing an appropriate termination point will be easier. Therapy should end when the stated goals have been achieved or when the client has done all he can do and is no longer moving toward these goals. It is not your job to figure out all of the other possible things he might benefit from working on, and it is certainly not advisable for you to stay stuck with him indefinitely. Rather, you can share with him your assessment of what is happening, invite him to join you in reviewing his progress, suggest other resources that may be available to him, and then say goodbye.

It would be most comfortable for both therapist and client if the actual point of termination were clearly indicated by some unmistakable marker, some event that would signal "now it is time," but it does not usually happen that way. Even in the best-planned terminations, there is an arbitrary quality. As they discuss the progress (or lack of progress) of therapy, client and therapist both know that termination is an option. Usually it is the therapist who gives her recommendations and the client who makes the final decision. He might have stopped earlier, or he might profitably continue longer; it is his choice. There will probably be some pain for him in terminating (we will discuss this and other emotional responses to termination in a later section), but there are gains as well—not only in terms of time and money saved, but in a sense of accomplishment, of a difficult task seen through to a good conclusion. It is the therapist's responsibility to see that the client does, in fact, leave therapy with these kinds of feelings—whether or not the therapist agrees with his choice to terminate.

Sometimes it is the client's decision to continue in therapy that leaves the therapist feeling uncomfortable. The client has done what he said he wanted to do, accomplished the goals he set for himself. Or, it seems clear that he will *not* achieve his goals; he is making no progress or is consistently sabotaging himself. The therapist feels pushed to "help" somehow but is not sure what kind of help the client really wants. This is the sort of situation in which reformulating goals, updating the therapeutic contract, is imperative. An explicit statement of the goals of therapy makes it possible to deal with the termination issue in the context of reaching, or being unable to reach, those goals. Be particularly cautious with the client who suggests a new contract as soon as you introduce the idea of termination; he may be looking for a rationale to keep the relationship going, and this need (rather than the ostensible goal he has suggested) may be the underlying theme throughout the rest of the treatment. Staying in therapy can indeed be appropriate for this sort of client, but dealing with his relationship issues may need to be formulated as an explicit goal.

Beware, also, of your own inclination to suggest that the successful client now turn to an exploration of this or that new issue: to what degree does your suggestion arise out of your own desire to continue the therapy? Salzman points out, "There is always some reluctance to terminate a patient's therapy without finding a replacement, or to terminate care for a well-understood patient and begin again with a new, untried and uncertain one" (1989, p. 227). It is only natural to experience this reluctance, to want to hang on to the client whom we know, who appreciates us—and who pays his bills! We need to remember to examine our own motives for continuing with a client and to make our recommendations on the basis of his needs rather than our own.

Hanging on to the relationship, whether by the therapist or the client, is not necessarily the most common termination error. Terminations can come too soon, as well as too late. Premature terminations can occur for a variety of reasons, some of which are unavoidable. We have already mentioned the financial considerations that can lead to early termination. People move away, job demands shift, life circumstances can change in ways that preclude continuing in therapy. Sometimes therapy must end even though both client and therapist would like to continue. Again, though, one should be cautious about accepting at face value such outside-of-treatment reasons for terminating. Clients (and therapists!) find it very difficult to say that they want to quit because they feel they are not getting anywhere or that they are afraid of moving into what may really be the central issue of treatment. It is much easier and more socially acceptable to use the excuse of running out of money, of no longer having time for therapy, or of objections from a spouse or other family member as a reason for quitting. When a client tells you that he is terminating for this sort of reason, you should review carefully your notes and recollections about the recent course of his therapy, as well as exploring with him the feelings connected with that decision. Similarly, you may need to confront yourself with your real reasons and feelings if you find you are thinking of terminating with a difficult client. It is often a good plan to discuss such a case with a colleague or supervisor, someone who is not personally involved in the relationship, before moving ahead in termination planning.

Whether you are talking with your client, with a consultant, or with yourself, frame your consideration of termination in terms of a range of desired outcomes. After all, there are many levels of success in therapy. Terminating at point X may be premature in terms of some set of long-range possibilities but quite appropriate in terms of more limited goals. This is particularly true in the case of the client who (a) has clear behavioral objectives and little awareness of or desire to deal with emotional issues; (b) has limited financial resources for therapy; (c) fears his own dependency needs and so is reluctant to become involved in long-term work;

or (d) seeks, consciously or unconsciously, to use therapy as a substitute for developing supportive relationships in the natural environment.

The ideal time for ending treatment is when both client and therapist sense that it should end, either because it has accomplished its purpose or because it would be better for the client to stop now even though the stated goals have not been reached or have been only partially reached. A good dollop of common sense is useful here: do not get so caught up in theoretical oughts and shoulds that you lose sight of the fact that you and your client are two people, working out ways for the client to get what he needs. He does not have to get it all; he does not have to solve all of his problems. He will continue to live and grow after therapy is over, and he may even enter into another therapeutic relationship some time in the future. Your job as therapist is to help him to explore his reasons for quitting, to understand and appreciate what he has accomplished in his work, and to anticipate what those accomplishments will mean as he goes on about the business of living his life. A clear termination decision made in this context will probably be both appropriate and therapeutic.

THE WORK OF THE FINAL PHASE

Even though the process of working through the termination phase will vary enormously from client to client, some patterns tend to occur again and again during this phase. Endings, after all, have some universal qualities and tend to call forth some typical responses. As with the middle phase, these responses—thoughts, feelings, and behaviors—become the stuff of therapy. The therapy relationship is a microcosm of the client's entire social existence, and in it he will replay his well-learned reactions to and interactions with his world-out-there. Ward points out that effective therapists encourage their clients to explore feelings about leaving therapy and leaving the therapist, thus dealing with the necessary business of ending the immediate relationship and, at the same time, gaining new insights about other relationships and their endings:

> A major strategy in this area is that of immediacy, or increasing the direct discussion of the client and counselor's feelings toward one another and toward the relationship itself. More than any other single indicator, the presence or absence of this increased attention to and working through of relationship factors discriminates between approaches that use the termination process most effectively as a facilitative or therapeutic mechanism in its own right and those that do not. [1989, p. 103]

The termination of therapy, then, can become an opportunity to work through one's whole way of dealing with goodbyes, with endings, and ultimately with one's own death. Many clients may not choose to explore all of these issues, of course, and you should respect their choice not to do so. But be alert to the possibility of dealing with them: understand each client's termination behavior in the context of the reality that, for him as for all of us, all parts of life eventually come to a close.

REPEATING OLD THEMES

As clients begin to realize at an emotional level that termination is approaching, they typically begin to bring up old themes and issues. This may be done in a defensive way: a covert message that "I'm not okay yet, so please don't leave me." Or it may occur in a spirit of review, integration, and even celebration: "I've changed here and here and here; I really am different than I was when we began." With either sort of process, the therapist's job is to support and clarify the work, to help the client make explicit what he is doing. If my client is desperately bringing up old issues in an effort to justify continuing in therapy, I will want to explore with him why it is so important to maintain our relationship. If he is sorting through his old issues for fear there may be something left undone, we talk about these fears. If he is reviewing in order to gain a better perspective on just what has happened over the course of treatment, I help him to do that and also encourage him to attend to his feelings as well as to his thinking. In each case, my aim is to assist him to integrate what he has accomplished with what he has yet to do and with what he may not wish to change.

"Termination," say Balsam and Balsam, "will represent a distillation of the themes that have arisen in the therapy, the situation that brought the patient to treatment in the first place, and the positive and negative aspects of transference and countertransference" (1974, p. 145). Whether or not the client brings up these themes explicitly, you may be sure that they are present at some level. He is working through the implications of living his issues with no therapy and no therapist to fall back on, and everything he says can be understood in that context. Every association, every insight, every emotional reaction is an interface between old and new, between the in-treatment situation and the no-longer-in-treatment situation. Material brought up in the session can, of course, be dealt with on its own terms, but it must also be seen in the context of the separation process. To the question, "What does this mean for a person with this kind of life situation and this kind of developmental history?" you must now add, "And what does it mean for a person who is ending a supportive/confrontive growth-producing relationship? What does it mean for a person who is moving from a dependent to an autonomous position?" The fact of imminent termination inevitably colors and flavors all the work that is done during each last-phase session; there is no way to change the subject or to undo that reality.

HANGING ON

We have already alluded a number of times to "hanging on," the reluctance of some clients to come to the end of their treatment. As a common and important therapeutic phenomenon, this behavior deserves a somewhat more detailed consideration.

For many clients, the notion of terminating therapy invites a feeling of neediness, a sense of wanting to cling to the relationship. They experience an almost panicky "something terrible will happen to me when I'm alone" feeling. This feeling, in turn, may cause them to prolong the therapeutic interaction. They may bring up old symptoms, reexperiencing them as if the work they have done in these areas had never happened. Or new issues may emerge with a strangely artificial or phony flavor. The same thing often occurs in microcosm at the end of an individual session when the client brings up an important issue with only a few minutes left in the hour, in order to hang on and prolong the contact. Again, the underlying concerns are those of separation and control: "Can I exist separately?" "Can I trust myself and my therapist to find a way to separate?" "How can I bear the pain of being alone again?" "Who will decide (control) when and how our separation will occur?"

Just as with ending-the-session behavior, hanging on at termination time needs to be confronted and worked through. The specific problem or symptom is less important than the separating; the problem is merely the vehicle by means of which the client plays out his need to maintain and control the relationship. It is important to recognize and respect both the reality and the intensity of those feelings while at the same time helping the client to grow past them.

Hanging on is not always a dysfunctional behavior, something to be worked through and gotten past. Sometimes it represents a realistic appraisal of the client's need for continuing support. For such clients, there are a variety of termination scenarios which may be more appropriate than simply coming to a final session and saying goodbye. Therapy can be tapered off, by scheduling sessions at longer and longer intervals. Or, a "5,000-mile checkup" can be planned for some months in the future, when the client will return to review with the therapist how he has handled his posttherapy challenges. Occasionally, a client will choose not to formally terminate but rather to move to "flexible scheduling" in which he will decide whether or not to call for another appointment.

You will surely have noted that these scenarios, particularly the last one, seem to violate the idea that clients should be encouraged to deal with the reality of ending the therapy relationship. Isn't "flexible scheduling" a kind of denial, a way of pretending that we don't have to say goodbye? In a sense, it is. In another sense, it is an accurate way of describing a situation in which a client is truly not ready to end therapy but chooses to deal with his issues on his own rather than working them through in treatment. The choice is not always one which I would prefer for my clients, but it is one which I must honor. It has the advantage of allowing the client to take a break from therapy and then come back, not as someone who terminated and then couldn't make it on his own, but as a person who has respected his own pacing and timing and is now ready to complete his work.

Endings are seldom pleasant and can be quite painful. They may be more often done badly than well. Therapy endings are no exception; regrets, second thoughts, "I wish I'd thought to…" seem to be a common experience for both therapists and clients. We therapists have an advantage, though: we, at least, have the opportunity to practice and to improve the way in which we deal with termination. An important part of this learning comes as we attend specifically to the emotions of the termination process. It is to these emotional responses that we now turn.

FEELING REACTIONS TO TERMINATION

Termination is a time of parting, of separation. It marks the end of a relationship which has been very important to the client, a relationship in which he has allowed himself to be touched and known in a way that he may never have experienced before. It is also a kind of graduation, the commencement of a new phase in the client's life. It can be an occasion for celebration, as client and therapist feel the satisfaction of a job well done. The emotions surrounding this event are often intense, and working these emotions through is literally the final task of therapy. *

SADNESS

A sense of sadness is the most common emotion connected with termination. We are sad when good things come to an end; we are sad when we must part with people who have been important to us. The ending of the therapy relationship involves not only the normal sadness of parting from someone who has been close but also the remembered and reexperienced sadness of earlier partings. The client has used his therapist as a stand-in for other important people in his history, for partners in other important relationships from childhood on; these transference relationships are also emotionally charged. Transference feelings are real feelings, and the transference attachment of client to therapist is a real attachment. It is both predictable and appropriate that the client experience some grief when it ends.

A major difference between this therapeutic grief and other experiences of separation and loss is that in therapy the client has the opportunity to talk through his feelings with the person he is losing, and that person is in a position to help him explore and integrate the feelings. The sadness and loss cannot be expected to disappear, but they can at least be made bearable; indeed, working through a separation in this way may help the client to manage future grief experiences in a more mature and less anguished way.

Another aspect of the sadness of termination is often a feeling of disappointment. "Is that all there is?" the client asks. "There isn't any magic? I'm leaving, and all of my pain and confusion haven't been taken away?" Most clients have entertained, at some level, the hope that through therapy all their problems will be solved, never to return. And as long as they stay in treatment, they can maintain the hope that the miraculous cure is just around the corner. With termination comes the realization that this will not happen, that "they lived happily ever after" is a rela-

---

* Balsam and Balsam, in their excellent *Becoming a Psychotherapist* (1974), describe the various affects that clients typically experience during the termination phase of therapy. I have learned much from their work, as the following discussion may indicate.

tive rather than an absolute description. If the therapist is skillful and the client willing, this can be another opportunity for significant growth; ideally, the client will come to accept not only the reality of pain and problems as part of living but also his own ability to survive without a lifetime guarantee of happiness. On the other hand, if the disappointment is not worked through, the client may become a therapy-hopper, going from one therapist to the next in search of that marvelous panacea that does not really exist.

ANGER

"Some clients worry that the therapist will be enraged, others are certain the therapist does not really care anyway. Some clients worry that they will fall flat on their face once separate from the therapist" (Kupers 1988, p. 55). Any or all of these concerns are painful and are likely to be defended against. And one of the most common defenses is to translate the worry into anger—anger at the unfairness of it all, anger at the therapist who is not making them feel better and who may even seem to be making it worse.

Therapists differ in their view of just how separation anger is aroused or maintained, but most agree that it usually occurs. One of the most obvious sources of anger for a client is his sense of being abandoned: "This person whom I trusted so much is dumping me. How can she do that? She has no right to leave me alone, especially when I may not be completely, permanently, and blissfully cured." At another level, the anger over being left may have to do with the sense that termination is too easy for the therapist: "It is not fair that I should suffer while the therapist does not." Clearly connected to this latter idea is the suspicion that Kupers alludes to: the therapist does not really care, after all. "She would not let me leave so easily, or so soon, if she really loved me and cared about me the way I thought she did. She has been faking all along, and I should never have trusted her." And so the anger builds.

There is another flavor of anger at termination, not so much directed at the therapist as at life in general. To the degree that a client experiences the separation as painful, he will feel frustrated; he wants something, and he cannot have it. Feelings of frustration, in turn, commonly vent themselves in anger. The client may direct his anger at the therapist, but he may also lash out at a spouse, a boss, or any other part of his environment which provides a handy target.

Termination anger is seldom a simple or uncomplicated emotion. As was suggested above, clients who have difficulty dealing with sadness or worry may choose to be angry in order to defend against their grief or scare. Other clients may be embarrassed by their tender or loving feelings toward the therapist and cover those feelings with an angry outburst. Finally, the anger itself may be experienced as unacceptable and be turned back against the self in feelings of guilt and shame.

In every instance, the job of the therapist is to help the client understand both his reaction—the angry feelings—and the source of the reaction. If the anger is derivative, covering some other feeling, the client needs to move through the anger so as to get to whatever is underneath. Similarly, the guilty client may need help in externalizing his rage, putting it out into his social environment rather than turning it back upon himself. Anger can be both energizing and empowering and is potentially a very useful source of strength. If we can help clients to use the positive aspects of their anger, rather than flying out of control or sulking or feeling guilty, we can again provide them with tools to help them through future separation experiences.

FEAR

There are many things for a terminating client to be fearful about. Probably the most common fear is that he will not be able to make it on his own, that something terrible will happen as soon as the therapist is no longer there to support him. The something terrible may be a slide back to the misery which brought him to treat-ment in the first place, some new crisis with which he will be unable to cope, or simply the sense of being alone and not knowing what the future will bring. Leaving one's therapist is not unlike leaving home for the first time, leaving the security of the known, the comfort of having some grown-up who is in charge or who can take over if one gets into a tight spot.

The very intensity of the client's feelings about termination may be a source of fear. He did not know he had gotten so attached or that he would feel this angry. It can be scary to discover feelings, strong feelings, that you did not know were there: "Where will it end? How long will I feel this way? Will it get worse?" A part of him feels new and strange and out of control, and he does not know what to do about it.

Along with permission to feel their fear and experience the therapist's sup-port as they do so, frightened clients need reassurance that they can deal with these feelings, that the intensity of the feelings will abate with time, and that such feel-ings are normal during the termination period. Simply knowing that other people react in the same way ("Oh, then I'm not weird?") does much to reduce the client's catastrophizing and to turn the fear experience into something which can be exam-ined and moved through. It is particularly important for the therapist not to give too much support, not to create the impression that she doubts the client's ability to deal with his own emotional business. Not only can such overreacting suck some clients right back into a dependent and helpless role, but it can actually increase the fear. The fantasy of a therapist who cares too much, who is overinvolved, is fright-ening in its own right. The client is already confused by his feelings and needs to know that his therapist is not confused by hers. The correct therapeutic course, then, is a blend of support, respect, and clear information: it is okay and normal to feel as you do; many people experience the same thing; and I am here for you to use as you help yourself through this part of your growing and changing.

GUILT

We have already mentioned the guilty feelings which clients may experience as a derivative of anger around termination. There are other sources of guilt feelings as well. Clients may feel guilty about sexual or dependency feelings toward the therapist. They may find themselves glad to be free of therapy and feel guilty about that. Or they may believe that they have hurt or disappointed the therapist in some way. Feelings that have to do directly with the therapeutic relationship are paradoxically easier and more difficult to deal with in therapy: more difficult because client (and therapist too) may feel embarrassed to talk about them and so tend to discount or suppress them; easier because, once brought out into the open, they can be explored in the here-and-now of that very relationship. New ways of being together, of relating and responding to the other person, can be tested out immediately rather than waiting until the next session for the client to bring back the results of the work he has done.

One last category of guilty feelings involves the sense of having said too much, having been disloyal to the significant others in one's life, or having exposed oneself too completely. The client may find himself wanting to flee the therapy situation, just get away and pretend that the whole thing never happened. Here the guilt of "I said too much" may be further complicated by competing feelings of attachment or gratitude toward the therapist or by anger at the therapist for having encouraged (or seduced) the client into too much self-revelation. Then the client may feel further guilt that he could be thinking such ungrateful thoughts.

PLEASANT AFFECT

It is a common failing in most writings about therapy and therapists that we tend to overemphasize problems and pain. Such a focus, I think, is unavoidable. People usually seek therapy because they are in some sort of discomfort, and the easing of discomfort is the most common signal that treatment has accomplished its purpose and should be terminated. Yet much of the experience of therapy can be exhilarating and joyful, and it would be foolish to ignore the good in our effort to anticipate and work with the painful. So it is with termination. There is a great deal of satisfaction for both client and therapist during the termination phase of a successful course of therapy. Ending the therapeutic relationship can mark a job well done, a moving forward into new and exciting possibilities. It can be a time for experiencing a feeling of completeness and competence. The client has indeed achieved something valuable. He emerges from a successful therapy experience with new tools, new skills, new confidence. He feels grounded and in charge of himself, perhaps for the first time in his life.

We know how to work with pain, rage, and fear. We help the client to change those feelings in some way or to use them to achieve some positive end. Some of us (a dwindling number, I hope) greet reports of positive feelings with a determined skepticism, refusing to take them at face value but rather poking and prying to find the bad things we are sure must be lurking underneath. Such an attitude may reflect the therapist's own unfamiliarity with and uncertainty about positive affect; at best it is a discount of both the client's ability to grow and the therapist's skill in facilitating that growth. Rather than discounting positive feelings, the competent therapist joins in celebrating them. She is not so naive as to ignore the possibility that other, less pleasant feelings may also emerge; but she is open to the reality of health and growth. She is quick to recognize and to reinforce evidence that the client has changed and does experience good feelings. In so doing, she may put herself out of business with this client, and that is what good therapy is all about.

THERAPIST FEELINGS

We have spent a lot of time discussing the affects that clients experience during the termination process, and occasionally we have touched briefly on the feelings of the therapist during this phase. The feelings of the therapist deserve more than just a passing comment, however. They are part and parcel of termination, and failure to recognize them and deal with them is probably responsible for more misman- aged terminations than any other kind of therapist error. "The therapist is unavoid- ably part of the treatment situation, both as therapist (change agent) and as him- self," says Baldwin. "He does not choose to be in or out, he can only choose to be aware or not" (1987, p. 27). We are real people, experiencing real feelings; our very genuineness is one of our most important assets in the practice of our trade. Ending a relationship with a long-term client is appropriately an emotionally laden process for us as well as for the client.

Just as the client often feels sadness at parting, so may we. Separation cuts both ways; we too experience the loss of a meaningful relationship. As we talk about termination and encourage the client to share his feelings, we too can acknowledge that we shall feel a loss and that we are sad about it. Talking about our own sadness and sense of loss is not merely acceptable behavior, behavior that will help us while doing the client no harm. It is an integral part of the separation process. It allows the client to separate cleanly from a real, whole human being, instead of drifting fuzzily away from a shadowy professional role-facade. And it does, also, allow the therapist to let go more cleanly and honestly.

Transference feelings are no less real because they spring from the client's transference; countertransference feelings are also real. Few therapists would argue against the position that a client's rage at his withholding therapist/parent must be worked through, as must other transference-based reactions, if the termination is to be a positive experience for him. It is less generally recognized that the therapist needs to deal with her countertransference reactions to termination: her fear, per- haps, that her client/child may not be able to get along without her or her anger that the client/child is abandoning her. It is seldom if ever appropriate to work through such countertransference issues directly with the client, but it is essential to recog- nize and work them through in some other setting. Especially for beginning thera- pists, it is a good idea to set up a case consultation with a supervisor or a colleague whenever a long-term client nears termination. This will allow you to explore your own termination issues early while they are still readily accessible and relatively unencrusted with rationalizations and other defenses.

There is one very real termination issue that therapists face but that clients are spared. For the therapist, a terminating client may mean the loss of status, security, or money. One is often tempted to hang on to a client well past the optimum termination point, simply because one needs business. Therapists wage continual war with worries that no new clients will show up to replace the ones who go away. This is especially true for therapists in private practice. We use our filled appointment book to reassure ourselves that we really are competent and that others recognize our skills. There is little that I can say about these reactions other than that they must not be dumped on our clients. We all suffer through them (any therapist who denies this probably needs to work out some additional issues!), and there is nothing strange or wrong in your experiencing these feelings. What is wrong is to try to soothe them by keeping your clients around longer than they need to stay. Not only is that bad for clients, but it is also bad for you. Again, find a supervisor or a colleague you can trust and deal with such feelings there; you will be much better able to work through termination (and other issues as well) with your clients for having done so.

One final problem that emerges over and over again for therapists is that of the kind of relationship (if any) they are willing to maintain with an ex-client. Clients and therapists both find themselves wanting to restructure the relationship, to continue but in a different way. While some therapists claim to be able to manage this kind of restructuring, to be just friends with an ex-client, I suspect that planning to do so before treatment has actually ended is usually a way to deny or distort what is actually happening in termination. It is another kind of refusal to end, an implicit recognition that one or both parties in the relationship are not ready to let go. Kopp's discussion of this issue really says it all:

> I find that attempting a social-personal relationship between myself and ex-patients never really works. No transference is ever completely resolved. Attempts to have a new kind of meeting have all the limitations of a parent and a child attempting to "just be friends." The shadow of the therapeutic alliance haunts attempts to move beyond it. There is residual doubling of role not unlike the usually disastrous incestuous efforts to have a parallel relationship *during* long-term intensive psychotherapy. [1977, p. 156]

I can only add that my own experiences as a client, as well as a therapist, support this position. Friendships with ex-clients, when I have ignored my own rules and attempted them, have had a curiously one-sided flavor; I have found it hard to stop being a quasi-therapist in my listening and equally hard to be open and vulnerable in my talking. And friendships with ex-therapists (this has happened once or twice) have left me feeling vaguely disappointed, as the relationship that had been focused almost exclusively on my health and growth suddenly changed into one in which the other person was free to be less concerned with and sensitive to me and more expressive of his own needs and wants.

But wait a minute! You really like this client. Does all this mean that you have to give up the possibility of ever having him for a friend? I believe, regretfully, that it does. And this brings us back full circle to the real sadness of termination: for the therapist, too, it is an ending.

UNPLANNED TERMINATIONS

Everything we have said thus far about terminations has assumed that the termination will be an orderly process, anticipated by both client and therapist, with ample time to work through all the issues that the separation may involve. Anyone who has done much therapy will realize, however, that this kind of planned termination is not always what happens. Therapeutic relationships can terminate in a variety of more or less abrupt ways, and many of these leave both parties feeling distinctly uncomfortable.

THE "NO-SHOW"

For less experienced therapists, a common problem is that of the client who simply does not show up for an appointment. He does not call to reschedule or let you know what is happening; there is just a curt message left with your answering service: "I won't be back; no, I'm not interested in rescheduling." Or, worse, just a gaping hole in your schedule, with no cancellation or any other word. Is he coming back, or not? Why didn't he show up? And what should you do about it?

Part of the answer here, of course, has to do with the kind of relationship you have established with the client. If you have been seeing him for some time and have a sense that you are working well together, the issue of no-show is very different from that with a brand new client or with an old client who has a history of manipulative behaviors. The established client is less likely to no-show, and when he does do so the event is likely to be highly significant in terms of his therapeutic issues. Going away, with no warning, is a dramatic and forceful way to convey a message to one's therapist. What is this client telling you? What is going on between you and him? What happened during the last session that may have provoked or frightened or disappointed him? One place to look for answers to these questions is in your own response to his not showing up. Do you feel angry? Relieved? Sad? Responsible? It is important to sort these questions out before your next contact with the client so that you can be clear about your own limits when you talk with him again. And you should definitely talk with him.*

For one thing, you need to take care of yourself; you need to know what is happening with him and between him and you. More particularly, you need to know whether he intends to see you again or whether he plans to terminate. Most important of all, the no-show is a therapeutic issue, which the client needs to deal

---

* The only exception to this statement that I can think of would be the client who has failed to show up on several occasions throughout treatment and with whom you have a contract that you will not initiate contact should this happen again.

with: it is a form of acting out which has been precipitated by some internal or external event. It's not an isolated incident, an odd but meaningless happening.

If a client of mine fails to show up, I call him and ask what happened and when he wants to reschedule his appointment. I also remind him that he will be charged for the missed appointment. If he says that he has decided not to return, I tell him that I believe it is important for him to have one more session during which we can discuss his decision to terminate and tie up any remaining loose ends between us. Ward lists a number of goals for such a final session:

> If the client is willing to engage in an exit interview, there are at least four possible positive client outcomes that may result: (a) reduction of as many negative influences as possible before the client resumes life without counseling, (b) resolution of critical issues to the extent that the client is able to continue counseling with the same counselor, (c) preparation of the client for gaining maximum benefit from referral to another "helper," and (d) increased likelihood that the client will reenter counseling or some other personal growth experience at some future date. [1989, p. 107]

Of course, the final decision to return or not lies with the client. I cannot force him to come back. I have found, though, that most clients will return for a final session. In fact, no-shows without notification are rare among established clients unless you have unwittingly created the impression that such behavior is all right with you. If you have established your ground rules clearly, the great majority of clients will respect them. When a client does not respect them, you may be sure that his behavior is a signal that something important is going on, something that should be attended to.

With newer clients, no-shows are less unusual (although, again, setting clear expectations will eliminate most such problems). A client may be shopping, setting up appointments with several therapists and planning to continue with only one. He may not have gotten exactly what he wanted in that first (or second or third) session and therefore decided not to come back; his failure to notify you of that decision is his way of expressing his disappointment or anger that his needs were not met. A spouse or other family member may have put pressure on him to discontinue treatment. Whatever the reason, it is still appropriate for you (or your secretary) to make contact with him and clarify the treatment contract. And again, he should be encouraged to return in order to discuss what happened and what he can do next in order to meet his needs.

The more experience you have as a therapist, the less you will have to deal with the no-show kind of termination. It is as if the client can sense the tentativeness and uncertainty of the beginner and, if it fits into his system, use that uncertainty to justify hanging on to his old ways of not getting what he wants. As you grow in confidence and learn to stop discounting your own ability, you will stop conveying a covert invitation to the client to join you in your self-discounting. In the meantime, you may have to suffer through the pain of a few no-show dropouts. And they are painful. The best that can be said is that they offer a fine opportunity for the young therapist to learn something about herself.

THE "ABRUPT STOPPER"

You and your client have had a run-of-the-mill session. Nothing awful and nothing wonderful has happened. Toward the end of the hour, the client drops his bomb: "I've decided not to come back after today." You're surprised and off balance; your attention is divided between reviewing the session and wondering what your mistake was and figuring out how to respond right now. And there's no more time left in the session to really deal with what is happening. What to do?

The first rule of thumb in this situation is: Do not extend the session in order to talk about continuing. "Doorknob terminations" are a favorite ploy of manipulative clients. Rather, let the client know that you are uncomfortable about accepting that decision without having a chance to discuss it and invite him back for a termination session: "I'm sorry that you didn't tell me sooner, because I think it's important that we discuss this. I'd like you to come back one more time. Please take a couple of days to think about it; if you do decide to come in, call me and confirm your appointment. I'll hold your time open until Wednesday afternoon." If the client does come back, the focus of the session should be termination; assuming that his decision to terminate still stands, do not work with him on any other issues. If he has changed his mind and now wants to continue, the "first no, then yes" behavior needs to be explored; it is almost certainly part of the dysfunction that brought him to therapy in the first place. And finally, if he chooses not to return at all, you have done what you can. The ultimate responsibility is his.

More commonly, an abrupt stopper will let you know at the beginning of a session that he does not intend to continue. In this case, of course, you can focus on termination issues then and there. There are many reasons for abrupt terminations, and some of them are legitimate: a sudden move, a changed and inflexible work schedule, unexpected financial problems. More often, though, the abrupt decision has to do with therapeutic issues. After all, appointment times can be changed to accommodate schedule changes, and reduced or deferred fees can be negotiated. The client should be given every opportunity to talk about what is really behind the termination. He should not be cornered or bullied into "confessing"; if the fiction of unavoidable circumstances is important to him, he should be allowed to keep it. Terminating his therapy with his defenses still working and his pride intact may make it easier for him to seek treatment again later on.

Paving the way for a later return to treatment is, in fact, the primary goal for the termination session with an abrupt stopper. One of the most effective ways to accomplish this is to reframe the termination as a vacation, a leave of absence, a timeout for integration. The client can be genuinely congratulated for the gains he has made, and his decision to stop at this point can be honestly supported as an integral part of his overall pattern of growth. He can be encouraged to monitor himself, to respect his own internal sense of when and if to reenter treatment: "This is the end of Volume I of your therapy. I don't know if there will be a Volume II or not; but if there is, you will know when to begin it." Supporting his decision in this way will sometimes have a paradoxical effect, nudging him to change his mind and continue. Or it may validate his decision, while at the same time leaving him the option of returning without losing face or feeling that he has failed in his attempt to be on his own.

THERAPIST-INITIATED TERMINATIONS

Early in this chapter, we commented that the termination decision ideally should be a joint one with both therapist and client in agreement. Occasionally, the therapist will terminate with a client before the client is ready. Usually there is plenty of time to work such a termination through before the last session actually arrives. In fact, lead time is a legal and ethical imperative. "Abandonment of a case without sufficient notice or adequate excuse is a dereliction of duty" (Furrow 1980, p. 37), and as such may make the therapist legally liable. Once in a great while, however, the therapist must deal with unforeseen circumstances: a major upheaval in her personal or professional life that necessitates abrupt termination of one or more clients. The therapist must make every effort to schedule several sessions with each client during which a coming separation can be discussed. It is not acceptable to suddenly inform a client that this will be his last session; it is even less acceptable that the client arrive for an appointment, only to be told that his case has been transferred to another therapist. Nor is notification of such a change by phone or mail an appropriate substitute for a termination session. If some personal crisis makes it impossible for the therapist to be really available for her clients, she may choose to let them know what has happened and reschedule appointments for a future date, providing them with names of other therapists they may see during the interim. In the extremely unlikely circumstance that one would be physically unable to respond even in this minimal fashion, clients should at least be sent a personal letter explaining what has happened and providing them with referral names. It would also be appropriate for the therapist to invite clients to write or call her, so that they have the opportunity to round off their side of the relationship.

AND, TO TERMINATE THIS CHAPTER...

Many, perhaps most, therapists have difficulty handling terminations. Perhaps it is partly due to our culture; as I mentioned at the beginning of this chapter, we Westerners do not deal well with endings. It is certainly odd when you think about it. Most therapists are relatively uncomfortable with terminations long after they have learned to manage initial interviews easily, and yet we end exactly the same number of therapies as we begin.

I suspect that we would all find terminations much easier if we were to fully recognize and accept the fact that we cannot (and are not expected to) finish with our clients. That is, we do not send them away completely problem-free, completely grown-up, completely through with their issues. Just as we must help clients to shed the illusion that perfection and unending bliss are reasonable therapeutic goals, so we must work to dispel that expectation for ourselves. Therapist and client both must recognize, moreover, that even if the stated and agreed-upon goals of treatment have not been completely reached, still progress has been made and the client is able to work out his life in ways that were not possible before.

The end of therapy and the end of treatment are not synonymous. Though it may seem when we say goodbye to a client that we are both ending his therapy, in reality the therapist is the only one who is really terminating treatment. The client will continue to work on his issues, using many of the tools and insights of therapy long after that final session. Some clients, in fact, discover their greatest therapeutic gains after therapy has terminated; it is as if breaking free of the therapeutic relationship provides the permission they need to let go of their old ways of being. Some simply need time to integrate, to bring together all that they have learned and experienced, and to make it a natural part of their everyday life. Some rediscover their earlier progress in the new, posttherapy context and are surprised at how differently they react to problems that once would have seemed insoluble; others literally continue the therapeutic process long after formal termination, as if they had actually taken some part of the therapist into their own personality structure. A letter I received from an ex-client more than a year after her therapy ended describes this kind of experience:

> I have grown and changed in many wonderful ways. A lot of the growth I see in me I can relate specifically to areas of work during the time with you....An amazing awareness for me—that really effective therapy is not just immediate in its obvious effects but never stops having positive and lasting effects, allowing us to ever be changing and growing...our work together is always present in me and helping me.

A therapist is a kind of gardener: we plant seeds here and there, tend them carefully, provide care and nurturing, encourage the young and growing plants to shape themselves and develop their natural interaction with their environment. When the plant is strong enough to get along without its gardener, the gardener moves on, knowing that the plant will continue to grow and flower and bear fruit. Our clients may endure some very bad weather; they may experience some long dormant periods; they may need help from a gardener again some day, but they do not stop growing when our time with them is done.

THE CLIENT IN CRISIS

7

This chapter marks a turning point in our discussion of counseling and therapy. Up until now, we have been talking about "generic" therapy, describing concepts and techniques that are appropriate across a wide range of therapeutic situations. While not every technique or approach will work with every client, none can be classified as being more appropriate in one sort of therapy setting than in another. Indeed, the appropriateness (or inappropriateness) of each of these concepts is more likely to depend upon the therapist—her theoretical stance, her comfort level, her degree of experience—than on the kind of client with whom she is working.

But now things are going to shift a bit. Crisis work, group work, therapy with couples and families all require some special skills and emphases, different from (though generally based upon) generic one-on-one therapy. The next four chapters will focus on these sorts of approaches. So here we go, beginning with crisis work. What, exactly, does that mean?

In the broadest sense, nearly every client who comes for therapy is in a crisis of one sort or another. Roberts (1990) describes a crisis as having three ingredients: a precipitating event that affects on the client, the client's belief that the event will be stressful or disrupting, and a lack of effective coping strategies—that is, strategies that have worked in the past won't work this time. And that is what much of therapy is all about: helping people to find new ways of coping, of relating, of problem-solving, when the old ways are not working any more.

Our common-sense understanding, though, tells us that a person in real crisis is different. There is a feeling of urgency, of danger, of need for action *now*. If something isn't done soon, someone will be hurt, something irreparably damaged. Typically, violence or potential violence is involved: to self, to others, or being victimized by the violence of someone else. The therapist is likely to respond to these danger signals with a heightened sense of responsibility. We feel pressured to fix things, to save the client, to make the pain and scare go away. Everything looms larger than life during a crisis period. The irony is that at the very time when we and our clients most need to make wise, carefully considered decisions, we are under the greatest pressure to move quickly.

While all clients, then, can in some sense be described as in crisis, it is useful to distinguish a particular kind of emergency situation as requiring "crisis intervention." No one is immune to these emergencies, by the way—any of us can be stressed by environmental events to the point where our coping strategies break down and we move into a psychological danger zone. "At times of stress," says Slaby, "neurotic propensities emerge that people did not even know they had. Sometimes these behavioral traits or symptoms reach psychotic proportions" (1989, p. 1428). This chapter is not about "crisis clients," as a special population, but rather about how to work with *any* client at those special times when he is experiencing a crisis situation.

BASIC PRINCIPLES

Today, more than ever, crises seem to be a part of everyday life. Large-scale disasters happen with numbing frequency; suicides, homicides, and other violent behaviors are a staple of the evening news. To add to the problem, governmental resources for psychiatric intervention are shrinking: there is more and more need for help, but there are fewer and fewer public dollars to meet that need. As a result, it is increasingly likely that you, as a general practice therapist, can expect to find yourself dealing with psychiatric emergencies and to have few backup resources to help you do so. You will need to know how to recognize a crisis (better yet, an impending crisis) and how to act so as to defuse the danger and shrink the problem down to solvable proportions.

One of the most notable characteristics of a crisis is its complexity and confusion. Everything seems to be happening at once; demands are coming from all directions; the client feels overwhelmed by the pressure of internal and external events. If she is not prepared, the therapist too may begin to feel overwhelmed. An important antidote to therapist confusion is a clear grasp of crisis theory: what is a crisis, how does it unfold itself, what are its separate stages and aspects? As we begin to unravel the various strands it becomes possible to think in terms of dealing with one bit at a time—usually much more feasible than trying to handle the whole mess at once!

Crisis situations do develop in a more or less predictable pattern, although it often requires hindsight to determine where one actually begins. The first phase of a crisis is not usually experienced as such; rather, it is experienced as a rise in tension or stress level, generally associated with some external happening. The external event may or may not be unpleasant, but the person must mobilize some resources, do something different from usual, in order to deal with it. So far, the system is working; if the new coping strategy is adequate, the crisis may be averted. But if the strategy doesn't work, we move into the second crisis phase: more tension, plus a growing feeling that we can't do anything about the problem. This phase signals the beginning of the crisis proper; it is at this point that the person himself is likely to recognize that he is getting in over his head. As all of his coping strategies continue to fail and he feels more and more desperate, the person begins to initiate emergency action—often some brand new behavior, one reserved for extreme situations. This is the third phase, the Big Push to deal with the problem. If it works, the person must then collect himself and return to his (perhaps somewhat altered) precrisis level of functioning. The crisis was not averted, but it was dealt with and is now past. If the Big Push does not work, the person moves into the fourth crisis phase: still greater tension, helplessness, feelings of inadequacy, disorganization, confusion, lack of control.

Although a therapist may enter this drama at any point, she is most likely to be called in for crisis intervention during the fourth phase. Phase 4 is the acute crisis phase, marked by the failure of the client's emergency coping system: the mechanisms have broken down, tension has peaked, and disorganization has set in. The time scale here can vary tremendously from one situation/client to another. A father, survivor of an automobile crash in which family members were killed, may move into the fourth phase within minutes of the accident itself. At the other extreme is the exhaustion crisis, in which the person may have been functioning for weeks or months in the second or third phase but finally has no more energy to maintain the emergency measures. An example here would be the single parent who works for months at two full-time jobs in order to pay off a massive debt and still provide for his children but who finally collapses into a suicidal I-can't-go-on-any-longer depression.

No matter what the time frame, however, all crisis situations have important common features. First, the final phase (the active crisis) is generally self-limiting, changing in some way within one to five weeks. People simply cannot sustain a crisis response for longer than this. Second, the nature of that change will depend on what is done during the final phase, rather than on what has happened in the past. Finally, people in an active crisis tend to experience an increased desire to be helped by others and to be more willing to accept such help than they are during noncrisis times. All of these characteristics of acute crisis point toward the importance of moving quickly in crisis intervention. There is a relatively short time during which (1) the crisis will continue to be acute, (2) present action will have the greatest effect, and (3) the client will be most open to being helped.

Moving quickly, in fact, is the common denominator in all crisis intervention approaches. "Quickly" applies to the initial response of the therapist, to focusing in on the primary problem, and to the overall length of treatment. With regard to initial response, it is best if intervention can be made within twenty-four hours of the client's request; delay of two weeks or more often means entirely missing the period during which the client is most open and available for treatment. Delay may also complicate the client-therapist relationship, as the client becomes angry about or resigned to the lack of response from those who might be able to help. Note, however, that "quickly" does not mean "hurried." Even as the therapist moves in quickly, she must appear calm and confident. Most clients will be reassured simply by the presence on the scene of someone who at least looks like she knows what she is doing, and the experience of reassurance and relaxing a bit is an important first step in actually solving the problem central to the crisis. Better, perhaps, to speak of responding quickly, but of acting decisively.

Clients in crisis do not want a leisurely, "tell me about whatever you want to talk about" approach. They want action, relief, a sense that something can be done. Foxman (1990) points out that there are two distinct parts to crisis work, first engaging the client's cooperation and then solving the problem. Decisiveness and self-assurance (not to be confused with smugness or authoritarianism) help the client to trust, to believe that this therapist can indeed make a difference and therefore is worth cooperating with. They also help in the problem-solving part, creating a business-like approach to a problem which is, by definition, solvable. The crisis therapist is relatively directive, helping the client to focus on the specific problem that is to be dealt with and to plan a strategy for making things better. With this kind of problem-solving approach, treatment does not ordinarily develop into long-term, depth therapy. Rather, three to six sessions usually suffice to move the client to a place where he can continue on his own (without the therapist, that is; one of the guiding principles of crisis work is to help clients develop and use social supports).

FIRST STEPS WITH A CLIENT IN CRISIS

Roberts gives a general outline of the steps involved in crisis work: (1) establish a working relationship with the client; (2) define the problem; (3) explore the client's feelings about his situation; (4) explore and assess his past attempts at coping; (5) develop new options; (6) help him to implement a plan of action; (7) follow up on what has been done (1990, p. 12). While this is an excellent overall plan and one which fits our discussion of crisis work, it does beg one important question: am I the appropriate therapist to carry out the treatment? The client in crisis is demanding help of some sort, and the therapist's job is to respond to that demand. However, our response need not be to work directly with the client; we can make a referral to another individual or agency, we can very briefly help the client mobilize his resources so that no further formal assistance will be needed, or—in circumstances of immediate danger to the client or others—we can arrange for voluntary or involuntary hospitalization. Our first job, then, is to get enough information to make a decision about overall strategy.

GATHERING INFORMATION

The kind of information you need in your first dealings with a client in crisis is different from the detailed symptomatic and historical information used in making a differential diagnosis, DSM III-R style (that will come later). First, you need the information that will allow you to make that immediate, practical, solution-oriented intervention.

While detailed history-taking is not necessary or even desirable for most crisis clients, it is nevertheless helpful to get some idea of what sorts of problems the client has faced in the past and how he has dealt with them. This information will help both you and your client to sort out patterns of response, to begin looking at what has worked and what has not worked for him during past periods of stress. It will also give you a sense of his normal state. Since the major goal of crisis intervention is to bring the client back to at least the level of functioning that he maintained before this present crisis, you must have some notion of what that level of functioning was. If the client was not doing well even before the crisis, that minimal level may be all that you can reasonably hope to achieve in your work with him now; alternatively, you may want to think of referring him elsewhere for more extended therapy when the immediate crisis has been attended to.

So, what will you focus on on that first contact? You need to know what is and has been going on and how the client has tried in the past to cope with the problem. You need to know who is involved—who are the actors in this drama? What is happening to each of them? What demands are they making on the client? And the final, critical question: Why now? Why is help needed today rather than tomorrow or last week? What is special and significant about the present situation that led the client to accept help at this juncture? It is the answer to this "Why now?" in all of its variations and permutations that will give you some of the clearest pointers for what can be done to begin solving the problems.

Notice that plural "problems." Most crisis situations, unfortunately, do not involve single, straightforward problems. People can usually take care of that kind of thing on their own! Crisis therapists are more likely to see multiple problems, layers of stresses and tensions and demands, complex intertwinings in which problem *A* has grown out of efforts to deal with situation *B*, which is in turn a result of demand *C*, and so on. Indeed, the multiple-problem crisis is often so entangled that the client loses track of just what is the most pressing demand, the source of greatest stress or conflict. Simply sorting things out, helping him understand and make sense of all that he is responding to, can be very therapeutic.

RESOURCES

Assessing the client's resources is a major focus of your early interactions with a client is crisis. Even as you invite him to tell his story, to share his perception of the nature of the crisis, you should be noticing what sorts of resources he refers to—and which ones he doesn't mention. Who are the significant people in his world, and which of these provide support for him? Of all the various kinds of resources that people can call on, social resources—people—are the most important in a crisis. Even if he does need professional therapy, his ability to use other people's help will affect the length of treatment that will be necessary, as well as predict the degree to which he will be able to allow the therapist into his personal life. "Successful management and treatment are facilitated by the patient's ability to acknowledge and use social support, especially the support of the psychotherapist, without feeling further guilt and shame" (Peterson & Bongar 1989, p. 578).

And what about other kinds of resources? What is his economic situation, the state of his finances? Does he have a job? What are his skills? Is he able to think clearly and solve problems? (It should be noted that a client who is using chemicals has, by definition, impaired thinking abilities. The client who is drunk or strung out on drugs needs specialized drug/alcohol treatment and should be referred to an appropriate agency; it is extremely unlikely that he will get the help he needs in a general-purpose setting.) If he has a good resource bank, one session of clarifying the situation and planning future action may be all he needs from you. If he falls into a middle range, a range with which you feel competent to work, you will still need to know which of these resource areas need building up and which ones he can now call on as he works to solve his immediate problems.

The purpose of this general crisis assessment is to decide how well the client is likely to respond to a situation-oriented cognitive approach. We want to know if, given a little professional help, he will be able to move ahead on his own, using the resources available to him, to solve his problems. And, while we are carrying out the initial assessment, we are also building a working relationship with the client. We are letting him experience us as a person and as a professional. We are giving him a chance to tell his story without being judged or shamed or pressured to take care of it on his own. We are hearing that story calmly, without being overwhelmed by it. Berman's advice to telephone hot-line workers applies to all crisis therapists: "From the very beginning, the counselor should sound calm and comfortable in the conversation, strong and capable in the counselor role yet gentle with the caller's feeling" (1990, p. 63). Presenting yourself in this way not only invites the client to believe that someone can really help him and to trust you enough to tell you what you need to know, but also provides a model that he can imitate as he begins to calm down and sort out his options.

CONFIDENTIALITY

As we have already suggested, one of the major strategies in crisis intervention is mobilizing the client's resource system. This may mean talking to other people in the client's world, alerting them to what is happening, and enlisting their support. For this reason, it is particularly important not to make early promises about confidentiality that may later have to be broken. Often, a part of the client's crisis involves some family secret (which may, in fact, be no secret at all) that he is worried others may discover. Rather than promising to help keep the secret, the crisis therapist will do better to make it clear that, while she will do her best not to use any information in an embarrassing or hurtful way, she must be free to do whatever needs to be done to protect the client and others with whom he interacts. This is most dramatically true when the crisis issues involve danger to the client or others.

"The usual rules for confidentiality do not apply when working with a suicidal patient," says Doyle. "Inform the patient that the suicide wish will be shared with whoever needs to know because the clinician wants the patient to live" (1990, p. 385). The same rule holds for clients who are threatening, verbally or otherwise, to hurt someone else. This is not just a clinical/ethical issue but a legal one as well; in most states, therapists are required to break confidentiality in cases of immediate physical danger and can be liable to prosecution if they fail to do so.

Beginning therapists are often concerned that refusing to promise confidentiality may prevent the client from sharing important information. In my experience, this is seldom if ever the case. The client may wait a little longer while he checks me out, but eventually he does talk. Generally my very insistence that he understand my own limits and that I will take whatever action I believe necessary (always, of course, informing him of my intentions) tends to make him more trusting of me rather than less so. If a client does not respond in this way, or if he seems overly concerned about confidentiality in general, this can have diagnostic significance. When secrets and trust are a major concern for a client, look for family issues such as power, control, sexism, and intimacy as having a bearing on whatever other problems the client may present (Petretic-Jackson & Jackson 1990).

THE CRISIS CONTRACT

The first crisis intervention session should end only when a crisis contract has been established: what will be done, and how. In building such a contract, "identifying goals and prioritizing values is the first step. The second step is determining what goals can be achieved, given the patient's current life situation and stage of life" (Slaby 1989, p. 1431).

Contracting is especially important early in the crisis intervention process for at least three reasons. First, the client in crisis is seldom clear about all the facets of his problem situation: he is confused and overwhelmed. Setting up a contract helps him to choose what he most wants to deal with and to focus his energies into solving at least that one part of his problem. It provides him with two essential ingredients for success: a sense of direction and a sense of hope that something can be done. A second reason for contract setting is the fast pace needed in crisis intervention. Clear contracting makes it possible to zero in quickly on a plan of action, one in which everyone involved can know what is expected of him. Which brings me to the third point: responsibility. The crisis client needs to take charge, to do something, to begin to resume control in his life. Making a contract underscores the client's responsibility—literally, his *response-ability* —and makes it clear that he is not a passive victim but rather will participate actively in remedying his situation.

"The contract," say Ottens and Fisher-McCann, "structures the limited therapy time, establishes treatment as time-limited and focused, and offers the client a realistic idea of what to expect" (1990, p. 88). To accomplish this, make sure that the contract you develop with your client specifies at least the following points: (1) the focus of the problem—exactly what is to be changed or solved; (2) the time limits—how long it will take to initiate change and how long you will be working with the client; (3) who else is to be involved and how; and (4) what are the responsibilities of the client and of the therapist. Once you have spelled out who will do what, with whom, when, for how long, and to what purpose, you have defined the framework of a good crisis work contract.

In essence, the whole of the first contact with a crisis client is an exercise in building trust in both directions—therapist for client as much as client for therapist. Your whole effort of assessment, evaluation, and contract building serves to inform you of how much and how far you can trust this client, just as the way in which you go about those tasks tells him much about how far he can trust you. And the more honest, solid trust there can be, both ways, the more effective your crisis interventions are likely to be.

MOVING IN

Our overall goals in working with a client in crisis are, essentially, always the same: help him to deal with his feelings, clarify the problem, identify options and resources, and take appropriate action. Put this way, it sounds simple. But when you are in the middle of it, with bad things happening or threatening to happen on all sides, it doesn't feel simple at all. You need a starting point, a way to move in and clear a space within which to work. As you do so, there is one fundamental principle, one rule that must be followed if your efforts are to succeed: treat the client with respect. No matter how confused, wrong, muddle-headed, or even just plain bad he may seem, he is a person who is handling his life as well as he can at that moment. Underneath the dysfunctional behavior there is always a positive purpose. Often the client himself has lost faith in his own value, his positive purpose, and a major part of your job is to restore that faith. "It is very important," says Foxman, "to give...respect, dignity and caring, as the client is especially sensitive to criticism, rejection, or insensitivity, implied or real, because of the client's own feelings of futility, inadequacy, and loss" (1990, p. 27). Your respectful presence is the first step in clearing a space for him to work.

By its very definition, a crisis leaves the client feeling overwhelmed and helpless. So much is happening in his life at such a high level of intensity that he can no longer hold things together. The coping strategies that have worked (more or less) for him in the past do not work any more, and he is left with a choice between floundering about doing useless or wrong things (that only seem to enmesh him further in the problem) or becoming immobilized. In order to turn the situation around, he needs first to back off and explore possible alternative solutions. The therapist's task is to find some breathing room for him so that he can begin to think again and can sort out the various resources and courses of action available. Listening to his story and helping him to put it into enough order to communicate it to you is the first step in helping him to back off and breathe. It is essential that you stay in tune with this story, allowing him to tell it in his own way; the content of the story is not the point here, but rather the process of his telling it. As he senses your commitment to understanding him and becomes involved in helping you to do so, he shifts ever so slightly out of the nothing-can-be-done hopelessness. Something *is* being done—he is making contact with you. Slaby (1989) talks about the importance of "peopling the empty space" in crisis work; as you enter the alien aloneness of the client in crisis, you lead the way for other supportive resources to follow.

COGNITIVE WORK

A direct implication of the problem-solving approach to crisis intervention is that much of the work will be very cognitive. Helping the client to think clearly, to explain what has happened and what he has done about it and how others have reacted, will also tend to shift him out of the helpless-hopeless downward spiral. As people slide deeper and deeper into crisis, their thinking tends to become ineffective and confused. They torment themselves with worried catastrophizing or berate themselves for having caused the problem, rather than trying to understand what is really going on. A major task for the therapist is to interrupt these destructive kinds of thinking and to help the client to replace them with clear assessment of what is happening and how that might be changed. We need to normalize the situation as much as possible: the client may have made mistakes, and so do all of us; his feelings are understandable and much like those of anyone else in the same situation. Reflect and summarize what he tells you, respecting his right to feel and believe as he does, but at the same time letting him know that you do not share his feelings: "I know that you feel very guilty about this situation and wish that you had done something about it sooner. It's normal and natural to feel that way, even though there may have been nothing that you could do. What is important now, though, is to look at what is happening *today,* so that we can figure out what to do to make things more bearable for you and your family." "Of course you feel angry; most people would. It's okay to feel angry, as long as you don't let your anger get in the way of figuring out what can be done to make things better." Notice that each of these responses contains three elements: acknowledging the client's feelings, reassuring him that these feelings are normal and acceptable, and then moving the focus from feeling to thinking. Notice, also, that we do not insist that the client switch immediately into trying to find a solution. They point him in the direction of thinking about the problem, of understanding it, as a step on the way to solving it, but they do not cut him off from telling his story.

A good way to get from talking about how bad and awful things are (which most crisis clients can do) to exploring the situation as a problem to be solved (which is more difficult) is to discuss what steps the client has already taken to deal with his problems. Every client in crisis has tried some things that have not worked; that is part of the crisis, the experience of old coping strategies failing to do the job. "What are some of the ways you've tried to make things better?" "You say that nothing helps—will you tell me some of the things, specifically, that haven't helped?' Not only do questions like these shift the client from a passive victim to an active (though unsuccessful) problemsolver, but they also yield information about the client's overall problem-solving skills. Find out not only what the client has tried that didn't work but also *why* it didn't work. This will again help the client to shift from "awfulizing" into constructive thinking; it is also often the case that an unsuccessful attempt at a solution can be turned into a useful strategy by modifying it slightly in one way or another (Ewing 1978).

In order for the client to come up with a plan of action that will work, he needs to have accurate and complete information about what is happening. And that is often difficult. A typical response to crisis is to acquire a kind of tunnel vision, a restricted view in which the victim is only aware of what is going on inside his head and right in front of his eyes. "Being caught up in the crisis itself limits the [client] to the here-and-now, whereas the therapist gives attention not only to the immediate crisis but to its meaning" (Whitaker 1989, p. 53). "What happened just before that?" is one of the most useful questions you can ask of a client; another is, "Who else knows/knew about it and what did they do?" As you begin to help the client reconnect with others (family members, friends, other professionals), you may want to ask them for information that will fill in the gaps and provide important antecedents to the client's story.

People in crisis do a great deal of blaming. They may blame themselves—even to the degree that their guilty feelings undermine any solution-engendering activities. Or they may blame others, feeling helpless and victimized by an uncaring or malevolent world. Just as the self-blamer needs to let up on himself, stop blaming and turn to solving, so the other-blamer needs to let up on others, accept his own share of responsibility and in so doing take back his personal power. Part of the goal of cognitive work is to help the client become aware of his own impact, both positive and negative: What is he doing (or not doing) that is keeping things from getting even worse? What could he do that would change things in *either* direction? A question that often helps clients toward a fresh perspective is, "What could you do, right now, that would make things worse than they already are?" The client may protest that making things worse is the last thing he would want to do; but if you can persuade him (just as a favor to you, because you're one of those weird shrink types) to take the question seriously it may lead him to a fresh awareness of how much he is actually doing right, how important he is in maintaining the status quo, or even that some potential catastrophic outcome might not be so impossibly awful, after all.

Still within the context of understanding what is happening, the client needs to think about his emotional reactions. Thinking about feelings is a new concept for many clients. They know how to think, and they experience feelings, but they do not put the two together. Teach your client to stand back from his feelings and to simply reflect on how he responds to his situation and how that response affects what happens next. Watching himself "from outside" may provide the shift he needs to move away from his repetitive and unproductive patterns into a more effective way of thinking and reacting.

AFFECTIVE WORK

With all of our emphasis on cognition and problem solving, we must not forget that all crises have painful emotional components. The client in crisis experiences intense feelings, and these feelings are a part of the crisis. The therapist must acknowledge and validate the emotional responses of her client. She can also provide him with an opportunity to experience or vent his feelings in a safe way. With her, it is acceptable and normal to be angry or scared or despondent and to talk about what those feelings are like. Berman advises telephone hot-line counselors that "the caller *is* who she is and *feels* as she feels, and the counselor needs to recognize and accept *that person* with *those feelings* at *that time* even though the person or feelings might not be acceptable to the counselor outside the call" (1990, p. 63). The advice holds for all crisis workers: regardless of whether you agree with the client's response, whether you yourself would respond that way, or whether you would choose for a friend someone who did so, nevertheless right now you need to support and accept the emotions and help the client to work them through safely. When there is a lull in the emotional storm, invite the client to think about what he has just been experiencing. When he can think about what he feels, he is not so much at the mercy of those feelings.

Some emotional responses are so common among crisis clients that we can expect them, be prepared to deal with them, and even probe for them if the client does not talk about them. I have already mentioned guilt as one such response. Clients may feel guilty about past or present behavior, about their (supposed) causal role in bringing about the crisis, about their negative feelings toward themselves or other people. They often fear that others will blame them too, will think them terrible or shameful people, will punish or abandon them. Another common feeling is ambivalence, which is often experienced as confusion. The client wants to hurt and wants to comfort; he wants to run away and he wants to stay and do battle; he feels triumphant (his dire predictions came true) and he feels miserable (he does not want those predictions to be true). He does not know what he wants or feels! The correct intervention here involves voicing both sides of the ambivalence and validating both: "Lots of times, when we're feeling rotten, we feel resentful toward people who seem happy and comfortable. Even when they reach out to us, and we really appreciate it, another piece of us would like to kick them." "Most people who are really brave are also scared to death—otherwise, it wouldn't take bravery to do what they do. It seems pretty normal to me that you would have found yourself angry and wanting to fight and wanting to run away at the same time."

When a child is in distress, his natural response is to go to a parent or other trusted adult for comfort. That response is so universal that it seems almost wired in; indeed, such a response would have obvious evolutionary survival value. It should not be surprising, then, that people in crisis have the same response tendency. They seek out someone they love and trust—what the analytic folk call an "attachment figure"—and find comfort in being attended to by that person. If they cannot find an appropriate attachment figure, they are likely to become angry, frightened, or to experience some other regressive emotion (Shulman 1990). This phenomenon has at least two implications for crisis therapists. First, attachment figures help people weather crises. As we shall see in the next section of this chapter, bringing in social supports is a primary strategy in crisis work, and one reason why it is so effective is that it often provides the missing attachment figure. Second, if there is no attachment figure in the natural environment, or until one can be found, the therapist can serve as a substitute.

Clients in crisis feel a loss of self-esteem, a threat to their sense of competence. Reluctance to admit that they have failed, that they can't handle the situation on their own, keeps many people from seeking help. Boldt, in his discussion of suicide and suicide prevention, suggests that suicidal people fear being labeled as mentally ill: the "social stigma of 'mental illness' has the effect of deterring the suicidal person and his family from seeking professional help, and from the social support and communications of relatives and friends" (1989, p. 10). The same is true for many other kinds of crisis; the very admission of needing help can make them feel even worse. In addition to admitting to their own weakness, there is a feeling of something given up: the loss of what-might-have-been and the longing for what-is-no-more. Even in crises which do not obviously involve grief and sadness, there is usually a sense of loss—loss of possibilities, loss of illusions. Sooner or later, all of us must grieve over the death of Santa Claus; the crisis client faces this loss in a particularly intense and poignant way.

While it is often helpful to encourage a client to talk about grief and sadness and loss, this is not always true. Invite the client to talk about his pain, but do not pressure him to do so. There is a kind of numbness that sometimes sets in to protect people from having to deal with too much, all at once, too soon. People experiencing a personal disaster may tell themselves that it can't be happening; they feel detached, dazed, unable to comprehend. "Denial of an overwhelming reality," says Slaby, "may be required at first to facilitate gradual acceptance of an event so tragic that it appears to be a bad dream. With time and support the reality can be processed sufficiently to allow planning for what may be required" (1989, p. 1431). Your client will surely need to talk about his feelings—some time, with someone. But perhaps not now, and not with you. Let him know that you are there, concerned and interested; then trust that he will know what is best for him.

Another common emotional experience of crisis is, of course, anxiety. How will it work out? What will I do? What will become of us? The sooner a plan of action can be worked out and implemented, the sooner this anxiety will begin to dissipate. Doing something about it is the best antidote for anxiety. With the dissipation of anxiety, however, may come frustration. The new plan is not working as well, or as quickly, as the client had hoped. Or he is finding it more difficult and demanding than anticipated. He does not like it; it is not good enough. An important part of the later phases of crisis intervention often involves helping the client to develop new, perhaps lower, standards of well-being, to do without some things he had previously taken for granted, to delay gratification until the situation works itself out. Developing and accepting these standards may take him back again through the gamut of crisis emotions: guilt, anger, ambivalence, loss and grief, the whole package. Hopefully, he will have gained both self-knowledge and coping skills in the earlier crisis work so that this set of feeling responses need not be as intense or as debilitating as his original emotional state, but it is no less real and no less demanding of therapeutic attention.

SOME GUIDELINES

Your job as a crisis therapist is to help your client to get along without you. Rather than learning to depend on his therapist for support, the client needs to learn how to find resources outside of therapy, in his natural environment. This is why virtually all crisis intervention theories stress the importance of reconnecting the client with his social support system—or, if he doesn't have such a system, helping him to create one. Slaby, for example, says unequivocally that "the goal in all emergency psychiatric interventions is to work with the patient in a family context (e.g., marriage, cohabitation, homosexual liaison)" (1989, p. 1431).

In a real sense, "the crisis client" includes not only the individual in the therapist's office but also the whole social network of which that person is the center. Family, friends, and co-workers are all potentially part of the solution, just as they are (overtly or covertly) part of the crisis. Although the identified client must learn to take responsible action to better his situation, that action can and should be supported by the other people in his life. Because crises are often emergencies that involve real danger to the client and others around him, we cannot afford a more leisurely approach in which he gradually learns to work with and accept support from his significant others through individual work with the therapist. To the extent that these significant others can be involved from the outset, the system itself can be helped to find and maintain a solution, thus freeing the therapist to act as consultant rather than trying to carry the full treatment responsibility herself. The first guideline, then, in crisis work is to expand the therapeutic unit. Bring in reinforcements; reconnect the client with the other people in his world.

A second guideline is to find a way to let the client tell his story. If he is readily able to do so, listen to him. Your respectful attention is the most powerful and effective initial intervention that you can make. "It is good to remember," says Berman, "that sometimes doing less is more, therapeutically speaking" (1990, p. 60). Explaining the situation to you, making you understand how things fit together, also helps the client to understand; it is the first step in the problem-solving process. On the other hand, the client may be in no shape to tell his story. He may be too overwhelmed, too angry, too confused. Once you have made sure that he (and others who are involved) is physically safe, your task is to calm and support him so that he can begin to think and to talk. While it may be necessary to get some of the initial information from someone else, the more of it that the client can give you, the better. Once you have heard it from his point of view and let him know that you respect what he tells you, then you can turn to others for additional facts and opinions. But the client's own story comes first.

Typically, the client in crisis is overwhelmed, stressed out, and not thinking very clearly. It may be that the therapist can see solutions or strategies of which the distraught client is not aware. Should she share these? Should she tell the client what to do? If the client is truly confused and open to suggestion and your suggestion is based on more than just your personal opinion or values, advice giving can be appropriate. Crisis intervention is short-term, action-oriented treatment; it is designed to get the client quickly to a place where he can begin to manage his own life again. Advice from someone outside the situation, someone who has experience with similar kinds of problems, can provide structure, direction, and a sense of hope that something can be done.

For other clients, though, advice giving is generally not helpful. These are the clients who are looking for easy, pat answers to complicated problems, answers that usually involve making somebody else change. Clients who have a long history of therapeutic contacts, or who are glib or hostile in their interactions with the therapist, are not likely to benefit from direct suggestions.

Another type of client for whom advice giving is not particularly helpful is the manipulative client. Such clients are adept at misusing advice, at acting on the advice in such a way as to prove that the therapist (and everyone else) is wrong and the problem is truly insoluble. Indeed, the crisis itself may have grown out of this client's unconscious desire to have an insoluble problem, one that will focus everyone's attention on his own needs. Giving advice, punishing, or scolding these clients often pushes them into further escalation of the problem. One of the best ways to recognize such a client is to tune in to your own emotional response to him. If you find yourself wanting either to rescue him or to kick him (or both!), chances are that he has indeed succeeded in hooking you. Step back and let yourself look past the surface at the vulnerable and lonely person underneath who is so desperate for attention. This need for attention, and the absence of effective ways to get it, has escalated the crisis to its present point, and getting attended to is what he must ultimately learn to do. Again, bringing in family and friends provide ways for him to begin.

Unless the crisis is one of anger and hostility, a common impulse when working with someone who is very upset is to move closer, to literally reach out to them. We therapists are not immune to this impulse; indeed, it may impel us even more strongly than most people, because we are trained to respond empathically to our clients. There are dangers in reaching out and touching, though, and we need to be aware of them. Parry warns us of touching not in response to the client's feelings, but to our own: "Often the helper is trying to avoid his or her own fear that he or she has nothing much to offer, that 'just listening' is not much good because—you guessed it—the feelings are unbearable. In this way, the physical contact becomes a collusion with the fantasy that no one has the capacity to bear the emotional burden" (1900, p. 75). The times when you are most tempted to comfort your client by reaching out and touching him may be exactly the times when you should refrain from doing so. Another problem with offering physical comfort is that we may get in the way of the client's getting that comfort from a more appropriate source. Remember, our job is not to make the client dependent on us for emotional support but to help him to get support from others. When I put a mother-ly arm around a weeping client, it may feel good to both of us, but it might be a more long-lasting, dependable feel-good if it came from that client's spouse or close friend.

I do not mean to suggest that therapists should never touch someone in crisis. There are moments when touching a client conveys more understanding, respect, and caring than words ever could. But because touch is so emotionally powerful, and because crises are times of intense emotion, there is danger in using it too often or with too little understanding of its effect. I can only reiterate what I said about touch in Chapter 5: when in doubt, don't. Much harm can be done by touch-ing a client at the wrong time or for the wrong reasons. Do not risk it unless you are quite sure that you know what you are about.

SUICIDE

Of all persons with whom a crisis therapist must deal, the suicidal client is perhaps the most demanding and the most frightening. You may hope that you won't have to handle this kind of problem, but chances are that you will—it comes with the territory in our profession. In fact, suicide problems have been on the increase in our society over the past decade, and there is no sign that this trend is changing.

Sooner or later, then, you will work with a client who is or threatens to become suicidal. Suicidal clients tend to push their *therapists* into a kind of crisis. Berman warns, "I would be aware that my own frustration at seeing a patient not respond could lead not only to anger but to a sense of hopelessness in myself that might be sensed by a patient" (1990, p. 93). When a client persists in his suicidal hints or threats, we often feel responsible and helpless; if those feelings are com-municated to the client, client and therapist can begin to feed each other's despair. When we find ourselves in this kind of situation, what we need is information, a set of coping strategies, and a way to accept and release our feelings appropriately. In this section we will attend to the first two of these needs; Chapter 11, on the Care and Feeding of Therapists, will contain some discussion of the third.

The therapist's task with a suicidal client has four parts: first, to recognize the client as actually or potentially suicidal; second, to assess the immediate danger (lethality) of the suicidal behavior; third, to understand some of the dynamics underlying the client's desire to kill himself; and fourth, to develop and implement a treatment plan.

RECOGNIZING THE SUICIDAL CLIENT

It should be stated at the outset that many, probably most, people have some suici-dal thoughts at one time or another in their lives. Begin by assuming that any client either is thinking or has thought about suicide, just like everybody else in the world.

Making this assumption will go a long way toward defusing the suicide issue and allowing you to talk about it more matter-of-factly with your client: "Most people think about killing themselves at some time in their life—have you?" Or, "When was the last time you thought about suicide?" If the client denies any suicidal thinking, you can accept the denial with mild surprise and then go on with the interview: "That's interesting; most people do think about it at some time or other." Most likely, your client will experience relief that here is someone he can talk with openly about suicide, someone who will not be frightened by or angry with him.

The person who says that he has not thought of suicide may or may not be telling the truth. Hendren says that "it is the rare severely depressed patient who has not had some fleeting thoughts of suicide. Therefore, total denial of suicidal ideation should be a red flag to the interviewer" (1990, p. 238). Many people feel guilty or ashamed of suicidal thoughts or fear that they will be prevented from carrying out such plans if they reveal them. The client who presents himself as hopeless, who is socially isolated or has recently lost an important relationship, or who has taken steps to tie up loose ends in his life (make a will, settle his business affairs) may be in serious suicide danger. Also of concern is the previously depressed client who now seems unaccountably at peace with the world (the peace may result from his having finally decided to end his life). If such a client denies any suicidal ideas, it is well to return to the topic gently or to find other ways to explore it.

Unfortunately, there are a number of beliefs about suicide commonly held in our society that are as misleading as they are difficult to eradicate. Table 7-1 lists ten such beliefs.

Notice that, in many instances, holding the belief would tend to make one less likely to suspect a given client of being suicidal. It is as if we have created a comfortable stereotype to protect us from the painful reality of how common suicide is among normal people. Perhaps the layperson can allow himself the luxury of such inaccurate beliefs; we therapists cannot.

An important part of recognizing the client who may be suicidal is knowing what sorts of life experiences and attitudes are most likely to accompany suicidal feelings. Roy tells us that successful suicides tend to be committed by "those who have suffered the loss of a love object, narcissistic injury, or who experience overwhelming affects like rage or guilt, or who identify with a suicide victim" (1989, p. 1416). If your client falls into one of these categories, you should be alert to the possibility of suicide, even if he denies thinking about it.

People who threaten or attempt suicide today do appear to be different from suicides of past decades in one major way. In the past, the suicidal person was likely to be overwhelmingly sad, often feeling guilty for some past behavior, often ashamed of himself and having very low self-esteem. While he may have been angry, the anger was directed inward, toward himself. "Today, the suicider's anger seems to have a greater degree of projected blame for their problems, rather than the previous feeling of culpability.... It is no longer, *I'm not okay, you're okay;* it's *no one is okay."* (Foxman 1990, p. 7). This anger makes the suicidal client espe-

TABLE 7.1 TEN COMMON MISCONCEPTIONS ABOUT SUICIDE

FALSE	TRUE
1. People who talk about suicide rarely commit suicide.	1. People who commit suicide have given some clue or warning of intent. Suidiced threats and attempts must be taken seriously.
2. The tendency toward suicide is inherited and passed on from one generation to another.	2. Suicide does not "run in families." It has no characteristic genetic quality,
3. The suicidal person wants to die and feels there is no turning back.	3. Suicidal persons most often reveal ambivalence about living versus dying and frequently call for help immediately following the suicide attempt.
4. Everyone who commits suicide is depressed.	4. Although depression is often associated with suicidal feelings, not all people who kill themselves are obviously depressed. Some are anxious, agitated, psychotic, organically impaired, or wish to escape their life situation.
5. There is very little correlation between alcoholism and suicide.	5. Alcoholism and suicide often go hand in hand; that is, a person who commits suicide is often also an alcoholic.
6. A person who commits suicide is mentally ill.	6. Although persons who commit suicide are often distraught, upset, or depressed, many of them would not have been medically diagnosed as mentally ill.
7. A suicide attempt means that the attempter will always entertain thoughts of suicide.	7. Often, a suicide attempt is made during a particularly stressful period. If the remainder of that period can be appropriately managed, then the attempter can go on with life.
8. If you ask a client directly, "Do you feel like killing yourself?" this will lead him to make a suicide attempt.	8. Asking a client directly about suicidal intent will often minimize the anxiety surrounding the feeling and act as a deterrent to the suicidal behavior.
9. Suicide is more common among the lower socioeconomic groups than elsewhere in our society.	9. Suicide crosses all socioeconomic groups and no one group is more susceptible than another.
10. Suicidal persons rarely seek medical help.	10. In retrospective studies of committed suicide, more than half had sought medical help within the six months preceding the suicide.

From C. L. Hatton & S. M. Valente, *Suicide: Assessment and Intervention* 2nd Edition. Englewood Cliffs, N.J.: Prentice-Hall, 1984, pp. 57-58. Reprinted by permission.

cially hard to deal with, as he is likely to be defensive, blaming, provocative, and generally indifferent to your attempts to draw him into therapy.

Suicidal clients are ambivalent. Part of them wants to kill themselves, while part of them wants to continue to live. If it weren't for that latter part, they would not be in your office; they would be dead or trying to get that way. Schneidman points out that a necessary condition for the seriously suicidal person is "a sharp and almost sudden increase of *constrictions* of intellectual focus, a tunnelling of thought processes, a narrowing of the mind's content, a truncating of the capacity to set viable options" (1989, p. 20). It is this constricting, this narrowing of possibilities, that allows the suicidal person to deny his healthier side. Suicide becomes a real possibility when there are no other choices, no way out of the pain. The therapist's office may be the healthy side's last option: the last, unlikely possibility that somewhere, somehow, something can change. Above all, then, we must help the client to keep options open and possibilities alive. As long as there are choices, there can be hope.

ASSESSMENT OF SUICIDE DANGER

There are four basic questions which must be answered in order to assess the likelihood that the suicidal client will actually carry out his intent. The questions should be put to the client calmly and matter-of-factly; the answers will help you to decide whether the client can be left to his own devices (in the context of whatever plan you and he will work out together) or whether more stringent measures (ongoing supervision or hospitalization) should be considered. The first of these questions has to do with method: has the client chosen a method for killing himself? If he knows that he plans to use a gun, take pills, or jump from a high place, he is in more danger than if he has just thought of suicide in a vague and general way.

Next, is the chosen method available? Does he actually have the gun or a stockpile of pills? Related to this is the question of specificity: has he clearly thought out exactly what he will do? The more specific and detailed his plan is, and the more available the method, the greater the danger.

Finally, is the chosen method likely to work? Taking half a bottle of aspirin or cutting one's wrists is less likely to result in death than shooting oneself or driving one's car off a cliff. You should be aware, too, of the very real danger of accidental suicide. While no actual figures are available, it is likely that a significant number of successful suicides occur among clients who intended only to call attention to their need for help. The victim of drowning or shooting may not have intended to die, but he is still dead; the lethality of the suicide attempt may have little relationship to the actual intention of the attempter.

If a person has attempted suicide (or even made a nonlethal suicide gesture) in the past, the dangerousness of his present suicidal thinking is increased. Contrary to folk wisdom (in this case, no wisdom at all), the history of a past suicide attempt is probably the single best predictor of present suicidal behavior (Roy 1989). Many people who eventually succeed in killing themselves do not do so on their first attempt; if your depressed client has made previous tries at suicide, no matter how ineffective they may seem in retrospect, he should be considered in serious jeopardy.

When is a person most likely to make a suicide attempt? There are several ways to answer this question, and one relates to previous attempts. Statistically, the risk of a repeat attempt is greatest during the three days following an unsuccessful try (Rosenbaum & Beebe 1975). In terms of the overall course of treatment, people are more likely to commit suicide when a depression has begun to lift or after having felt better for a short time. We can speculate that this may be related to the amount of energy available. People in the depths of depression have little energy for taking any kind of action. Or it could be related to the dread of slipping back into despair once they have experienced something better. Whatever the reason, suicide danger increases rather than decreases during the initial improvement phase of a depression.

Obviously, external forces also affect suicidal behavior. The outbreak of suicides during the Great Depression of the thirties may repeat itself in any economically unstable period, when people see their financial security and sense of vocational achievement melting away. Student suicide rates increase dramatically around final exam time. And drug and alcohol use greatly increases the likelihood that a person will kill himself. By far the most important external event, in the context of suicidal behavior, is the loss or potential loss of a significant relationship. The popular songs that moan "I can't live without you" reflect a sadly common belief among many people; loss of lover or of parent are among the most common triggers for suicidal behavior.

In short, there are a variety of criteria that can be used to determine the degree of risk for a suicidal client. Some of these are statistical; others are a matter of clinical judgment and assessment. There is no formula, no sure way to decide that this client will while that client will not. Patterson et al. have developed a scale, the "SAD PERSONS" scale, for assessing the degree of suicide risk for a given client. Table 7-3 shows this scale, together with their suggested guidelines for action when using it.

While such lists and tables are highly useful, ultimately there is no substitute for clinical experience. In the meantime, the beginning therapist is well advised to make ample use of supervision and consultation when working with a potentially suicidal client.

THE MEANING OF SUICIDE

In order to work successfully with a suicidal client, it is useful to have some idea of what it feels like to be suicidal. What is the frame of reference of someone who wants to kill himself? What is the real meaning behind the suicide message? Many books and articles have been written on this topic, and we will not try to condense all of them into these few paragraphs. Rather, let us look at a few outstanding themes.

Suicide has often been described as an angry or aggressive behavior, and anger seems now to be even more the predominant mood of the suicidal person than it has been in the past. It is the final, unanswerable response to an uncaring

TABLE 7.2 THE *SAD PERSONS* SCALE

Sex	1 if client is male, 0 if female
Age	1 if client is 19 or younger or 45 and older
Depression	1 if present
Previous attempt	1 if present
Ethanol abuse	1 if present
Rational thinking loss	1 if client is psychotic for any reason (schizophrenia, affective illness, organic brain syndrome)
Social suppport lacking	1 if these are lacking , especially with recent loss of a significant other
Organized plan	1 if plan made and method lethal
No spouse	1 if divorced, widowed, separated, or single
Sickness	1 especially if chronic, debilitating, severe

Guidelines for action with the SAD PERSONS Scale:

Total Points	Suggested Action
0-2	Send home, with follow-up
3-4	Close follow-up; consider hospitalization
5-6	Strongly consider hospitalization, depending on confidence in the follow-up arrangement
7-10	Hospitalize or commit

Adapted from W. M. Patterson, et al., "Evaluation of Suicidal Patients: The SAD PERSONS Scale." *Psychosomatics*, vol. 24 (1983), pp. 342-349. Used with permission.

and unfeeling world, the ultimate revenge against life itself. Yet the suicidal client may not be consciously aware of his rage. For him, the overwhelming feeling is one of despair. Here are no options left, no hope. There is no way that things could possibly be better; every option ends in pain and misery. "With rare exceptions," says Boldt, "suicide is constrained by an urgent and intense need to relieve an intolerable life situation" (1989, p. 6). Even the rage he feels becomes unbearable, and suicide appears to him to be the only way to relieve his pain while at the same time lashing out against those who have caused it.

The suicidal client may imagine that his suicide will punish, control, or gain power over others. Or he may hope for atonement, to sacrifice himself or make restitution for some otherwise unforgivable behavior. Sometimes a grieving person hopes for reunion with a loved one after death. Or he may imagine that his suicide will simply bring respite, escape, a long sleep free from pain. Ask the client what he imagines will happen, to him and to others, after his death: "much can be learned about the psychodynamics of a suicidal patient from his or her fantasies as to what would happen, and what the consequences would be, if indeed he or she were to commit suicide" (Roy 1989, p. 1416).

While the feeling of despair is pervasive, coloring every event and every relationship in the suicidal person's life, there is usually some specific happening that triggers the acute crisis. The event may be one which would seem tragic or debilitating to anyone, or it may be one which appears rather trivial to an outsider but is experienced by the client as overwhelming or as the last straw, the final insult in a series of painful, humiliating, or hopeless situations. It is important, then, to understand not only what has happened but what the meaning of those events may be to the person experiencing them. It is not the bad grade on a test, the reprimand from a boss, the breakup with a lover per se which triggers a suicide; it is that event in the context of the person's emotional world. The client defines his experiences, reframes them so they fit into his map of the world, and then acts and reacts on the basis of those definitions rather than on the basis of the event itself. If your lover leaves, you may begin to make plans to go out and meet new people; the suicidal client may, instead, understand that now he is forever alone, deprived of all companionship. Talking with him about a new relationship will at first have little meaning, for within his emotional frame of reference there is no such thing.

The death of others has particular significance to a suicidal person. This is especially true in the case of one's parents. Suicidal people are often preoccupied with the death of a parent. Symbolically, when the parent dies the child loses all possibility of being nurtured and cared for. The significance of a parent's dying can be seen in the anniversary reaction, in which the client's crisis is triggered by the anniversary of the parent's death. Anniversary reactions can also be connected to the death of a spouse, a child, or a sibling; they are particularly significant if the dead loved one was also a suicide. It is wise, in assessing a suicidal crisis, to ask about traumatic events that have occurred around this date (that is, the date of the present crisis) in the client's past. Sometimes the link is not the actual date of someone's death but rather the client reaching the same age as the loved one who died or the client's own child reaching the age that the client was when he was bereaved. Whatever the link, identifying it will again give you some sense of the meaning of the event for your client.

WHAT TO DO

All the understanding in the world will not help a suicidal client unless it is coupled with a course of action. The overall strategy has several steps that will be utilized with every client. First, you must establish a relationship with the client that will begin to meet his need for help. Second, gather information about what is going on, assess the immediate danger, and decide on a strategy. Third, put that plan into effect. Last, evaluate how well the plan is working and be prepared to cycle back to step two if necessary.

That is all very well, you may be saying, but it still looks pretty vague. What are these strategies that may be employed? Let's start with the most drastic ones and work backward.

The client who is in clear and immediate danger of harming himself (or others) can be hospitalized. You should be familiar with hospitalization procedures in your area and have a working relationship with at least one physician who has admitting privileges in whatever facilities are available. You should also know the law having to do with involuntary hospitalization (commitment) and how to implement such procedures. Obviously, voluntary hospitalization is always preferable to commitment, but should you find yourself working with a client in acute crisis and clearly at risk, you do not want to have to take time out to read up on what you can or cannot do.

Another option open to you is referral for psychiatric evaluation and possible medication. You should be able to recognize the kinds of symptoms most likely to respond to drugs—antidepressants, tranquilizers—so that such referral is not just a knee-jerk reaction to any mention of suicide. You should also be familiar with how such medications affect people, so that you can give your client some idea of what to expect from his medication. (Of course, the psychiatrist or general practitioner prescribing the medication should do this, but it does not always happen that way.) A good rule of thumb is to suggest psychiatric evaluation if you think there is any possibility that the client might benefit from medication in addition to other therapy. It is irresponsible and unethical for you (or anyone else) to treat a client without medical supervision when that client might otherwise have sought and obtained needed medication.

Referral for evaluation has another benefit for both you and the client. It allows you to consult with another professional about the situation. Two heads are usually better than one, especially if the consultant is not feeling scared and responsible (as therapists with suicidal clients often do). Peterson and Bongar point out how debilitating one's own response to the suicidal client can be: "It is also of critical importance to note the intensity of the clinician's own personal reaction to the patient's suicidal communications, for it has been noted that countertransference feelings of anger, anxiety, and lack of control are common when interviewing suicidal patients" (1989, p. 573). Use your colleagues to get advice, discuss options, and talk about your concerns. Not only are you likely to get some new ideas, but also their emotional support will help you to be more effective in working with your client.

If you need support, then your client needs it even more. Remember that suicide is nearly always a two-person event. The suicidal person is joined, in fact or in fantasy, with some significant other; the suicide itself is directly related to that relationship. Since it is a two-person event, whenever possible the significant other should be brought into the therapy; this can be done in fantasy when it cannot be accomplished in fact. Suicidal clients can be helped to talk to their spouse or emotional partner about their intentions; they can be encouraged to create a dialogue between themselves and the dead or distanced other whom they "cannot live without"; they can be asked to write letters to their children, to be read after their death, explaining what they have done. The more social contact that can be maintained, the less likely it is that the suicide will actually be carried out.

Support can come from other people in the client's life, as well. Another set of options open to you is to enlist the help of members of the client's real or potential support network. Various combinations of people from the client's family, friends, work group, church, etc., may be brought together (along with the client himself) to discuss the fact that the client has been having suicidal feelings and is at definite risk. This group can then develop plans for immediate supervision/support as well as help the client to find longer-range solutions.

Whatever else you may or may not do, a key element in the treatment of suicidal persons is talking about suicide. Usually, the suicidal client will find it easier to talk to you about his feelings and intentions than to talk to others in his life, because you are not a part of the web of relationships within which the suicidal feelings have developed. You are neutral; you are neither the object of his revenge nor someone who must be protected from his pain. Hendren gives six guidelines for helping a client to talk about suicide: (1) let him tell his own story, while still maintaining structure in the narrative; (2) use language appropriate to his age and general background; (3) use tact in talking about sensitive matters—but do talk about them; (4) use natural transitions, within the context of his story; (5) allow him to express his feelings; and (6) express your own understanding and empathy (1990, p. 236). Talking about suicide, and about death in general, is not often socially acceptable behavior. The therapist, while respectful and tactful, does not pussyfoot or use polite euphemisms. She wants to know, and wants her client to know, just what will happen if the client carries out his intention. One purpose of this line of questioning is to help the client differentiate between his suicidal fantasies and the realities of his situation. Another is to allow him to vent his pent-up fears and feelings: talking about it may give him some measure of relief, so that he will not be impelled to act it out.

Be very sensitive to the nonverbal communications of the client and bring them explicitly into the discussion. A deep sigh, a gallows laugh ("Well, I can always drink myself to death, ha-ha..."), leaning away and withdrawing eye contact are all statements about the client's experience and intent. If you are not clear about the meaning of such communications, ask: "I've noticed that whenever I mention your ex-wife, you fold your arms and cross your legs and begin to swing your foot. What does that mean?"

One of the most important presuicidal communications is the missed appointment. Unlike some other clients, with whom missed appointments may be dealt with at a later time or during the following session, the suicidal client's missed appointment should be responded to immediately. Not only may such a response prevent an actual suicide, but it also deters the client from deciding that since the therapist did nothing, she really does not care about him or take him seriously.

Ultimately, the plan of action with a suicidal client will involve a contract to live. Some variant of a no-suicide contract is essential to successful working-through of a suicidal crisis. The final, and most desirable, form of such a contract is a commitment on the part of the client not to kill himself (or anyone else), either accidentally or on purpose, for any reason whatsoever. There are many workable variants. For instance, the client may insert an escape clause having to do with suicide or euthanasia in the case of a painful terminal illness. The client who is unwilling to make a long-term commitment to life may contract to live for some shorter period of time, after which the contract will be renegotiated. (Be sure to follow up on such a contract, even though the person may no longer be your client. Due dates for no-suicide contracts can be anniversary events triggering a fresh crisis.) Another workable variant is the contract to get in touch with the therapist (or some other person who is party to the contract) if the client believes he is about to kill himself. These short-term contracts give you some working space to deal with the crisis. The client who refuses to make such a contract may be genuinely unable to do so, in which case some form of supervised care should be arranged for him. He may also be manipulative. In my private practice, I will not work with a suicidal person who refuses to make some sort of a no-suicide contract. Once this is made clear, most clients address quite seriously the task of deciding how long they are willing, right now, to choose to live.

CONCLUSIONS

Crisis intervention is perhaps the most demanding and stressful area in which a therapist can choose to work. Clients in crisis need a lot from their therapist—time, energy, resources, ingenuity—and they often do not give much back. They may return to a level of functioning which seems to us pretty minimal and unsatisfying. Or they may simply disappear, leaving us wondering if our efforts made any difference at all. The ones that we do know about are likely to be those for whom we were unable to do enough—the hospitalized, the jailed, the broken family, the suicide.

Crisis workers need to develop strong professional support systems. They need people to talk with about clients, to get angry with, to weep with, and to celebrate with. It is very important not to underestimate this need, and we will return to the topic in Chapter 11.

Keeping ourselves alive and effective as crisis workers requires that we get support. It also requires that we know what we are doing—even when we do not! Especially when the crisis worker is confused and frightened for her client, she needs a clear plan of action, a set of specific options for herself. She needs to know as much as she can about how other professionals work with crisis clients; she needs to be aware of all the resources available in the community. In short, she needs to know that she is doing the best that can be done. Secure in this knowledge, her failures will bring sadness rather than guilt; and her successes will be celebrations indeed.

GROUPS AND GROUP THERAPY

8

As long as there have been people, there have been groups. People are social creatures; they form groups naturally and inevitably. Why, then, not make use of this grouping tendency in psychotherapy—why not work with groups of folks, all at once? It's a logical notion, and perhaps the most surprising thing is that group work took so long to gain acceptance in the therapeutic world. It is generally thought that the earliest instance of group work took place just after the turn of the century, when a doctor named Joseph Pratt worked with tubercular patients in groups and noted that their mood and attitudes improved. The significance of Pratt's work was not noted, however; it wasn't until thirty years later that J. L. Moreno began experimenting with psychodrama groups. And group work really hit its stride during World War II as psychiatrists looked for ways to treat larger and larger numbers of soldiers needing mental health services.

In this chapter we will first take a look at some of the characteristics of a therapy group and how these characteristics work together to create a climate in which clients can help each other to grow. We'll then turn to the special concerns of the group therapist: how to get started with a group, how to work in a group setting, and how to deal with some of the problems that can occur in a group.

CURATIVE ELEMENTS OF THE GROUP

According to Ohlsen et al. (1988), clients typically bring five sorts of problems to a group: unfinished business with significant others in their lives, self-defeating beliefs and behaviors, crisis management, faulty or insufficient information about themselves or the problem situation, and learning to manage developmental or life-passage issues. With each of these problem areas, the group can provide some very special kinds of help. The support, attention, and collective wisdom of other group members, and the opportunity to try out new and old behaviors in the protected arena that the group affords, are valuable commodities not to be found (at least not in the same way) in individual therapy.

Advocates of group therapy are fond of pointing out these ways in which groups provide experiences and possibilities not available in other kinds of therapy. They talk about group energy, support, momentum. Some sound almost mystical as they try to describe the way in which group members use each other in their process of growth and change. This kind of mystique, while it may sound wonderful, is not much help to the beginning therapist. You need to know what a group does and how it does it in order to capitalize on those effects. A number of students of group work have attempted to specify the ways in which a good group is useful to its members; among the clearest of these is Yalom's (1985) discussion of the "curative factors" in group therapy. I have made use of many of his ideas in the following pages. As we move through the list, it will probably be helpful for you to keep asking yourself two questions: Do I want my group to operate in this way? And, if so, what can I do to enhance this particular effect in the group?

IMPARTING INFORMATION

One of the most obvious ways in which a group can be more effective/efficient than individual therapy sessions is in giving information. That is what schools are about; that is why most formal teaching goes on in classes rather than in individual tutorial sessions. If you have information that you want clients to know about, it is common sense to say it once to several people rather than to repeat it again and again to one person at a time.

Even in settings where all of the formal therapy is on an individual basis, groups may be used in this informational way. Some agencies request that clients attend a group class before beginning therapy in order to acquaint themselves with the philosophy of the agency and/or the possible goals which therapy may help them to reach. Others may run classes in assertiveness or relaxation training or communication skills, which clients attend concurrently with their individual therapy.

In the therapy group, information may come from the therapist or from other group members. You may teach some skill—how to paraphrase, for instance, or how to become more aware of body sensations—and encourage members to practice the skill right there in the group, perhaps pairing up to coach, monitor, or provide practice partners for each other. A member may recommend a book that he found helpful or alert the group to a community resource. Through both formal and informal teaching, group members and leader share important information with each other.

SOCIALIZING TECHNIQUES

Along with information, many clients need to acquire simple social skills. They have been more or less socially isolated (as both cause and consequence of their other difficulties). They do not know how to listen to others, do not know how to share their thoughts and feelings appropriately, do not know how to assess or use the feedback they get. Unable to interact with others in any but superficial ways, they have few opportunities to develop appropriate social behaviors, to compare their ways of acting and reacting to how others act and react, or to update their old ideas about themselves and others.

The group setting gives people a chance to develop and practice social skills. The therapist may, as I mentioned above, give information about communication skills and then involve the group in structured exercises in which they can practice what they have learned. Or she may simply comment on social behaviors as they occur naturally in the group, encouraging members to communicate openly, to give clear feedback, and to begin to notice verbal and nonverbal messages from others.

Even without formal attention to social skills, group members need to learn to communicate with each other in new and more open ways. This involves more than just telling their stories, however important that storytelling may be. "Openness," says Corsini, "is not related to horror tales or confessions of 'sins,' but rather, the willingness to examine what is even more central, more sensitive, and potentially more hurtful: a close examination of one's viewpoints" (1988, p. 21). It is almost as if learning to communicate with others helps one to communicate honestly with oneself. And change in one member begets change in another; as one person risks a more honest examination of himself, others will begin to do the same. The communication skills developed in the group will probably help most members improve social relationships outside the group as well. As they become more confident in their ability to make good contact with other group members, and more fully aware of and confident with themselves, they will be increasingly able to use their confidence and skills in a whole range of social interactions.

INSTILLATION OF HOPE

"I did it; you can too!" is a standard advertising pitch used to sell everything from diet plans to carpenters' tools. It works. The audience sees Jane Doe standing there in her size-nothing bathing suit (or in front of her lovely new handcrafted whatzit) and thinks, "Wow, maybe I could..."

The same phenomenon, though not so blatantly engineered, happens in groups. Through watching and hearing about what others have accomplished, each member is invited to hope that perhaps he, too, can work through his problems and achieve his goals: "If so-and-so, with all of the mess in his life, can end up feeling good about himself, why not me?" "Mary says she was so depressed she wanted to kill herself, and look at her now. Maybe there's a chance that I won't have to feel bad forever, after all."

Hope, the belief that things can be better, is an essential ingredient in therapeutic success. Without hope, there is no energy to do the work, the hard work, of therapy. Why put myself through even more pain and suffering, unless I think some good may come of it? The invitation to hope may be direct and overt as members encourage and support each other's efforts. It may be a more subtle influence, coming simply through the obvious, visible changes that are occurring in one or several members. However it happens, it is an important curative factor.

Closely related to the instillation of hope is the phenomenon of universality. Many clients enter therapy with the conscious or unconscious belief that they are the only one who has ever been in this particular situation. Nobody else has ever felt just this way, has ever had these kinds of problems. Often, there is a sense of shame: "I'm worse (more stupid, more selfish, more angry) than anyone else around." Ashamed to let others see how bad he is, the client sits in a cocoon of secret misery and guilt. Gradually, as he listens to the other group members, he begins to realize that he is not unique, that others feel the same kinds of feelings and experience the same kinds of pain.

Part of the curative aspect of this kind of sharing is expressed in the old saying "misery loves company." There is a great relief simply in knowing that one is not alone: other parents are troubled by their children's behavior; other couples have sexual difficulties; other people feel trapped and helpless in jobs or at school. Beyond the simple relief of sharing, knowing that other people experience the same kinds of shameful feelings or desires makes it easier to break down the barriers, to talk about and work on that which had been too awful to let anyone else know about. Ohlsen suggests that this community of experiencing leads to what is perhaps the most curative factor of all: "the genuine self-respect [clients] experience as they struggle to discuss painful material, find that they can do it, and discover the extent to which they are admired by fellow-clients for doing it" (1988, p. 165).

ALTRUISM

As people share what has been kept secret, they also share their needs: the need for love, nurturing, forgiveness, support. Group members can and do meet these needs for each other. Although this is of great help to the needy member, it may be even more helpful to those who give. An important task for the group therapist, then, is to point out, encourage, make opportunities for helping activities on the part of group members.

Clients are often so locked into their own pain and distress that they lose awareness of their ability to be helpful to others and of the satisfaction they get from helping. They lose their sense of social interest, the awareness of being bound into the social web, of being part of the stream of human interaction. It is this kind of connectedness, this ability to share in the joy and in the pain of others, which makes us truly human.

As a person's personal problems grow, it is inevitable that his connectedness to others becomes distorted. He may withdraw from those around him as he feels increasingly angry, hurt, or ashamed. He may smother his genuine connectedness by desperate attempts to hang on, to keep others around. He may simply stop being aware of what is happening outside of his own painful internal processes. In any of these cases, the group provides a road back. It surrounds and bombards the person with evidence of the presence of others who feel, hurt, laugh, and care. It offers a person the chance to reach out, at first tentatively, and give something of himself to someone else. In so doing he breaks through the shell and begins to feel connected. He is a part rather than apart.

COHESIVENESS

The giving and the receiving that occur in groups are really inseparable, like two sides of a coin. One cannot occur without the other, and both are curative. I cannot give unless there is someone who will take from me. In a deeper sense, I cannot give unless I am also willing to take; connectedness flows both ways. Just as people in pain may lose the ability to give to others, they may also lose the ability to receive. They have been hurt so often, or they feel so rotten and unworthy, that they are no longer open to caring contact. Learning to let others in, to be warmed by the warmth and concern of another human being, can be as frightening as it is exhilarating. The group offers the chance to relearn acceptance and closeness. It is a safe place to experiment with trust, with loving and being loved.

As the safety and cohesiveness of the group begins to grow, it builds upon itself. The more I trust, the more I am willing to risk; and as I discover that my risking does not end in disaster, I will risk yet again. Others watch and listen; encouraged by my experience, they too decide to risk. The process is not always an even one; there are setbacks, down times, ruptures in the fabric of cohesiveness. These heal, and with healing comes an even greater sense of the strength and safety of the process. The collection of people becomes a group, and the group becomes my group, *our* group. We belong together; we support each other. We care, and in caring we cure.

TRANSFERENCE

It is a given in therapy that whatever the client is doing out there to perpetuate his problems, he will also do in the therapeutic relationship. This is even more apparent in group work where the client has a whole constellation of relationships with which to reenact his maladaptive responses. "The emotional relationships established between and among the members and to the therapist," says Borriello, "are related to the unique past developmental histories of each member and the therapist" (1990, p. 80). Clients set up the same kinds of no-win situations with fellow group members as they have set up with teachers, colleagues, relatives. In terms of transference, they now have not only the therapist as a transference target but also a whole family. Old business with mother, father, siblings, and other significant childhood figures can be played out in the group.

Just as in individual therapy, the group offers a setting for redoing the relationship, finishing the unfinished business, playing out the old trauma to a new and healthier conclusion. Yalom points out that group members need to work through not only the distortions in their relation to therapist/parents, but also—vis-à-vis fellow members—"other interpersonal issues; competitive strivings with their peers; conflicts in the area of assertion, of intimacy, of sexuality, of giving, of greed, of envy" (1985, p. 46). All adult relationships are, in one way or another, derived from early family relationships. After all, that is where we first learn that other people do exist and that we have to discover ways of getting along with them. In a psychoanalytically oriented group, much attention may be paid to early learnings, to exploring the unconscious processes that underlie the here-and-now relationships in the group and that lead back to primary and primitive family experiences.

Even in more present-time-focused groups, there is an assumption that whatever happens in the group reflects, in some way, what is happening elsewhere. (Conversely, what is happening elsewhere socially will be brought into the social structure of the group and acted out there.) Interactions and transactions between members are not simply taken at face value; the therapist concerns herself with the broader implications of each member's behavior. If a member makes a critical comment, for instance, he may be invited to experiment with a new kind of response to the person he has just criticized; or he may be asked who else in his life he feels critical toward. The leader might suggest that he criticize everyone else in the group, that he tell the group what happened when he expressed criticism as a child, or how he feels (felt) when he is (was) criticized.

The unique contribution of the group setting, then, lies in the client's ability to recreate and reexperience old or troublesome relationship patterns within the group itself. The therapist (and other members, too) provide feedback, confrontation, and encouragement to explore these patterns.

IMITATION

In the course of developing new ways of relating to others as well as to oneself, clients often find themselves stuck. Sometimes this stuckness signals an inner conflict, an old belief system or emotional reaction that needs to be worked through. Sometimes it is simply a result of not knowing what else may be possible, of never having seen things done differently. The group provides many examples of different ways of responding, and this can help clients find new options. Simply imitating the behavior of another group member can lead to important and powerful new insights.

Clients not only imitate end-product behaviors ("I could respond to my mother the way you responded to Liz when she said she was angry"), but also pick up techniques of working through, of doing their own therapeutic work. Seeing a fellow member cry or watching someone ask to be held gives permission and encouragement. The client who would need many individual sessions before he allowed himself to express strong feelings may do so much more readily after several others in the group have dealt with rage or fear. Group members often comment on the common-theme phenomenon: as one person brings up a particular issue, others discover their own version of that issue. The whole session may focus on feelings of loneliness, on dealing with frustration, or on sexual fears or fantasies. It is partly imitation but something else as well: the work of the person sitting next to me can help me to recognize my own needs and to find new ways of meeting them. The group as a whole, by supporting this kind of creative imitation, helps me to move into new areas more deeply and more meaningfully than I might otherwise have done.

CATHARSIS

Catharsis is usually understood to refer to the expression or the venting of strong feelings. Once thought to be useful in and of itself as a sort of emotional house-cleaning, it has lately come under considerable criticism. Corey, for instance, points out that "some group leaders measure the efficacy of their group by the level of catharsis, and members can be exploited by a leader who has a need to see them experience intense emotions" (1990, p. 37). Behavioral therapists, in particular, insist that catharsis alone, with no corrective follow-up, can serve to reinforce the very maladaptive behaviors that the client needs to change. It might be more appropriate (though more cumbersome) to refer to the curative aspect of catharsis as the "corrective emotional experience." As Yalom describes it, this corrective emotional experience in group therapy has five components:

1. A strong expression of emotion that is interpersonally directed and is a risk taken by the patient
2. A group supportive enough to permit this risk taking
3. Reality testing, which allows the patient to examine the incident with the aid of consensual validation from the other members
4. A recognition of the inappropriateness of certain interpersonal feelings and behavior or of the inappropriateness of certain avoided interpersonal behavior
5. The ultimate facilitation of the individual's ability to interact with others more deeply and honestly

Again, the group setting allows a more intense expression and experience of the kind of emotional learning that is expected to occur in many other therapeutic encounters. Rather than risking, checking out, and getting feedback just from the therapist (who is, after all, expected to respond differently than most of the other people in the client's life), the client can discover how a variety of people react to his behavior. He can experience both positive and negative responses, and he can take in feedback from several people at once. Through the mechanisms of transference, he can begin to examine how he filters and translates those reactions so as to maintain his old patterns which are no longer working for him.

BUILDING AND MAINTAINING THE GROUP

Few therapists acquire a ready-made group; our first task is usually finding the people who will be in our group and preparing them to make the best possible use of the group experience. In this section we will talk about both of these concerns, as well as some of the basic rules for getting your group going.

INITIAL INFORMATION

Experts differ as to how much prior information a therapist needs about prospective group members. Some group therapists prefer to take a fairly detailed history and do specific goal setting with each client before he enters the group. Others believe that this kind of information is more useful to both the client and his fellow group members if it emerges in the context of the work he does in the group setting. And still others are more concerned with the match among members than with any general rule-out or rule-in characteristics.

There does seem to be some agreement, though, that certain kinds of clients will do better in groups than others. Corey, for instance, says that "individuals who have a need to monopolize and dominate...hostile people or aggressive people with a need to act out...people who are extremely self-centered and who seek a group as an audience" are not good prospects for group work (1990, p. 89). People who have these characteristics can benefit from groups—indeed, it could be argued that they are the very folks who most need those curative elements that the group provides—but they are hard to work with, take longer to learn to be good group members, and have the potential for sabotaging the overall process of the group. For these reasons, it is a good idea to be very cautious about introducing them into a group, especially if the group is just being formed or if the therapist is relatively new to the challenges of group work.

Obviously, as you gain experience in leading groups, you will develop your own guidelines for what sort of prior information is most helpful to you and how you will use it in screening prospective group members. In the meantime, your most important concern must be the well-being of your clients, and there are some things that you do need to know ahead of time in order to protect that well-being. Most of these are things that you would ordinarily ask a client about during the first stage of individual therapy; the need to make a group screening decision will push you to move more directly into gathering the information than you might if you plan to stay with individual treatment.

1. *Medical status.* Is the client on any kind of medication? What is his physical condition? Is he under a doctor's care, and has he had a recent physical examination? Group work can be very intense, and you need to know if there are any potential health complications—asthma, for instance, or a history of heart problems.
2. *Reality orientation.* Some psychotic clients do reasonably well in groups, and some groups can benefit from the presence of a seriously disturbed member. Some do not. This may have more to do with the leader's comfort and skill level than with the actual behavior of the client, so your first task here is to decide how you feel about including such a member. Probably, for beginning

group therapists, the best rule is to exclude seriously disturbed clients if you are at all uncomfortable about having them in the group.

3. *Concurrent treatment.* If the client is in treatment with another professional, you must get the client's permission to share information about the client with that professional. Exchange of information is essential in order to ensure that the two treatments are compatible. If the client is unwilling to give such a release, he will have to choose one or the other treatment; to continue him in both would be unethical as well as countertherapeutic.

4. *Illegal activities.* Although you can (and should) request that the group treat all group discussion as confidential, you cannot guarantee that this will happen. A client who is, or has been, engaged in illegal activities (selling drugs, for instance) may incriminate himself in the group. Moreover, his revelation of such activities can create unnecessary problems for other group members who may be torn between conflicting values: to report a crime to the proper authorities or to maintain the confidentiality of the group. Unless the group is a special-client offenders group, it is probably best to exclude people involved in illegal behavior; to do so, you need to know about such behavior before the group actually meets.

5. *Relationships with other members.* Ideally (except for couples' groups or family cluster groups), it is best if new group members are not involved in outside-of-group relationships with each other. Practically, this is not always possible. In order for you to do your job, you do need to know if such relationships exist—that Richard and Vince are employer and employee, for instance, or that Carol and Jay used to be lovers. Both client and therapist must be able to veto such group membership if it feels wrong to them. Vince must be told that his boss may be in the group or Carol that her ex-lover may be there. Both may be given the option of excluding themselves. The therapist also may decide that having both parties there would not be in the best interest of the group as a whole. Dealing with this kind of situation can be tricky, as it involves potential breach of confidentiality, but it is very important. One way to handle it is to ask each potential member to make a list of anyone now living in the area with whom he would be unwilling to share group membership. Just making such a list, by the way, can produce useful therapeutic material.

The client has a right to know if people who stand in significant relation to him are likely to be in his group. What else do prospective members need to know? Screening is a two-way process; people need to be given enough information to opt out of a group if it will not meet their needs. In giving them this information, don't assume that they understand what group therapy is about and how it works—even if they assure you that they do know. Groups differ greatly from each other, and even if a client has been in a group before, it may have been very different in structure and purpose than your group will be. Also, many people get information about group therapy from friends (who may have gotten it from *their* friends) or from the media; what will happen in your group will probably not bear a very close resemblance to the therapy groups portrayed in the daytime soaps!

The prospective group member should be told what will be expected of him in the group and how he is likely to benefit from participating. He should have a general idea of the techniques that will be used and what risks there may be for him. He must understand that his participation is voluntary, that he does not have to follow the suggestions of the leader or other members, and that he may leave the group if he wishes. Procedures for leaving should be explained; many groups request that a member who decides to leave the group discuss the decision in the group rather than simply leaving without saying goodbye to the other members. As is true for individual therapy, he should be informed about what kinds of records (notes, tape recordings) are being kept. In particular, he should know about any research that is being carried out in the group and must give his permission, in writing, for such research. He should know what kind of confidentiality will be expected in the group; he must be aware that complete confidentiality cannot be guaranteed, and he should be explicitly informed of the areas in which the therapist is required to break confidentiality. Finally, he should know that any member may be removed from the group if the leader decides that he is harming or being harmed by other members.

SETTING THE STAGE

Most of us want our groups to be self-curing. We want the members to be helpful to each other. We are aware of the danger of becoming too directive, too powerful, of making interventions that would be more therapeutic if they came from another group member. So we make a conscious effort to sit back, to let the group develop at its own pace and in its own way. At the same time, we do have some responsibilities in setting the stage, creating an arena in which these self-curative activities can take place. Foremost among the characteristics of such an arena is safety. If a group member is to open himself to the risks of self-examination, with all the anxiety that comes with it, he needs a protected environment. "To participate freely," says Combs, "group members need to feel safe. Such security is generally more difficult to establish in groups because participants can easily be threatened by other members of the group, and the leader has less direct control over events" (1989, p. 129).

The control that the leader does have over group members, though indirect, is considerable. In selecting members, in setting the structure of the first meeting, and in providing both a model for participation and a powerful source of verbal reinforcement, she influences the norms of the group. The group begins to establish norms from the first moment it convenes. It begins to develop implicit and explicit rules for what will and will not go on in the group. The obvious guidelines of time and place and length of meetings, for which the group leader is explicitly responsible, are only the tip of the iceberg here. Much more powerful and pervasive are the unstated rules: who will speak first about what; will members address each other directly or only through the leader; are interruptions permitted, by whom, and of whom (in some groups, members will interrupt each other but will not interrupt the leader). Such norms, once established, can be changed only with great difficulty; it is as if they take on a tenacious life of their own. Making sure that the group norms are therapeutic or, at least, do not interfere with the therapeutic process is perhaps the most important early job of the therapist.

Norms may be established either explicitly, by stating them directly as rules or guidelines for the group's operation, or implicitly, by example. If there are some guidelines that are very important, things that you may need to refer back to as the group progresses, it is probably wise to get them out on the table at the first meeting. The leader may request, for instance, that people not leave and return to the group (for a cigarette or a bathroom break) but rather wait until a scheduled break time. Some leaders have a no-gossip rule: "We do not talk about people. If you have something to say, say it *to* the other person. If the other person is not in the group, put him here in fantasy and talk to him." Another frequently observed norm is that of the check-in or survey: the session begins with each member making a brief statement about how he is feeling and/or what he wants to get out of the group interaction this time.

Members may ask questions about norms: "Are we expected to let you know ahead of time if we cannot make it to a session?" "Is it okay to bring snacks to share with the group?" If you are truly neutral about these issues, it is fine to let the group decide; but if you have an investment in one particular outcome (not wanting members to be munching on goodies while the group is working, for instance), it is best to be straight about it. Many an unwary leader has tried to manipulate a group into choosing to do what the leader has already decided, with disastrous results.

In one area, though, you most emphatically must not make the "rules" yourself. This is the area of individual goal setting. It is very important that group members do set specific goals for themselves—even more important, perhaps, than in individual therapy. Without specific goals, the group can get lost in a quagmire of interesting but aimless interactions, where nothing is accomplished and everyone ends up frustrated. The therapist can help members clarify their goals and is certainly responsible for setting aside a time during the first or the second meeting in which each member will have a chance to talk about them. But the actual choice of a goal or goals is the client's responsibility. Do not let your enthusiasm, or your overinvestment in "doing it right," trap you into a power struggle over what is or is not a good goal for a group member. If he has chosen unwisely, he (with the help of the group) will find it out for himself and can then move on to something more workable or rewarding.

Be aware, though, that you can never be completely neutral, no matter how hard you try. Consciously or unconsciously, you (being human) will reveal your own preferences and prejudices, in the matter of goals as well as of norms and general group routine. And be sure that the group will notice! Remember "imitation" in the list of curative elements? The leader is a prime target for imitation. New members, uncertain of what is expected of them, will look to you for cues as to how they should behave. Some leaders prefer to withhold imitable behaviors as much as possible, after the initial structuring has taken place, so that members will be forced to come up with their own ways of working in and using the group rather than becoming dependent on the leader for direction; others are willing to foster some initial dependency in the interest of getting things moving and providing members with an early positive experience. As is so often the case, the best guideline here is probably your own comfort zone. Whatever level of activity/structure allows you to work most comfortably will also free up your energy and attention for more important group concerns.

The arena in which you can make the most beneficial use of imitation is that of process activities. It is your job to make sure that group members use their process, and the power that process can have over each member, in a therapeutic way. "Sensitivity and therapy groups, especially, have the capacity to exert a tyranny on individuals. As people begin to identify with one another, the group develops a tremendous power to coerce its members... Present theory suggests that such coercion will...result in client resentment or resistance" (Combs 1989, pp. 126–127). By your personal example even more than by specifying appropriate and inappropriate behaviors, you will teach your group members how to guide and help each other without being coercive. Deal with group members as you would like them to deal with one another. If they see you attending to and taking seriously the remarks of every member, they are likely to do the same. If they see you refusing to join in scapegoating or in laughing at jokes that are inappropriate, the scapegoating and the inappropriate jokes are likely to diminish. Groups whose leaders are willing to self-disclose, to make physical contact with members, and to express feelings freely will have members who are willing to self-disclose, to touch each other, and to express their feelings.

THERAPEUTIC GUIDELINES

The therapist, says Yalom, has two basic modes of presentation or roles in a group: she can be a technical expert and she can be a model-setting participant. Everything that you do in your group will be a variation on one of these themes. As a technical expert, you may give information, ask questions, provide direction; you may use techniques such as guided imagery or fantasy, making the rounds, psychodrama, sculpting, or role reversal. As a model-setting participant, you will use your own internal processing and responding to help members to work through their issues, to deal with each other honestly, to discover their own potential for relationship and growth. In both of these modes, you will be honest about yourself, responsible *to* but not *for* the members of the group. "The basic posture of the therapist to a patient must be one of concern, acceptance, genuineness, empathy. Nothing, no technical consideration, takes precedence over this attitude" (Yalom 1985, p. 112).

NOTICING PROCESS

As the therapist attends to and shares her own responses to group members, she
sets an example for them to do the same. Gradually, the focus begins to shift from
a discussion of what has been happening to members outside the group to what *is*
happening to them *in* the group. "Processing the awareness of members' here-and-
now experience aids group members in understanding how others view them
and/or feel toward them; and, in turn, form relationships with them" (Ohlsen et al.
1988, p. 85). This is the heart of group therapy. The interpersonal behavior of the
client within the group is an extension of his behavior with the other people in his
out-of-group activities. As he examines the within-group process (which, occurring
here and now, is available for discussion, confrontation, and feedback from therapist and other members), he will begin to make connections, to see those same patterns in his other relationships. As a consequence, both in-group and out-of-group
behaviors can begin to change.

Group members usually find it difficult to shift from focusing on content
issues to focusing on the group process. Beginning group therapists have the same
difficulty. It is easy to get caught up in a problem-solving session around Jerry's
spending habits or Ellen's seeming inability to finish school assignments on time,
and to lose sight of how Jerry or Ellen or the other members are dealing with each
other. Is Jerry's pulling his chair into a corner a nonverbal request that someone
notice and invite him back into the group? If so, who responds to the request? Is
Ellen setting herself up to be criticized or punished, and who in the group is ready
to do the criticizing? A group member may seem uninvolved, an event may appear
to be a simple coincidence—and appearances are deceiving! Nothing that goes on
in the group is unimportant or accidental. "There are no innocent bystanders in the
here-and-now of the group," warns Borriello. "Whatever happens in the here-and-
now of the group, happens because all members and the therapist in their unique
individual ways sanction it" (1990, p. 79).

The best way to train yourself to be aware of process in the group is simply
to think "here-and-now." As you think in this way—about what is going on for
each member, and for yourself, at this moment—the actual words being spoken
will begin to fade in importance. What will begin to speak to you will be the
voice tones, the expressions, the body language, and your own visceral response
to all of these nonverbal events. Corey recommends that the therapist talk about
her internal responses as a way of helping the group learn to deal with process.
Of all forms of self-disclosure, he says, sharing one's feelings about the group
process is the most productive. "For instance, if you have a persistent feeling
that most members are not very motivated and are not investing themselves in
the session, you are likely to feel burdened by the constant need to keep the
meetings alive all by yourself, with little or no support from the participants.
Disclosing how you are affected by this lack of motivation is generally very useful and appropriate" (1990, p. 59). Group members can be expected to attend to
and talk about the same kinds of responses in themselves, to begin to be more

interested in how the group deals with an issue than they are in the issue itself. They will learn to notice what people are saying about themselves and their relationships through the process of telling their stories and of responding to the stories of others.

INTERVENTIONS

The more experience you have with groups, the more confidence you will feel in identifying process patterns. You'll almost surely be tempted to share these insights with the group. It is fun to point out what people are doing with and to each other; it is satisfying to score a bull's-eye! Why not, you may ask. After all, people begin to grow and change as they recognize their styles of interacting with others. Isn't it your job to tell them what you see?

The problem with telling them is twofold. First, people will hear process feedback most clearly when they are ready to listen; often you will notice a pattern before the people engaging in the behavior are themselves open to dealing with it. Second, process interventions tend to be much more powerful when they come from group members rather than from the leader. Even though it feels good to be wise, and to have the members of your group be impressed with how insightful you are, those members need to learn to provide their own insights and to do without your wisdom. The hard fact is that the more you seem to be doing for your group, the less they will probably benefit from your leadership. They need to depend on themselves, and on each other, for feedback, and you need to find a way to back off and let them do so.

Sometimes, of course, you will and should make interventions. To sit and say nothing makes you an observer, not a participant; you are not being paid for just observing! Most of your interventions (at least those made in the role of technical expert) will be made so as to focus attention back on the group process. McKenzie (1990) warns that we need to encourage and lead our groups to move into productive interactions but at the same time must take care not to get too far ahead, to push them too fast or expect them to take risks that are too great. Keeping the group functioning as a group, making sure that individuals are not left behind or excluded or scapegoated, is more important than helping one member do a major piece of work. The therapist, from this point of view, is a kind of verbal sheep dog, nipping at the heels of members who stray too far from the appropriate focus. Process comments directed toward the overall functioning of the group need only describe what you actually see: it doesn't matter so much whether you understand what it is you are pointing at, so long as you point at it directly and ask the group what is happening. You might notice, for instance, that throughout an animated discussion of "how can I ever pay all my bills?" one member has been quietly looking at the floor. You intervene: "I notice you haven't said anything, Pete, and you look worried." Pete may respond, "No, I'm not worried. I'm pissed off that these guys are bitching about money when they spend more in a week than I earn in a month." The fact that you mistook Pete's anger for something else is not particularly important; you have succeeded in bringing the focus back to the immediate interrelationships within the group.

CONFRONTATIONS

Simply calling attention to what you see, with or without a tentative label, is a first-level intervention. It is often all that is needed. Relating a specific behavior to a general pattern goes a step further. It invites each group member to examine that pattern, and his own part in it, and to wonder where else he may be doing the same thing. Some of these patterns are so common, so universal, that it is useful to carry them in your head as ready-made templates, hypotheses; you are almost sure to find an application for them. One such is displacement, in which a person directs his response to someone other than the one with whom it was originally experienced. Randy may feel annoyed with Bill, for instance, but instead of dealing directly with Bill he makes a sarcastic response to Joan. Another is indirection: two people relating to each other through a third person or in some other disguised way. Giving person A a compliment on his new this-or-that, when I really want person B to notice *my* new that-or-this, is an example of indirection. A third common pattern is isolation, which involves responding to a comment or a behavior as if it occurred in a vacuum, ignoring the context. Isolation behaviors derail the group process and often set the isolator up to be ignored or criticized by the group.

A second-level intervention can point out such patterns directly or can involve a self-questioning technique: "When Julie told Tom how to discipline his son, it seemed like nobody was interested in what she had to say. I wonder what was going on." "I'm curious about what happened just now when Randy sounded so abrupt with Joan, right after Bill criticized him." Such implied questions encourage the group members to generate the interpretation rather than waiting for you to provide it.

These kinds of interventions are, essentially, confrontations. Confrontation is simply an intervention that invites (sometimes quite strongly) the group member to think about his behavior, to consider it from a different angle, to notice that he has other options. Confronting a member is a very powerful move and must be used sparingly and with great care. Done carelessly, or out of frustration or anger, it can be destructive to both the group member being confronted and the group as a whole ("After what happened to Tom, I'm sure not going to stick *my* neck out!"). The group leader is likely to underestimate just how powerful her confrontation will seem to the confrontee; for this reason it is a good rule to make your first confrontation of a pattern or a person gentle and tentative, leaving plenty of room to back off or soften what you have said if there is a negative response. Later, when trust and comfort have grown—or when you have determined that the soft confrontation is ineffective—you may choose to be more forceful.

Knowing how to confront, though, may be less important than knowing when confrontation is appropriate. Egan, almost twenty years ago, developed a set of guidelines for when to use confrontation in groups; it is as valid now as it was then. You'll find Egan's recommendations in Table 8–1.

TABLE 8–1 GUIDELINES FOR USING CONFRONTATION IN A GROUP SETTING

1. Confront in order to manifest your concern for the other.
2. Make confrontation a way of becoming involved with the other.
3. Before confronting, become aware of your bias either for or against the confrontee. Don't refrain from confrontation because you are for him or use confrontation as a means of punishment, revenge, or domination because you are against him. Tell him of your bias from the outset.
4. Before confronting the other, try to understand the relationship that exists between you and him, and try to proportion your confrontation to what the relationship will bear.
5. Before confronting, try to take into consideration the possible punitive side effects of your confrontation.
6. Try to be sure that the strength or vehemence of your confrontation and the areas of sensitivity you deal with are proportioned to the needs, sensitivities, and capabilities of the confrontee.
7. Confront behavior primarily; be slow to confront motivation.
8. Confront clearly; indicate what is fact, what is feeling, and what is hypothesis. Don't state interpretations as facts. Don't engage in constant or long-winded interpretations of the behavior of others.
9. Remember that much of your behavior in the group, such as not talking to others, or expressing a particular emotion, can have confrontational effects.
10. Be willing to confront yourself honestly in the group.

From *Face to Face,* by G. Egan. Copyright © 1973 by Wadsworth Publishing Company, Inc. Reprinted by permission of Brooks/Cole Publ. Co., Monterey, Calif. 93940.

Lest you begin to feel overwhelmed by all of these rules, by the impossibility of remembering everything while simultaneously noticing all that is going on in the group, reassure yourself. First, much of what has been said in this section is a review of what you, as a good individual therapist, already know how to do. You are already behaving in these ways, often without awareness of your own skills and techniques. Second, it is permissible to make mistakes. In fact, it is not only permissible but it is inevitable. Missing something, doing something wrong (or not doing it as well as you would have liked), and owning up to your own shortcomings is also therapeutic.

PROBLEMS

Every group has strengths, expected and unexpected curative abilities which emerge with or without the therapist's intervention. Every group also has problems. It is a common pitfall for beginning therapists to fret about these problems, rather than to see them as necessary raw material for the group to work with. Stumbling blocks can also be steps to climb on! If you see a group problem as unrelievedly negative, you may miss the opportunity to turn it into a learning experience. One way to avoid this kind of error is to know ahead of time some of the most commonly occurring group problems, to be aware that they do occur in lots of groups (and aren't unique to yours and therefore your fault), and to have a sense of how to deal with them constructively.

Over the years, students of group process have identified a number of individual behavior patterns that, if they are not handled well, can be hurtful to the group process. Without exception, people who engage in these behaviors do so because they need or want something from the group but have not learned how to get it in an appropriate way. As we discuss the problems that they present, it is important to recognize that helping the group to deal with them also involves helping them to deal with themselves; that a true solution to any group problem implies that everyone gains.

AIR TIME

In any group, the amount of time available for each person is limited by the number and the talkativeness of the other members. Some groups have air time problems: some or all of the members do not feel they get enough time or attention. People respond to this problem in a variety of ways: some become demanding, some whine or sulk, some withdraw into helpless silence.

Dealing with air time inequities is not just a group therapy task, but a life task. As with all group phenomena, the process within the group is a reflection of the members' general coping behavior. The therapist's task, then, is not so much to distribute air time evenly among the members as it is to help them recognize how they themselves address the task of getting attention, of being heard, of making interpersonal contact. If the therapist intervenes to make things "fair," she will short-circuit the struggle that can lead to awareness—awareness of patterns, of expectations, of the possibility of change.

Confrontations around air time, therefore, should direct attention to the how and the why of what is happening. If you choose to draw a quiet member into the discussion, do so in a way that will invite both that member and the rest of the group to examine how he and they contributed to his exclusion. If there are one or two people who tend to monopolize the group, it is better to help the group itself deal with them than to use your leadership power to give the others more time.

Remember that many people will occasionally want and need to assume a more passive role in the group. It is not always helpful to talk; sometimes listening quietly or even withdrawing into one's internal business is the best strategy for a group member. While it is not good for someone never to talk, it is therapeutic for members to know that they can occasionally use the group as a place to hide, as a timeout from pressure, or as just a comfortable, supportive, and demand-free environment.

MONOPOLIZING

Our discussion of air time has already highlighted two problem roles, monopolizing and passivity. People who monopolize take up group time by monologing, interrupting, continually demanding that the group focus on them. Members may become anxious or resentful or bored, but (especially early in the life of the group) they may be reluctant to address the problem directly. Unlike choosing to withdraw, observe, just be quiet for a while, monopolizing is seldom if ever a constructive behavior—except as it draws attention to the underlying neediness of the overtalking member. Here again, the group needs to be encouraged to deal with the problem and to do so in a way that lets the whole group take responsibility for what is going on: "We've spent nearly an hour discussing Mark's situation. How did we decide to give him all our attention today?" "I notice that Kathy has been doing most of the talking. How are we all encouraging her to do that?" Similarly, the group needs to be invited to change the monopolizing pattern, if they are uncomfortable with it: "Rose, you've been shifting around in your chair a lot while April has been talking about her job. Will you tell April what's going on for you?" One way to invite people to be clear and open about their feelings in this kind of situation is to describe your own reaction: "I'm uncomfortable with the group's taking so much time with Mark, and I'm wondering why I keep helping us to do it. I think maybe I'm afraid of hurting his feelings. Is anyone else experiencing this kind of reaction?" Comments like this legitimize dealing with the monopolist's behavior and with his response to being confronted openly. They serve not only to address the air-time problem but also as examples of process focusing, which is the major task of the group.

RESCUERS AND VICTIMS

Some group members, with the best (conscious) intentions in the world, can be quite disruptive of others' therapeutic processes. These are the rescuers, folks who leap in too soon with advice, sympathy, or defense. The rescuer may see himself as an assistant therapist (or may, with or without awareness, be competing with the therapist for the role of leader). He may have learned to get a great deal of personal satisfaction from "helping" other people. He simply may not understand the importance of being allowed to work through an issue on one's own, to express strong feelings, to discover one's own solutions. Rescuers, by interrupting these processes, get in the way of therapy; yet other members often find them hard to confront. After all, they are only trying to help.

Confronting a rescuer is important for both the group and the rescuer himself. Being a rescuer is, in the long run, singularly nonrewarding. Perpetual rescuers nearly always find themselves also playing the role of martyr. Somehow, nobody really appreciates what the rescuer has done; they don't notice, or they seem actually resentful. The rescuer is confused, angry, sad—and so, in order to feel better about himself, he looks around for somebody else to rescue. And so the cycle continues. The therapy group is one of the few settings where there may be enough support and patience to help the rescuer to come to grips with how self-defeating his behavior really is. He probably won't like the confrontation (most of us don't enjoy confrontations much), and he may refuse to understand what his fellow members are telling him. But over time, and with the group's help, he may be able to break out of the pattern and find some other way to make contact with people.

In terms of group needs, confronting and limiting the rescuer's activities makes it easier for others to get on with their work; when done caringly by the therapist it also sets a permission-giving example for other members. Early confrontations will probably focus on the needs of the person being rescued: "Dan needs to deal with his problem himself right now, rather than listening to someone else's ideas." "Give Mary a chance to deal directly with Chuck." Later, you may choose to make a process comment that will help the rescuer to examine his own perceptions and expectations: "What does it do for you, Gerry, to always be the one who helps people in the group?"

Rescuers often find a natural partner among the group members, someone who makes contact by needing to be rescued. These people fall into a helpless victim role, telling endless stories about how badly they have been treated or how unsolvable their problems are. They often invite members to try to rescue them but manage to sabotage the rescue attempt in some way. The result is the classic "Why Don't You...Yes, But" pattern described by Berne (1964) in which one or more members take turns offering advice while the victim maintains his position by explaining why nothing that is offered will work for him.

Probably the best way to deal with this pattern is simply to let it play itself out, and then ask the group to describe what has happened. With a minimum of prompting, clients usually recognize their roles and will identify the process the next time they see it being played out in the group. When this happens, the helpless victim (like the rescuer) can be encouraged to explore his own payoff in maintaining this position and to find new options for getting what he wants from the other members.

DISRUPTING AND SCAPEGOATING

Most of the problem people we have discussed tend to be more or less disruptive of the group's process. Some individuals are even more overtly disruptive: they become aggressive, they interrupt (verbally or nonverbally), they make inappropriate comments. No single solution is available for dealing with disruptive persons. The closest thing to an all-purpose solution is to discuss with the group what the disruptive person is doing and how the other members are responding. Ultimately, if the disruptor is unable or unwilling to change his behavior, you may have to ask him to leave the group. This is an extreme solution and should never be used before the group has dealt with the problem openly. Of course, it is much more desirable that a discussion of everyone's responses may help the disruptor to change and help the group to find new, constructive ways of supporting him.

One last problem should be mentioned here, and that is the process of scapegoating. Occasionally a group will collectively decide to make one member the target for its anger, frustration, or disappointment. Nothing that person does is right, and everything that goes badly in the group is his fault. The scapegoat does not consciously choose to disrupt the group process though he is often someone for whom the kick-me position is a familiar, though painful, way of interacting with others. Scapegoating is as bad for the rest of the group as it is for the victim; it allows them to avoid their own role in creating and maintaining problems. The therapist needs to be alert to the scapegoat syndrome and take steps to block it from being played out in the group. Again, asking members to take a look at what is going on, and to think about what they are really wanting to accomplish with their behavior, is generally the best kind of block: "Everyone is criticizing Jim today." "We all seem to have agreed that Lucy is to blame for this situation. How did we do that?"

The behavior of problem people in the group can provide useful material for the group to focus on. Looking at such behavior as material to work with, material that is highly relevant to the very things that brought each person to the group in the first place, will help you not to become frustrated and impatient. When problem behaviors do not respond to the process approach, the leader's response must be one of setting limits, of framing the interaction so as to keep one or two individuals from sabotaging the work of the whole group. Usually, members will respond positively to process comments and will gradually replace their disruptive or maladaptive behaviors with new and more appropriate ones. When this does not happen, you will have to provide protection for the group by setting more explicit limits. As you do so, remember to acknowledge the feelings that underlie the problem behavior and help the person to talk about those feelings. Also, be sure to provide suggestions as to alternative behaviors that are acceptable in the group; don't just say "don't," but also say "do, instead." Finally, remember that the limit-setting confrontation is likely be embarrassing or upsetting to the person. He may need some help in dealing with his embarrassed or resentful feelings.

A FEW LAST THOUGHTS

Working with groups provides the therapist with a wealth of possibilities. There are so many things to notice, so much going on, so many different places to intervene. In fact, working in a group setting almost guarantees stimulus overload; there is no way that a single person can take in and deal with all of the information available at any given moment.

Since you cannot deal with it all, you will have to make choices. You will have to ignore some things in order to respond to others. In this chapter, I have introduced some high-priority guidelines for the sorts of things that experienced group leaders have found to be important.

In order to further condense this list, let me end with my own set of basic priorities. You may not always want to follow them, but they will be a useful set of rules for you to check in with occasionally. First, attend to the group dynamics. What is the process? Look underneath the content, at who talks to whom, when, in what tone, and with what consequences. Second, review the explicit and implicit contracts. Are people getting what they came for? If not, how is the group failing to help them meet their needs? Third, step back and examine your own role in the group. How do you feel about what is happening? Whom are you angry with, scared of, disappointed in, protective of? What do you want to get out of leading the group, and how are you getting in your own way? Consultation can be invaluable here; it is extraordinarily difficult to back off far enough from our groups to be really objective about how we ourselves are contributing to the process.

The biggest mistake that beginners tend to make with groups is that of trying too hard. It is better to do too little than to try to do too much. Groups do, in and of themselves, have enormous curative potential. If your only function as leader were to be to create a framework within which members could come together regularly, this alone would be therapeutic for most of those members. Again there is a paradox: the more leadership skills you acquire, the less you will need to use them. Lean back, relax, trust the group to teach you at least as much as you teach them, and enjoy the ride. And your group will prosper.

COUPLE THERAPY   9

Margaret Mead, one of the foremost anthropologists of our time, wrote the following in 1949: "The American marriage ideal is one of the most conspicuous examples of our insistence on hitching our wagons to a star. It is one of the most difficult marriage forms that the human race has ever attempted, and the casualties are surprisingly few considering the complexities of the task" (p. 342) Now, almost half a century later, the casualty rate has grown enormously, but we continue to expect and demand a great deal from our primary partnerships. We expect our partner to be our lover, our best friend, our major source of social and economic support. In spite of the many social changes of the nineties, marriage is still the context in which most of us have hoped to raise our children, manage our dreams and our disappointments, and learn to grow old. Having achieved independence from our parents (often with great difficulty), some of us scarcely pause to enjoy our autonomy before we plunge into a new and even more demanding kind of relatedness. Others of us embark on a series of relationships, each more or less monogamous, each with at least the potential to be long-term, and each ultimately ending in disappointment for one or both partners. In each new relationship we must learn all over again how to give and take, to be strong and to be weak, to trust and yet protect ourselves. We hope—and sometimes promise—to maintain this relationship for decades to come, into a future in which we cannot even imagine what kind of people we, or our partners, will become. Mead is still right: the surprising thing is that it works as well as it does.

Even when it does not work out so well, when frictions develop, and the rosy ideals of first love crash on the rocks of reality, we do not want to give up. We may try to talk things out (if we are female) or patiently wait for things to improve (if we are male). Beck points out that gender-linked communication styles are one of the basic trouble spots of heterosexual partnerships: women tend to believe "the marriage is working as long as we can talk about it" while many men believe "the relationship is not working as long as we keep talking about it" (1988, pp. 83–84).

But, in spite of these miscommunications, couples do keep on trying. They talk to friends; they plan secret strategies of their own; they look for advice in sex manuals, at marriage encounter workshops, and from inspirational articles. Sometimes they seek professional help, a third-party expert who will turn things around and make them better.

The couple therapist, of course, cannot make things better. What she can do is help the couple themselves to find new ways of working and living together. She can encourage them to listen, to think, to experiment, to risk. From her standpoint outside the relationship, she can see patterns that the couple themselves are aware of and can invite the couple to step back and look in a different way. This ability to see things from the outside, and thus gain a new perspective, is the major advantage that the couple therapist has; we need to guard it well. We can never be completely objective, because we inevitably bring our own beliefs and values (about gender roles, and partnerships, and what is fair or not fair) into our therapy. But we can at least acknowledge those beliefs: "It is important that the clinician be aware of his or her biases, values, and attitudes. Acknowledging what these biases are goes a long way toward keeping them from unconsciously influencing a couple" (Wiseman 1990, p. 31). A useful warning signal in this area is the impulse to provide an answer or a solution to the couple's dilemma. If we think we know what they should do, we are likely being influenced by our own personal values. For we really don't know the answers; we are not a grab bag of ready solutions. Even if we really do have a sense of what the couple ought to be doing differently, we are often wise not to share that information. The most successful solutions must come from the partners themselves. The therapeutic function in couple work is that of observing and directing process, of protecting the clients by insisting that each observe the ground rules of fair fighting, and of supporting the whole endeavor with a confident certainty that new options are possible.

Shack suggests three overall guidelines for couple therapists: "(1) make clear what behavior is expected of the couple and why, (2) recognize minimal changes in behavior or attitude, and (3) be realistically positive in supporting and encouraging these changes" (1989, p. 54). Shack's first guideline, making clear what behavior is expected, has to do with setting up the ground rules; this protects each of the partners as they begin to explore the painful areas of their relationship. Recognizing minimal changes can counter the couple's tendency to notice only major breakthroughs and to become discouraged when these major changes don't occur. And being realistically positive reinforces new behavior and underscores the possibility that change can occur.

THE FIRST STEPS

Beginnings are often awkward with couples as well as with individual clients. The couple does not know what to expect, and each partner may be vacillating between a hope for vindication ("therapy will make my partner see what s/he is doing to me") and a fear of new demands ("they'll decide it's all my fault"). Anxiety is high, and trust is low. The therapist, especially if she is inexperienced, may be dealing with anxieties of her own: "Will I be able to work with these people?" "How do I teach them to use therapy appropriately?" "Will I get trapped into their system?" Having a clear sense of how to get organized for therapy will help everyone in the room to get past the initial awkwardness and into the treatment process.

It is probably best to begin by settling the administrative details of your working together. Clearly state your expectations about appointment times, fees (who will pay, how much, and when, plus any arrangements for insurance payments), missed sessions by one or both partners, etc. Problems that come up in dealing with these arrangements will be valuable indicators of communication issues between the partners, so this early part of your session has important therapeutic implications as well.

Once the housekeeping details have been taken care of, the next order of business is to let each partner know what you know about them and how you know it. Since one partner will probably have made the first appointment, it is essential to balance the ledger by sharing with the other partner just what was said. This brings the second partner up to date and may allay some suspicions about how much tattling or blaming has already taken place; it also allows the partner who made the initial contact to clear up any misunderstanding between you and her or him about what was communicated.

Reviewing the original contact, letting both partners know what you think they are asking for, is a natural way to lead into a discussion of what therapy will be like. Part of your responsibility as a therapist is to teach your clients how to work in therapy. While it is impossible (and probably not even desirable) to spell out everything that may happen over the course of treatment, you can and should provide some guidelines for their behavior. Ables has suggested the following list of client responsibilities: "to be willing to voice one's complaints and needs, to use one's assertiveness and anger for the protection of self-interests, to be willing to listen to and try to understand the spouse's position, needs, and feelings, as well as one's own, and, ultimately, to negotiate differences" (1977, p. 75). As an astute therapist, you will recognize these as guidelines not only for working in therapy but also for maintaining a healthy ongoing relationship: they are simultaneously means to an end and the end itself.

Once you have laid out some of your expectations about the way you will work together, you may move into the assessment phase. You can proceed directly to history taking, exploring how the relationship came to be and what has happened since it began; or you may choose to focus on the specifics of what is happening now. We shall discuss these assessment options in more detail in the next section.

ASSESSMENT

Knowing that you don't have the answers, and refusing to try to supply them, can help the therapist to stay out of the couple's pathology. But therapists need to know more than what *not* to do; we need to be able to figure out what kinds of interventions are likely to be most effective with a given couple. In order to do this, we need information.

HISTORY TAKING

As you begin to listen to each partner's account of how they came together, and what has happened since then, you are likely to hear two very different stories. One of the first things to remember, in gathering a relationship history, is that "there is no one truth as to why the relationship broke down: only two people's experiences" (Wiseman 1990, p. 27). To be sure, each person will probably have both a public and a private version: the public version is the one that exaggerates the partner's faults (just a little) and tones down one's own mistakes (only a bit), while the private version is the one we don't even like to look at very closely when we're all alone. Even those private versions, though, won't agree. People do experience events differently depending on where they stand during the event. Over the course of successful couple therapy, each partner's experience comes closer to that of the other, as they learn to step outside of their own private worlds; that's part of what couple therapy is intended to accomplish. If the therapist makes a premature judgment as to who is "right," she is likely to make this convergence more difficult for both partners to accomplish. Instead, she is wise to focus on understanding just what those two sets of experiences are, remembering that there is no need, at this point, to attempt to reconcile them.

Experts differ as to the usefulness of an extended and formal history-taking procedure in couple work. Some therapists prefer to focus right away on the couple's here-and-now process, encouraging them to begin talking and negotiating with each other in the context of the issues which have brought them to therapy Others use the first several sessions to gather detailed information about the couple's past history, both before and after they began their partnership. In addition to providing a basis for planning one's strategy with a particular couple, this information-gathering process can help to allay the couple's anxiety by giving them a relatively nonthreatening task that they can work on together and (at least at some points) agree about. In other words, the first session can provide them with an experience of success with each other and with the therapist.

Whichever of these two positions you adopt, or whether you find a comfortable middle course, your early sessions with the couple will be largely devoted to finding out what is going on for them—where things are going well and where things are going badly. You will be gathering information about the interpersonal dynamics of the relationship. All humans have three basic interpersonal needs: inclusion (in a long-term relationship, this translates into questions about commitment), control, and intimacy (Hof & Treat, 1989). Ask yourself which of these needs is not being met for which partner, and how that lack plays itself out in their relationship.

"A couple's ability to change," say Hof and Treat, "is a function of their responsivity (response-ability) vs. reactivity (re-activity)" (1989, p. 14). People who are able and willing to respond to each other, rather than react against each other, have a much better chance of successful negotiation of differences; they can listen better, take the other's point of view, and consider acceptable compromises. Reactive couples, in contrast, are so bound up in the need to defend themselves that they dare not listen well or allow themselves to consider other viewpoints than their own. Assessing responsivity and reactivity is a major aspect of the overall evaluation process.

TREATMENT PLANNING

Throughout all of your early interactions with a couple, you will need to be thinking about an intervention package, a therapy plan. One useful mind-set, proposed by Pittman, is to ask yourself, "What, above all, is the change this couple must prevent? What is there in this couple's structure that is so precious that it must, at all costs, be protected?" (1987, p. 19). Keeping in mind that both members of the couple are (probably, but not necessarily, out of awareness) protecting something that feels valuable to them will help keep you from getting hooked on the same snag that has hung them up. You can steer them in the direction of replacing the threatened "possession," or of finding new and healthier ways of protecting it, instead of blundering in and adding to the sense of danger and threat.

It is because of that sense of danger and threat that couples who seek therapy are likely to be experts (usually at an unconscious level) at enmeshing and confusing a relationship, muddying the waters so that, no matter how hard each is determined to try, they both go away hurt, disappointed, and angry. The therapist who leaps into this arena armed only with good intentions stands a fair chance of getting snarled in the same kind of relationship.

Your specific treatment plan will depend, of course, on the therapeutic style that is most comfortable for you. Some couple therapists work in a relatively structured way, taking charge of the interaction and letting the couple know clearly that the therapist will decide what sort of therapeutic activity is in their best interest as the therapy progresses. Groome, for example, advises: "The therapist needs to take control from the beginning, so that feelings of confusion change to hopeful feelings, and become manageable for the couple. Paradoxically, the therapist's task is to create control in order to give it back to the couple" (1989, p. 23). This kind of stance tends to be particularly effective with couples who are invested in fighting, bickering, getting in the last word—who have somehow decided that being "right" is more important than being happy with each other.

Other therapists, with other couples, prefer to provide a space in which the couple can interact more spontaneously with each other, acting as a kind of referee who will ensure that they fight fairly as they work out their differences. Even with this more laissez-faire approach, though, effective therapists do need a sense of direction so that they can encourage the couple to explore in areas most likely to bring about changes in the relationship.

Hollander-Goldfein suggests: "As each partner states her or his perceptions of the marriage, the overt or covert battle over who is right is played out. In response, the therapist needs to dispel the illusion of an absolute truth and validate each partner's experience" (1989, p. 66). Plan your strategy so as to accomplish these first therapeutic goals, and the rest will follow naturally. Stand back far enough to see the overall pattern of the relationship, so that you yourself won't fall into the trap of looking for an "absolute truth." Assess the nature of the conscious and unconscious contracts; evaluate and reevaluate the couple's motivation for (and fear of) change; and look for ways to build on their strengths. As you combine these general rules with your own stylistic and theoretical preferences, a treatment plan will begin to emerge.

THE ART OF COUPLE THERAPY

In the previous pages we have concentrated on the goals of couple therapy and on the activities leading into the therapy process. Now we turn to the process itself: the actual tasks of the therapist as she works with a couple. We will look first at some general guidelines and then turn to some techniques specifically relevant to the problem-solving process with couples. We will identify some of the more common problem behaviors that couples need to learn to change. Finally, we will briefly discuss some special situations that frequently arise during the course of couple work.

GENERAL GUIDELINES

One of the first tasks of the couple therapist is that of joining each partner. This joining essentially involves forming a therapeutic alliance; it requires that the client experience the therapist as trustworthy and competent. In individual therapy we talk of establishing rapport, and this is usually accomplished with relative ease. Couple therapy is more complicated because joining with one partner may create distrust in the other. The goal is to join with both, to be seen as caring about each one while taking sides with neither.

The therapist's own attitude is a key factor here: if you do not secretly take sides, favoring one partner over the other, you are more likely to create a balanced relationship with them. That is easier said than done, however; it seems to be a natural social characteristic to make judgments, to choose a favorite, to assess rightness and wrongness whenever we notice disagreement between two people. The couple you are working with is likely to further complicate things as they vie for your support. Each may be convinced, consciously or unconsciously, that you will in fact act as judge and jury and that if you are allied with one of them you must by definition be "against" the other. Goldberg notes that "each of the agents in chronic conflict operates from an arbitrary moralistic structure that implicitly suggests that the other agent is supposed to act in particular ways" (1977, p. 21). Your challenge is to avoid getting caught up in this same implicit moralistic process, holding your "shoulds" in abeyance while you get to know each partner. One thing that I have found helpful here is to remind myself that, no matter how it may look on the surface, *both* partners are in pain. There are no winners in couple dysfunction; both lose. And both want the pain to stop. No matter how different the perspectives, no matter how entrenched the roles or the defenses, it is a safe assumption that each partner wants change—and fears it, too.

Joining can be accomplished in a variety of ways. Most obvious are the conversational ones: listening carefully to each partner's story, making sure that each has a chance to speak, choosing your comments and questions so that each will know you have understood what they are saying. More powerful, though, are the nonverbal behaviors: your facial expression as you listen to each, your movements and gestures, the amount of air time you give to one or the other. One of the greatest dangers is that of accepting the couple's initial definition of one partner as the problem or the sick person in the relationship. Even if the "identified problem" person may agree that he or she belongs in such a role, you must leave room to balance things out: acknowledge that the specified behaviors are *one* of the serious problems that the couple will need to deal with. You can also intensify your nonverbal bonding with the accused partner by sitting closer to her or him, or by mirroring his or her body position. This will allow you to preserve the possibility of joining, while avoiding a premature verbal challenge of the information the couple is presenting.

The next major therapeutic task is to engage the partners in talking with each other, instead of to or through the therapist (Hollander-Goldfein 1989). Talking to each other is the appropriate mode for problem solving; talking to the therapist is more likely to involve destructive behaviors like blaming or criticizing one's partner. As partners talk to each other, the therapist can observe the communication patterns in vivo. Rather than describing what did happen, they show the therapist what is happening. Thus they present both diagnostic information and material for immediate working-through.

Often, asked to talk to each other about their issues, partners will object: they have talked about it so often already, they have nothing more to say. An appropriate answer is to agree that they have, indeed, talked about things a lot, but that this will be different because there is a third person with them now; the therapist will be there to help them learn more about the nature of their talking together and to help them develop some new skills in dealing with each other.

Typically, partners will respond to this sort of intervention by beginning to talk to each other but will turn back to the therapist after only one or two transactions. They can be redirected to the task by an encouraging "Tell her/him about it" or "Good, now tell your partner the same thing." Notice that by using this redirection technique you avoid the need to criticize anyone for doing it wrong; in fact, you can reinforce them for sharing information and feelings even as you turn them back to deal with each other.

Occasionally it will be important to one partner that the therapist know or understand some part of the overall situation, and telling the partner (while the therapist listens and gets the information indirectly) will feel frustrating and uncomfortable. Don't get into a power struggle over the issue of who someone must talk to. Instead, go ahead and listen to the story, and then respond by inviting the storyteller to tell the partner how he or she felt when "that"—whatever the story was about—happened. If the story contains specific reference to feelings ("...and when I found out that he bought all that stuff without telling me, I was so angry and hurt that I..."), you can bring the other partner in by asking,"Were you aware of how he/she felt about that?" and reengaging them in a discussion of the feelings. Nonverbally, continuing to look at A while A talks about B, rather than looking back and forth between the two, helps to prevent the formation of a two-against-one coalition. Finally, if all else fails and one partner insists on talking to you rather than to her or his partner, you may choose to direct a comment about the speaker to the (often silently colluding) nonspeaker: "Kevin seems very upset about this." Or, "I notice that Carol finds it more comfortable to tell me what she feels than to tell you about it."

The therapist is responsible for slowing down the exchange between the couple so that each has a chance to talk, to hear, to think about, and to respond to what the other says. As they begin to talk about their feelings, this slowing down becomes even more important. "The therapist often needs to walk a thin line, creating an environment for honest feelings to be expressed on the one hand, and guarding against their inappropriate expression on the other" (Rice 1989, p. 159). Couples often find it hard to stay on track with an issue, particularly when strong feelings are involved. They sidestep, change the subject, switch to a safer topic. The therapist needs to bring them back to the issue at hand, setting a model for accepting what is said, and the emotions with which it is said, whether or not one shares that belief or feeling: "Stan, I didn't hear you answer Laura's question." "Betty, Carl just told you how he feels when he hears you yelling at the kids. Will you let him know that you heard what he said?" "Tom will be better able to hear what you think about that, Sue, if you first make sure he knows that you listened to him and understood what he told you."

Some couples need even more than this kind of gentle guidance. They literally do not know how to listen to each other, nor do they know how to let the other person know when they have been listening. In such situations, a technique known as "therapist processing" is useful: the therapist listens for the partner and interprets to the partner what the other partner has said. This way the speaker hears the message reworded (thus getting proof that someone has heard), perhaps picking up pointers on how to express ideas and feelings more clearly and getting an opportunity to correct any errors the therapist may have made in her paraphrase. In the meantime, the listening partner hears the message twice and can respond to either the original or the therapist's rephrasing of it.

As the partners learn to talk, and listen, to each other, they will be most concerned with content: "Do I agree with what you are saying?" "Are you being fair and accurate in your description of what happens between us?" "Are you going to understand what I tell you, and are you going to try to argue with me about whether or not I am right?" The therapist, in contrast, needs to be much more interested in *how* things are said, in what patterns, with what effect on both speaker and listener. "The therapist," says Groome, "must be able to move beyond the content to the process: how they interact with each other, what feelings are being alluded to, who protects whom, when and why, etc."(1989, p. 28). Noticing, and commenting on, these process issues will help the couple to break out of the old patterns, to begin to understand how they continue to do the same dance whatever music may be playing.

Another generally useful technique with couples is the assigning of homework. Couples may work issues through in the therapy session only to go home and fall back into the same old nonfunctional behaviors. Giving them a specific assignment helps them to solidify the gains made during the session and to translate those gains to the home environment. Interestingly, the homework need not always involve interacting in the newly acquired way. It can be very effective to ask the couple to go home and deliberately do it the old way—the way that doesn't work. Doing it wrong on purpose turns out to be a very different animal than doing it wrong because you don't know any better or don't know how to change! Most couples, after dutifully carrying out a "go home and relapse" assignment, are enormously relieved to be allowed to treat each other in the newer ways—the ways that would have seemed impossible before therapy began.

It is a good idea to insist that the homework assignment be written down by both partners before they leave the session. If there is no concrete record, partners are likely to forget just what the assignment was, or to disagree about how it is to be carried out. Even if you choose not to assign specific homework, you may want to ask the couple to write down toward the end of the hour the main things they got out of that session. Differences and similarities between their perceptions, or between theirs and yours, will give useful information for them to discuss and for you to consider in your ongoing treatment planning. In fact, "write down, without comparing notes, what you think were the most important things that happened in the session; then discuss the differences and similarities between your two sets of perceptions" is a pretty good all-purpose homework assignment for most couples, at most stages of therapy.

PROBLEM SOLVING

Couple therapy, whatever else it may involve, is a problem-solving process. Problems are what bring the couple to treatment in the first place: something is not going well, and the couple has not been able to find a solution on their own. Although the therapist cannot, and should not, solve the problems for the couple, it is imperative that she believe solutions are possible. She helps them to identify what they have tried to do to solve the problems, thus shifting the focus from blame and criticism, and consistently operates from the premise that there are always new and unexplored options.

IDENTIFYING THE PROBLEM

More often than not, couples whose relationship is in trouble don't really know what the problem is. They know where it hurts, what they are afraid of or angry about, but somehow when they try to deal with that hurt or scare directly, everything gets confused and out of control. They get sidetracked, defensive; they bring up old issues; the more frustrated they feel, the more they lash out in all directions. Helping them to focus on a single problem (even if it isn't the most important one) and solve it, before moving on to another issue, is a major therapeutic accomplishment.

The notion of working on a less important problem is a very useful one at the beginning of the problem-solving process. It is easier to give a little on a minor issue, to allow one's partner the benefit of the doubt, to be generous or forgiving. And success in negotiating a minor issue allows each partner to hope: maybe my partner is willing to listen to me, maybe we can find a way to compromise—maybe this counseling stuff can actually work! In order to clear a space for this preliminary "negotiation training," the couple is asked to make a conscious decision to live with things-as-they-are for a short time (this assumes, of course, that violence has not been a part of the problem and that all family members are protected from actual abuse). Wiseman suggests that the therapist encourage the partners to "tolerate 'not knowing' for a limited period of time, in the interest of making a wise decision. He or she often repeats throughout the intervention, that deciding may be a matter of uncovering a decision that is already deep within the individual but that he or she has not allowed him or herself to know up to this point" (1990, p. 11). Besides giving the couple a chance to learn some negotiation skills in a less affectively charged context, putting the major problems on hold can help them to reappreciate some of the positive parts of their relationship, things that they haven't been able to see because of the emotional dust stirred up by their struggling with each other.

A basic problem-solving principle is that the solution must involve doing something rather than not doing something; this is true for the minor as well as the major problems in a relationship. Nobody can stop a behavior without putting some other behavior in its place; conversely, when you start the replacement behavior, the old behavior has to stop. Getting rid of an undesirable behavior, then, becomes a secondary goal while starting a desirable behavior is the primary goal. Many (perhaps most) couples come to therapy with a good idea of the secondary goals: "I want her/him to stop nagging, spending too much money, going out with other men/women, ignoring my needs, etc." The first step in solving a problem is to identify what the complaining partner would like the accused partner to do instead.

As the couple begins to think in terms of "doing" rather than "not doing," the idea of multiple solutions becomes a possibility. There are lots of things that my partner can do instead of the one thing that I hate; some of these would be better than others. What I most want may be something that you are unwilling to give, and vice versa, but we may be able to find some second choice that would be at least acceptable to us both and certainly an improvement over what we have been doing. Ultimately, each partner learns to ask the other, "What do you need from me in order to give me what I want?" and to ask her or himself, "If I give this in order to get that, will it be an okay exchange?"

So begins the negotiation process. The couple learns to talk about primary (doing) rather than secondary (not doing) goals, and each partner is encouraged to think of several acceptable primary goals rather than a single nonnegotiable one. At this point, change becomes a possibility. Getting this far is not a trivial accomplishment; it requires that each partner be clear, with her- or himself as well as with the other people in the room, about wants and needs, likes and dislikes. This kind of honesty can be quite threatening, especially when one or both partners are afraid that their partner will use the information as a weapon rather than a tool. It may require many sessions to arrive at the point at which honest negotiating can take place.

FINDING ANTECEDENTS

Early in therapy, each partner is often confused about what really causes their conflicts. Even though things happen the same way, over and over again, it feels as if the trouble comes out of nowhere—suddenly, bang! we're at it again, both angry or hurt or scared, not knowing how we got here but knowing it's as familiar as it is painful. Learning how to anticipate, and thus avoid, these familiar and hurtful interactions is an important treatment goal. When I understand that my doing X typically results in something that I experience as unpleasant, I will be able to decide whether X-ing is really worth the unpleasantness.

A common reason why partners do not understand these cause-and-effect patterns is that they do not recognize the beginning moves as part of the sequence. Marvin and Martha relate a blowup: Marvin sat down after dinner to read the paper, only vaguely aware that Martha was banging dishes and cupboard doors in the kitchen. A few minutes later she stood in the door, crying, and accused him of being inconsiderate and lazy. He responded angrily. The drama ended with Martha sobbing in the bedroom and Marvin slamming out of the house late for his bowling tournament (in which he did badly because he was so upset).

For both Marvin and Martha, this sequence began at the end of the evening meal; and each found the other's behavior unreasonable and inexplicable. In order for them (and the therapist) to understand what happened, the antecedents must be identified. There are always antecedents. Nothing can occur that has not been preceded by something else. If neither the therapist nor the couple is able to specify an antecedent, its existence can nevertheless be asserted. Moreover, the antecedent itself has antecedents; the roots of a pattern can be traced back. When this kind of search has been done a few times, a pattern will begin to emerge. Marvin may have been late for dinner, or Martha may have been thinking resentfully about the evening out he had scheduled that night, or Martha may have been fighting the budget and worried about the purchases she had made and hadn't told Marvin about. The possibilities are endless. The content is usually not particularly important in determining the pattern. What usually emerges is a sequence of feelings and responses to feelings. When these feeling patterns are recognized and the couple is willing to deal with them as such, the actual content issues become much less crucial and the problem begins to be solvable.

VULNERABILITY

Dealing with feelings honestly means being vulnerable. I can maintain my behavior and attack the behavior of my partner for weeks; I can even weep or scream at him or at the therapist and still stay safe behind my defenses. However, once I start letting people in on how I really feel, what really makes me sad or glad or mad or scared, my defenses are shattered. Before I do that, I need to be quite sure that both therapist and partner will respect my feelings and not use my weaknesses against me. It is the therapist's job to protect partners against attack or blackmail, providing a forum for discussing such behaviors if they occur (or if someone fears they may occur), and occasionally helping a partner to develop new and more constructive defenses if the other partner continues the attack. Balancing the vulnerability by encouraging both partners to share feelings will help each to feel supported by and supportive of each other.

While the therapist must maintain neutrality throughout the process, and most particularly must nôt take sides when emotional issues are being worked through, this does not mean that we somehow turn off our own feelings. "The self of the therapist must always be present as a feeling human being, 'in touch' with her or his own emotional experiences. This requires self-awareness, comfort with strong affect, and the resolution of personal barriers to the expression of emotion" (Hollander-Goldfein 1989, p. 112). Being real with our feelings, secure in knowing that we will not be injured by strong emotional expression, we create a safe zone for the couple to learn the same kind of security. With this kind of safety, deeper and deeper sharing becomes possible; and with the sharing come new understandings and new ways of being together.

THE NEW SOLUTION

Problem solutions, like new clothes, need to be tried on to find out whether they fit. Not infrequently, a bargain or agreement or compromise will turn out to fit well for one partner but to be less than satisfying for the other. Ables has pointed out that both partners must be asked how the new agreement is working, but special attention should be paid to the partner who has made the major behavior change:

> The spouse who modified his or her behavior should have all this fully acknowledged and receive positive reinforcement. However, to determine how satisfactory the solution is, it is extremely important to ask this spouse about the

change. What was the degree of struggle? What was the personal cost? A solution that works well for one spouse but not the other, even though he or she complies, is no real solution. [1977, p. 113]

As the couple learns to listen to each other, to attend to and respect feelings, they will discover a whole new arena for communicating and problem solving. This is an exciting time, and there is often a kind of euphoria, a sense of "everything is wonderful and we'll never have troubles again." The belief that it is all solved forever is a comforting one; couples may deny the existence of other, related problem areas in their desire to maintain the belief that their relationship is now perfect and problem-free. Again, they must be cautioned to expect setbacks. New areas of conflict can and will appear; the real value in the therapy process lies not so much in solving the present problem as providing the couple with tools to use in future problem situations.

COMMON PATTERNS

The guidelines we have been discussing thus far are useful in most if not all couple therapy situations. We now turn to some more specific areas of concern in working with couples.

BLAMING AND COMPLAINING

As has been mentioned, many couples come to therapy with a great need to blame and complain about each other. It may be necessary to allow a certain amount of tattling to go on; just as a child may need to tell his side of a story and know he's been listened to before settling down to find a new way of dealing with a situation, so partners may need to know that the therapist understands how things seem from their point of view. The therapist must learn how to listen for and empathize with the feelings underlying the complaint, without taking sides or deciding that one person's viewpoint is either right or wrong. It is not a good idea, though, to allow the couple to engage in prolonged blaming and complaining interactions with each other, as these can be quite emotionally abusive. When angry complaints need to be directed to the partner, the therapist can mediate: "Instead of allowing the couple to step immediately into their maladaptive communication with its attendant frustration and diminished self-esteem, I often substitute the paraphrase at the beginning of the intervention.... Through paraphrasing...the poison or toxins can be taken out of what one person is trying to convey to the other" (Wiseman 1990, p. 24).

Complaining can be used as a springboard to problem solving, if the therapist consistently redirects attention to the specifics of what is happening and the internal experience of the complaining partner. The useful data in any complaint has to do with exactly what did happen and how the complaining partner was affected; information about how many times it has happened in the past, or how bad the partner is for doing it again, is largely irrelevant. Repeatedly asking the complaining partner to identify *exactly* what the partner does that is bothersome and *exactly* what alternative behavior would be preferable, shifts the process from helpless whining or angry blaming to a search for new ways to get needs met.

TERMINAL LANGUAGE

Stuart (1980) uses the expression *terminal language* to describe adjectives or nouns that place a partner into a category, as opposed to *instrumental language* which describes modifiable events. Terminal language defeats the purpose of therapy in that it suggests that the partner *is* some way and thus cannot change. The husband whose wife is a neurotic, for example, or the wife whose husband is a liar has little choice but to learn to live with the neurotic or the liar or leave the relationship.

Spouses who use terminal language need to learn to describe the behavior that the partner engages in and then begin to identify ways in which their own actions contribute to that behavior. Once such patterns are recognized, each can then look for ways in which changing his or her own behavior will help the other to change. Again, the focus shifts from assessing who is bad or sick or at fault to finding new patterns that will be more satisfying for both partners.

RED FLAGS

Over the months and years of living together, fighting the same battles over and over on a series of changing battlefields, couples develop tender spots. They know each other's weaknesses, know just what word or gesture will pierce the armor and get to the vulnerable target. Often this knowledge is outside of awareness, so that the hurtful words will seem to just pop out in the heat of the moment. The therapist needs to bring this behavior into awareness, to red flag it. Then the partners can be asked whether they want to resolve the issue or simply to punish the partner for past behavior. If their choice is resolution, they will need to agree to avoid the low blows which only serve to escalate their conflict.

While some red-flag behaviors are idiosyncratic to a particular couple, others are common to many marriages. One such category is the negative noun or adjective which we have already characterized as terminal language. Another is the sentence that begins with "You always" or "You never." Besides being inaccurate, always and never statements also have a quality of unchangeability, of hopelessness. They invite furious arguments about the truth or falsehood of the "always" or "never," replete with examples and counterexamples which totally avoid the task of detailing the specific trigger, the specific problem behavior, the specific feeling response, and the possible alternatives at each point in the sequence.

DOUBLE BINDING

The phenomenon of double binding was originally described in the context of parent-child interactions, but it also appears in chronically unhealthy relationships between adults. The three primary characteristics of the double-binding situation are: (1) a message is delivered which will call forth a "wrong response," no matter what that response may be; (2) the receiver is not allowed to question the meaning of the message or comment on its double-binding quality; and (3) the receiver is not allowed to change the subject or leave the interaction—he or she is "bound" into it. A typical double bind is the "go away closer" transaction, in which one (usually verbal) component of the message is a request for closeness while another (usually nonverbal) component is a demand for distance. Nora may tell Nathan, for example, that he never wants to cuddle with her any more; when he responds by putting his arm around her, she pulls away and says that she doesn't want him to patronize her. If he tries to point out what has happened, her response is, "That's right, blame it on me again!" and if he moves away she can use this as additional evidence that he does not want to be close.

Double binders beget double binders; often the only defense against double binding is to double bind in return. Nathan, after a few exchanges like the one described above, may begin (perhaps without full awareness) to approach Nora only when she is busy or preoccupied or otherwise emotionally unavailable. When she pushes him away, he too has replenished his stock of ammunition for the next skirmish. Thus is created an interlocking double bind pattern, which is virtually impossible for the participants to sort out without help from a noninvolved observer.

Dealing with double binding requires that the therapist insist on unraveling the pattern without getting tangled in details. The technique of looking for antecedents is useful, in that it may uncover a preceding double binding transaction that is interlocked with the one already identified. Mind reading is expressly forbidden: attributing motives to the offending partner is one of the surest ways to create a new double bind or cement an old one. "What did you feel?" and "What did you want?" are key questions for both partners; the feelings can be accepted and the wants understood quite apart from the unanswerable question of who actually started the whole thing.

FUSION

While some couples' difficulties have to do with not being able to interact with enough closeness to satisfy one or both partners, others experience the opposite kind of problem: they are too close. They are fused, unable to think of themselves as individuals apart from their partner. Such fusion, in turn, invites a whole host of troublesome consequences: inability to tolerate differences, fear of abandonment, a feeling of being smothered (to name but a few). For such partners, a major therapeutic goal is that they experience their separateness.

"We" statements are among the best indicators of the fused relationship. The partner who frequently talks about what we wanted or how we felt is signaling his inability to think of himself as separate from his spouse. He is also demonstrating his belief in mindreading, as if he, through the closeness of the relationship, actually does know what his partner thinks and feels. Knowing, he doesn't need to ask;

in the most dysfunctional of fused relationships he will argue with his partner if the partner expresses an unexpected feeling or want. "I know you so well," he seems to be saying, "that you cannot possibly feel different from how I believe you to feel. Therefore, if you tell me you feel that way, you are either mistaken or lying." Needless to say, double binding is rampant in these relationships.

Changing the "we" language is the first step in dispelling the mind-reading myth and separating the fused couple. The therapist needs to confront this situation patiently, as it will happen again and again. And the confrontation needs to be framed carefully, so that it will not fuel the other partner's tendency to accuse, blame, or mind read in return. Simply describing the process and the false assumption underlying it, and inviting the partner to change his language whenever an inappropriate "we" statement occurs, can go a surprisingly long way toward moving couples into nonfused ways of thinking and behaving.

RESPONSIBILITY

A final relationship phenomenon to be commented on here is that of overresponsibility. Spouses who are overresponsible tend to see their mate as faultless and to blame themselves for all or most of the bad feelings in the relationship. Overresponsibility is common in the codependent partnerships currently dealt with so often in the pop-psych and self-help literature. Overresponsible partners know that they should do better and that they "make" their partners feel unhappy and behave badly. The partner may helplessly protest that this is not so or may be quick to acquiesce in this uneven assignment of blame. Whichever way the pattern goes, the therapist's job is to help each person take the responsibility for his or her own feelings and behaviors, while giving up responsibility for the partner's feelings and behaviors. Nearly all the tools and techniques we have described in this chapter may be needed to accomplish this task; surprisingly, partners are often even more reluctant to give up blaming themselves than they are to stop blaming their spouse.

SOME SPECIAL SITUATIONS

SEXUAL DYSFUNCTION

The treatment of sexual dysfunction has become an area of therapeutic specialty, requiring specific training in techniques not used in other kinds of therapy. It is my position that sexual dysfunction therapy should not be attempted by therapists who have not received this advanced training.

In working with couples, however, it is important to know whether their sex life (or lack of it) is an important part of the problem. This requires some amount of sexual history taking, and the couple therapist must be able to gather sexual information accurately and with a minimum of embarrassment for the couple.

Dealing matter-of-factly with sexual matters can, in and of itself, be therapeutic. "Beginning counselors will find that simple, uncomplicated procedures, such as giving permission to enjoy erotic pleasure and reviving sensual satisfactions of the courtship days, are often effective, as is reassuring couples that fantasies, whatever their nature, are normal and indeed useful in obtaining sexual pleasure" (Freeman 1982, p. 50).

In is particularly important that the therapist be sensitive to her own comfort level when discussing sexual issues. Feelings of constraint or embarrassment will quickly convey themselves to the clients and may heighten their sense of shame, anger, or guilt. Freeman continues: "It should be recognized that beginning counselors or practitioners should use only those techniques with which they are comfortable, and about which they have conviction. It is quite in order for the counselor to limit himself or herself in this way" (p. 50).

If careful questioning reveals that the problem is primarily one of sexual dysfunction, the couple may be referred to a physician or to a qualified sex therapist. If, as is more likely, sexual dysfunction is only a part of the overall relationship problem, you may make some initial suggestions and observe the couple's response; if these first interventions are not helpful, it is probably wise to recommend concurrent treatment by a sex therapist. Although some therapists have been concerned about possible interference between two kinds of couple therapy going on simultaneously, there seems to be no evidence in opposition of such an arrangement; other experts firmly support the practice.

GAY AND LESBIAN COUPLES

Increasingly, gay and lesbian couples are publicly defining themselves to be in committed relationships and are dealing with each other and the world from that position. Changing attitudes and values are beginning to allow such couples the right to treat themselves, and be treated, like any other couple. As gay and lesbian relationships begin to be "normalized" in society, they begin to show outwardly the same stresses and strains of any other couple learning to live together—stresses and strains that have been there all along but have been driven underground by the biases of the heterosexual majority. And they, like their heterosexual counterparts, are turning to mental health professionals for help in dealing with their problems.

The question of how to work with a gay or lesbian couple reveals, on the surface, a kind of naiveté: why should we work with such couples any differently than we would work with anyone else? They experience exactly the same kinds of problems that we have been describing in these pages and respond in the same ways to the interventions that we have suggested. Gays and lesbians are people in relationships; they are couples first, and gays or lesbians second.

Having said this, though, it would be equally naive to pretend that there were no special areas of concern to be dealt with in working with a gay or lesbian couple. The first of these, and without question the most critical, is your own attitude toward homosexuality. If you are uncomfortable with or disapproving of gays and lesbians, then you have no business attempting to work with them. There will be no way that you can disguise your discomfort; and even if you can, it will surely interfere with your ability to be honestly and openly present for the couple. You cannot make a valid contract to help someone achieve a goal that you yourself disapprove of; and your clients deserve a therapist who can truly respect and value their relationship.

Quite apart from the specifically sexual concerns that gay and lesbian couples may bring to therapy (and what was said in the previous section is as valid for these couples as for any other), homosexual people do experience problems as a result of their sexual orientation, and these problems do affect their relationships. Despite the changing legal and social climate, gays and lesbians are still targets of discrimination and persecution. They are overtly or covertly barred from pursuing their careers; they may be discriminated against in housing, in religion, in recreational activities. There are innumerable reasons why a gay or lesbian couple may be wise to conceal their relationship. The strain imposed by having to hide or lie about being in a relationship is considerable, even when both partners agree about the conditions under which deception is necessary; it is even greater when one wants to "come out" while the other is not willing to take this step.

In-law problems plague many relationships but tend to be even more troubling for gay and lesbian couples. Some people are unwilling to tell their parents about their involvement with a same-sex partner; others, who have attempted to be open with parents, find themselves rejected or expelled from the family of origin. Another, and equally troubling, problem involves dealing with one's children: "Can I share the fact of my sexual orientation with my child?" "How will he or she feel about my partner?" "If I am open about my relationship, will this create social or psychological problems for my child?" "And, if I don't have children now, shall I have one—and how will I deal with the consequences of that decision, whichever way I make it?" These are issues which lie at the heart of a gay or lesbian relationship and need to be addressed openly.

Society provides significant support for heterosexual relationships; even the nonmarried, "living together" relationship is now generally accepted in most communities. All the world loves a lover: men and women can hold hands and embrace in public, kiss each other goodbye at the airport, cuddle in a movie theater, call each other by pet names. Not so for gays and lesbians; the ordinary demonstrations of affection that others take for granted are either forbidden to them or allowed only under threat of disapproval or worse. It is the absence of positives, though, rather than actual negative sanctions, that takes an even greater toll in gay and lesbian relationships. The social glue that holds heterosexual marriages together, from insurance benefits to the wedding ceremony itself, are simply not there. The gay or lesbian couple, if they are to venture out of the homosexual ghetto, will need to learn to survive the silence of indifference or hostility from the rest of the world.

And you, the therapist, unless you are a gay or a lesbian yourself, are a part of that "rest of the world." There are serious differences of opinion as to whether "straights" ought even to attempt to work with gay and lesbian clients. Those who argue against it maintain that the nongay therapist simply cannot understand what it is like to be gay in a heterosexual society. Some go further, asserting that the straight therapist's unconscious homophobia makes it impossible for her to avoid discounting and devaluing a gay relationship. On the other side of the ledger, it can be argued with equal persuasiveness that a "gays work with gays" policy (which, logically, would have as its corollary "straights work with straights") only leads to more fractionalizing: blacks can only work with blacks? physically handicapped with physically handicapped? alcoholics are the only people qualified to treat alcoholics? maybe left-handed people should only be treated by...

But I digress; this is not a book about social philosophy. There is really no rule that will tell you whether it is appropriate for you to work with gay and lesbian couples. That decision has to come from you, from your honest confrontation of your own values and biases. Again, supervision and consultation are your best resources. Say Rigby and Sophie:

> If [gay and lesbian] clients are to receive the ethical treatment to which all clients are entitled, it is important that...therapists explore their own attitudes and work with supervision groups or unbiased consultants, to overcome the tendency to view sexual preference in oversimplified terms that neither reflect reality nor help clients toward self-understanding and self-acceptance...therapists must be able to freely explore with clients the entire array of feelings around sexual identity, guilt, loyalty, religious and family concerns, and so on—without prejudging what outcome is best for any client. [1990, p. 171]

And this advice, by the way, holds true for the gay or lesbian as well as the heterosexual therapist.

THE EXTRAMARITAL AFFAIR

Either spouse's involvement in an extramarital affair during the couple therapy process vastly reduces the likelihood that therapy will improve the relationship. The partner involved in an affair has already established an escape hatch, another person to be with in case the marriage does not work out, and thus need not have the same level of commitment to the marriage as does the other spouse. The marriage may have already assumed second-best status, and therapy may be a kind of ritual that must be performed in order to separate without guilt.

Discovering that one's partner is having an affair is one of the events that often brings a couple to therapy. Few things have more power to disrupt and traumatize a relationship. The couple who present with a newly discovered extramarital affair need first to be reassured that their distress is predictable and appropriate. "They need to know that the emotional and cognitive disequilibrium they experience is a normal response to the crisis and, what's more, is likely to continue to a lesser degree for several months. Far from alarming the couple, this knowledge usually allows them to relax somewhat their frantic and futile efforts to achieve a hasty return to pre-crisis normalcy" (Westfall 1989, p. 170).

More difficult to deal with is the situation in which the therapist discovers, during the course of treatment, that one of the partners is secretly involved in an ongoing extramarital relationship. There are few rules that must be followed in therapy without exception, but this is one of them: the therapist must not become a coholder of the secret of an ongoing affair. "In accepting the secret the therapist, wittingly or unwittingly, becomes involved in a deception—she is expected to feign ignorance of the secret information in the presence of those who do not know and in so doing becomes secretly allied to her informant" (Carpenter & Treacher 1989, p. 117). At the moment this secret alliance comes into being, effective therapy ends. The partner having the affair must either end it or tell her or his partner what is going on, so that they can deal with this problem in the same way that they would deal with any other major relationship difficulty.

If the partner is willing to end the affair, and commit her- or himself to working on the relationship, it may not be necessary that the other partner be told about it. However, keeping this (or any other) major secret is certainly not desirable and should not be done unless there are overwhelming reasons for not disclosing. It is far better that the partner confess and deal with the consequences of her or his behavior. Helping the couple to rebuild the trust level to a point where they can begin to work through their feelings and negotiate a new set of relationship contracts will be the primary therapeutic task.

If a partner is unwilling either to disclose or terminate an extramarital affair, you may suggest that one or both spouses be seen individually. Most often, the partner who has no outside involvement will be the one who will agree to this arrangement; and she or he is quite likely to end up working out a way to end the old relationship and say goodbye to the other partner. It is appropriate for the therapist to warn such a client that this may happen, and to determine whether they see such an outcome as acceptable, before involving them in individual treatment. It may also be advisable, since you are the holder of an important secret, to refer the noninformed partner to another therapist.

SEPARATION THERAPY

I mentioned that the partner who is involved in another relationship may be using couple therapy as a way to move out of the original relationship. It is also possible that one or both partners, even though not extramaritally involved, may be overtly or covertly wanting to separate. They may view such a separation as either temporary or permanent; it is a mistake to assume that moving apart for a period of time is always a first step toward a more final separation. "Sometimes," says Rice, "a period of living apart may even be necessary to get the message of dissatisfaction across; in this case, the 'separation' is not necessarily seen by the initiating partner as a prelude to divorce" (1989, p. 153). People may have many reasons for seeking couple therapy when they have already decided to separate: they may want to learn how to use the time of separation as a way to come back together, to find someone to take care of the partner after they leave, to prove that they did everything possible to save the relationship, or to deal with their own feelings of grief and loss and guilt over the breakup.

The couple considering divorce or separation will need help in moving through their decision-making stages. There are five major steps in the process of making any major decision, and these are quite relevant to the decision of a couple to separate:

1. Appraising the challenge (what are the risks if I/we don't change?).
2. Surveying alternatives (have I/we considered all possible alternatives?).
3. Weighing alternatives (which alternative will best meet my/our needs?).
4. Deliberating about actual behavior (will I/we actually do what we think we need to do?).
5. Adhering to decisions despite negative feedback. [adapted from Turner & Strine 1985, p. 487]

The decision to separate affects not only the couple themselves but other family members as well. Separation therapy often expands into family therapy, as the children (in or out of the home) are helped to deal with the implications of their parents' new relationship. Even when children are not physically included in the therapy, the separating couple will usually need help in working through both practical and emotional issues having to do with the family as a whole—everything from finances to holiday visits to who gets to take the family dog.

Deciding to end a relationship does not necessarily mean that couple therapy has failed. As Rice points out, "many of the couples who come in initially for marital help will go on to divorce; the therapist who measures his or her success rate by how many couples stay together is likely to feel like a failure much of the time" (1989, p. 158). As therapists, we need to remind ourselves that sometimes a separation or a divorce is the best possible outcome for both partners; some relationships are simply too painful or too pathological to be worth maintaining. Nevertheless, parting is painful, and much of the emphasis in separation therapy will be on change and risk and loss. Ideally, the end product of such therapy is two people who are able to respect each other, to appreciate what was positive in their relationship, to work together constructively as coparents, and to move out into the remainder of their lives as whole and autonomous individuals.

IN CONCLUSION

Whether the therapy process ultimately ends in strengthening or dissolving the couple relationship, one thing is certain: the therapist's role and behavior must change over the course of treatment. At first, she will be an active intervener in the partners' interactions. She will instruct, interpret, and interrupt; she will determine the pace of the therapy process and will often prescribe activities to be carried out between sessions. Having deliberately placed herself in the center of the relationship in order to bring about changes, she must then find a way to extricate herself, for her job will end only when she is no longer needed. From directing the first efforts of the couple, she will shift to coaching them, and from coaching she will move to simply giving feedback about what they are doing (Stuart 1980). Finally, she must separate from them entirely.

The separation need not be an abrupt one, however. It is often useful to invite couples to return for a reporting session several months after they have terminated therapy. This allows them to review the changes they have made, to get a "booster shot" to strengthen their new behaviors, and to receive well-earned recognition from the therapy (who knows better than anyone else what they have overcome) for their accomplishments. Couples may also be reassured that they can return for further help at a later date should the need arise: like so many kinds of contingency planning, just knowing that they can go back often helps the partners to avoid having to do so.

Couple therapy can be exciting and fun. There is always something going on; the difficulty is in deciding what to focus on and what to let go by. The couple therapist really has three clients: the two spouses and the relationship itself. In dealing with one of these three, she must necessarily miss something that is occurring in the other two. As with all other kinds of therapy, mistakes are inevitable. Yet there is a resiliency about couples, an ability to bounce back from errors of omission or commission, that is reassuring. On the other hand, couples can seize upon a therapeutic error and use it to confuse and confound the process to an incredible degree. Perhaps in no other kind of therapy (with the possible exception of family therapy, which also involves people in relationships) is a small intervention likely to have such far-reaching and ongoing consequences. It is a roller coaster ride and, like other roller coasters, it is not to everyone's taste. But if you do like it and choose to continue with it, you can count on having an interesting career. You may be frustrated, disappointed, triumphant, or apprehensive, but you definitely will not be bored!

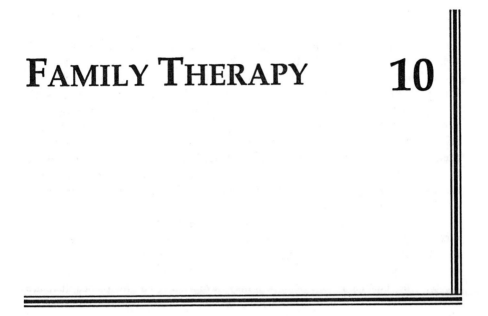

FAMILY THERAPY 10

Families, and the ways in which we work with them, are changing. First, the families themselves are changing. Since the seventies we have seen the emergence and growth of a bewildering variety of family structures. While the Mom-and-Dad-and-two-kids family has not disappeared, it certainly is no longer the rule. Single-parent families, blended families, his-hers-ours families are far more common; even multiparent families, communal families, and gay and lesbian families are seen with some frequency.

Second, the kinds of problems that families bring to counseling have changed. A few decades ago families seen in counseling almost invariably fell into one (or both) of two categories: (1) the family with a severely disturbed or damaged child: these children were schizophrenic, autistic, developmentally disabled—they were clearly and obviously sick; (2) the family in which one or both parents were neglectful, abusive, and/or incompetent; these families were chaotic, disorganized, usually multiproblem families, and the children were the victims of the parents' inadequacies. These kinds of families can still be found in therapists' offices, of course. But a growing acceptance of psychotherapy as a means of achieving health and harmony in the family, as well as a whole new set of family stressors brought on by cultural changes, have brought a variety of other patterns to our attention.

Chief among these patterns—and deserving of special attention—is the abused parent family. As our youth-oriented culture has flourished, many parents have become increasingly confused about the limits of their authority: their right to make and maintain family rules and to discipline their children. In such families "obedience" is a questionable virtue, if not a downright character flaw. Parental rule is replaced by a kind of quasi-democracy, and parents, by trying too hard to be fair to their children, allow themselves to be verbally and sometimes physically abused.

As families have changed, our ways of understanding and intervening with them have changed as well. We are unlikely now to think in terms of a single "sick" family member, of "good" or "bad" parents and their effects on the children. The work of such seminal thinkers as Bateson, Haley, Jackson, and Selvini-Palazzoli have led us to look at the family as a dynamic system in which each person responds to and is responded to by every other person. Says Dallos: "It is helpful to regard each person's actions in a family as based upon a set of constructs or premises which are not merely individual but have evolved out of the family dynamics. Since these premises are also seen to be shared, no one individual is regarded as holding unilateral responsibility for the circumstances that have developed, including the current problems" (1987, p. 140).

As families evolve their unique ways of being and interacting with each other, they become tightly interacting systems. Their patterns become well-established, taken for granted by all members, maintained by interlocking layers of perceptions, expectations, and habit. Communications are redundant, so that cutting through one maladaptive message path may have little or no effect since there are so many others leading toward the same outcome. Each member feels powerless to change, because whatever change he might make must (in order for him to feel safe) be matched or validated by changes in someone else—and he's quite sure, based on past experience, that those someones aren't going to change.

Trying to understand a family system in terms of a linear, causal model leads only to frustration. The family therapist must learn to think circularly, in terms of ongoing, interactive loops. She is alert to the ripple effect: the reverberations that a change in one family member will set up in all the others. She is sensitive to the feeling of stuckness, of helpless impotence, that members of an entrenched and malfunctioning system experience, and she attempts to enter that system in such a way that its self-reinforcing patterns will be disrupted and it will be forced to find a new and healthier equilibrium.

Watzlawick uses a vivid metaphor to describe what has to happen if an unhealthy family is to change. He asks us to imagine

> two sailors hanging out of either side of a sailboat in order to steady it; the more one leans overboard, the more the other has to hang out to compensate for the instability created by the other's attempts at stabilizing the boat, while the boat itself would be quite steady if not for their acrobatic efforts at steadying it. It is not difficult to see that in order to change this absurd situation at least one of them has to do something seemingly quite unreasonable, namely to "steady" less and not more, since this will immediately force the other to also do less of the same (unless he wants to finish up in the water), and they may eventually find themselves comfortably back inside a steady boat. [1978, p. 36]

As soon as either of the sailors stops doing what he has been doing and starts doing almost anything else, the situation will change. Yet to do anything different feels terribly risky, if not downright destructive. When a family is in this kind of a fix (and most of the families seen by therapists are), the therapist's job is to help someone—anyone—to make a change, thus enabling the others to change too.

GETTING STARTED

Family therapy, like any other sort of therapy, moves through beginning, middle, and ending phases. The beginning phase is a getting-to-know-each-other process in which therapist and family check each other out, decide if they can (or want to) work together, and come to some initial agreement on what problems are to be solved. "The help giver," say Dunst, Trivette and Deal, "must develop a relationship with the family in which he or she becomes a trusted confidant....It is a partnership that creates the medium for effective work with families" (1988, p. 52). So far, no different from individual therapy. The big difference, of course, has to do with the fact that in family therapy the client is several people. A major task for the first few sessions is what is known as "joining." Therapy proceeds most efficiently when each person in the family feels "joined" by the therapist: listened to, cared about, and taken seriously. Failure to join one or more family members almost always leads to the therapist being seen as taking sides "for" this person and "against" that one. The family will almost always expect you to take sides. They will have defined one or two members as "wrong" or "sick" or "bad" and in need of fixing and will expect you to see things in the same way. Dallos describes one family who took this set of expectations to an extreme:

> Prior to their second session the mother in one family phoned to cancel the session. She explained that they could not attend "because they were having family problems." This apparent absurdity exposes a fundamental dilemma in the practice of family therapy in that few families attend intending to have "family therapy". Instead, almost invariably, one person is designated as the root or cause of their problems. In many cases this understanding may be the exclusive area of agreement in the family. [1987, p. 136]

It was greatly surprising to this family that the "family problems" they were having might be an appropriate concern of the therapist, since they had nothing to do (in their perception) with the behavior of the "sick" member that the therapist was supposed to "fix." If the therapist were to go along with this point of view, accepting the designation of member X as "the problem" and joining with the others against X, she would be reinforcing the very pattern which is keeping the family stuck. Rather, it was imperative that she join X as well as all of the others. Failure to do so in such cases almost guarantees that the therapy will be at best inefficient and at worst ineffective or actually harmful to the family.

How do you "join" a family? The definition says it all: you listen to, care about, and take seriously each family member. You want to hear each person's beliefs about why they are here with you; you want to know where it hurts for each of them and what they have done or are doing about it. You most definitely are *not* interested in playing judge or jury, elevating one member at the expense of another, or even—at this early stage—finding a solution to their problem. You want to know what is happening, but even more important is *who* is happening, how, and from each person's point of view. If you are genuinely invested in learning about these things and give yourself permission to find out, then the joining will more or less take care of itself.

Finding out about a family is both easier and harder than finding out about a single client. Harder, obviously, because there are more people to know about and more data to collect. Easier because the family will act it all out before your very eyes if you allow them to do so. Notice what people say with their nonverbal behaviors as well as with their words. Who sits next to whom? Who talks for whom? Who obeys? Who looks away? Who is attentive? There will be much more going on than you can possibly hope to take in, so just sample that which catches your attention—and ask about it! Part of your job is to bring into the open what has been hinted at and skirted around; this can best be done by calling attention to the nonverbal messages and requesting a translation.

Sometimes family members will be able to provide that translation—the "meaning" of the behavior—and sometimes they won't. All families operate according to three sets of rules: (1) the ones everybody knows about and can state to the therapist; (2) the ones they seem to be unaware of but will agree about once someone else points them out; and (3) the ones they don't or won't recognize but that still shape their behavior. Asking person A what person B meant when she/he did X ("I notice that Suzie slumped down in her chair while you were talking, Dad. What do you think she is trying to tell us?") is a way for you to find out about all three kinds of rules.

Most family therapists advocate a particular kind of questioning process, known as "circular questioning," at some time during the joining phase. In circular questioning, every member of the family is asked about something that happens between two other family members. Asking everyone about the behavior or the interaction not only shows interest in and attention to each person's opinion but implies that the behavior being examined is important. "Neutrality is maintained...by the therapist's conveying to each family member that he or she considers them competent and that any behavior they display is for good reason" (Gelcer, McCabe, & Smith-Resnick 1990). When you are allied with everyone, yet remaining neutral, you have in fact joined with the family.

Not only does circular questioning help in the joining process, but it also begins to break down one of the most common rules that govern dysfunctional families: the rule of nonsecret secrets. Nearly all distressed families have "secrets" that everyone knows, in one way or another, but that nobody is allowed to acknowledge. "Very often," say Carpenter and Treach, "such secrets, although known by all, are never discussed and family members pretend that they do not know, not only to outsiders but also to each other. It is for this reason that it is sometimes asserted that there is no such thing as a secret in a family—they all know" (1989, p. 119). Nonsecret secrets gum up communication, interfere with trust, and create feelings of confusion, resentment, and guilt. Getting the secrets out into the open is one of the first steps in bringing families back to health.

Another task for the early sessions of family therapy, also quite compatible with the joining process, is that of giving information. Family members have lots of questions: How bad is my family? Can things get better? Is it really my fault? What will you, the therapist, do with us? Some of these will be answered explicitly and some implicitly. One point that needs to be made clearly and explicitly has to do with protection: it is not acceptable for any member of the family to hurt himself or anyone else. Abuse of any sort—physical or sexual or psychological—will not be tolerated. If it has been occurring, it is now over with; it will not start again under any circumstances. You, the therapist, will take whatever steps are necessary to ensure the safety of every family member.

Questions about how bad off the family is and whether it can be helped to change usually are best answered implicitly (which is how they most often are asked). The family is hurting, or it wouldn't be here. You think they can be helped, or *you* wouldn't be here. Trying to reassure them that things can change is likely to have the opposite effect, making them wonder if you are perhaps just trying to reassure yourself.

On the other hand, it may be quite helpful to predict some of the less comfortable things that may occur during treatment. I often talk about the way that family members learn to protect themselves and each other; how those learned protections get to be so habitual that they seem like the only way to act; and how later, as people grow and change, the learned protections can get in the way of folks getting what they want. I say that part of our job in therapy will be to get those old habits out and look at them again, and that this may be uncomfortable, embarrassing, or even painful at times. I expect that I will make mistakes, and that one or more people in the family may get angry at or disappointed with me, and that is what I tell them. Predicting the negative makes it acceptable, part of the treatment plan; it gives me more leverage and flexibility as a therapist. It also gives the family permission to act naturally—to get mad or be upset with or scared of me. Finally, it models "telling it like it is," which is precisely what most families need to learn to do.

TREATMENT PLANNING

In order to get somewhere with a family, you need to have some idea either of where you want to be or where you want not to be. Sometimes the dysfunction will be clear and the remediation obvious: The children have been given too much power, and the parents need to reclaim their authority. Or, the father has abdicated his responsibility as an adult and joined the children, so that the mother is functioning as a single parent; Dad needs to be Dad again. Or, a tyrannical grandparent is running the family while the parents feel enraged and act helpless; the parents need to take control of their own household.

Beware, though, of placing too much confidence in your own hypotheses. After all, that's all that they are—hypotheses. Dunst, Trivette, and Deal remind us that "there are no right or wrong family functioning styles, but rather differentially effective styles that are likely to be employed in response to different life events and situations" (1988, p. 52). It's not at all unusual for a family to surprise and startle a therapist by finding a solution of their own that works for them and looks quite different from what the therapist thought was needed. It's probably a lot more sensible to base your change hypothesis on an analysis of what needs to be different than to aim at some particular end product. In other words, you can help a family get somewhere other than where they are without specifying where you think that somewhere is. Choosing which new way is the family's job.

Knowing "where they are," though, also requires a hypothesis about the process a family system uses to maintain a set of behaviors that cause them pain. As you begin to understand how the system keeps itself balanced (in a painful way), you can begin to upset that balance. You will be able to see the pattern much more clearly than the family members, because you stand outside of it. The family can only understand within the context of how they experience themselves, and that experience is shaped by the very patterns they need to change. "Because the family is a system that has a long history of interaction, it also has a long history that dictates the type of actions and reactions....generally these action and reaction patterns within a family can recur even in different contexts and are sometimes transmitted from one generation to another" (Gelcer, McCabe, & Smith-Resnick 1990, p. 66). Creating disequilibrium in a family system invites—indeed, often demands—change in the system. Without a hypothesis you are likely to mire the family even more deeply in their dysfunctional patterns and increase their distress and confusion rather than alleviate it.

In general, family system hypotheses have to do with the structure of the family, the communication process of the family, or both. Structural hypotheses focus on such things as family hierarchies, alliances, and boundaries. Communication process hypotheses focus on the way in which information flows among members. Communication process therapists are most particularly interested in the meanings of behavior and understand behavior (particularly symptomatic behavior) as a way of communicating nonverbally.

In developing hypotheses about change, it is important to remember that no family operates in a vacuum. Extended family members, friends, neighbors, and outside authorities may exert important influences on family process. "Ask about the power that other professionals and social agents may have in relation to the family," warns Madanes. "The therapist needs to plan how to influence these sources of power so that they will collaborate instead of interfering with his endeavors" (1984, p. 119).

Finally, remember that hypothesizing about change works best when it is done stepwise. It is not necessary and often not even desirable to try to predict *all* of the changes a family can benefit from; you don't need to plan for everything all at once. Making one single change and making it solidly will prepare the way for the next one and frequently will make planning for the next one relatively easy. Here's another aspect of the "you don't need to know exactly where you are going" rule: sometimes neither you nor the family can know where they need to go until all have experienced some in-between places.

THEORETICAL APPROACHES

Historically, we can identify three major theoretical approaches to doing therapy with families. Each approach has its own typical strategies and is based on a particular set of assumptions. Practically speaking, in the therapeutic climate of the nineties, these three approaches often seem to blend together, and most therapists borrow from them all. In terms of your understanding of where the different strategies and conceptualizations come from, though, it's helpful to put them in their individual contexts.

Early family therapies were more or less straightforward educational experiences. One family member (usually a child) was creating a problem for himself and the other family members, and the family came to treatment in order to learn how to make the problem member change. Family therapy often involved teaching more appropriate parenting skills, helping family members utilize all their potential resources, and improving communication. While it was recognized that the most obvious problem in a family was not necessarily the most troublesome one in the long run and that the family was an entity in itself—rather than just a collection of individuals—therapists tended to approach problems fairly directly and to take at face value the consensus of family reporting about the problems. Gradually, therapists began to suspect that more was going on in these dysfunctional families than met the eye and to look beside, or under, or away from the identified problem. Bowen (1978), for instance, brought in extended family members—especially grandparents—in order to deal with the unquestioned rule structure that is handed down from generation to generation.

The first major break from a generally logical approach came with the advent of structural family therapy as developed by Minuchin. Minuchin (1974) became interested in the ways in which families divide themselves into subgroups, how membership and nonmembership in those subgroups is determined, how the subgroups communicate with each other—in short, how the family is structured and how that structure affects the family's ability to function healthily. Out of this interest came a system of family therapy that manipulated and shifted the substructures and the membership within the substructures in order to rebalance the out-of-balance family. Commonly occurring maladaptive substructures were identified (the family in which one member of the parent substructure has joined the sibling substructure, for instance), and techniques were created to help families reorganize themselves.

Systems theory and the study of paradox gave rise to the third major approach to family therapy: the systemic approach. In this approach the family is viewed as a semipermeable system with all of the mathematical characteristics of a system. Therapists such as Haley, Watzlawick, and the Italian group spearheaded by Selvini-Palazzoli use concepts like feedback loop, runaway, homeostasis, and second-order change to describe how the family system functions so as to maintain its members' maladaptive behaviors or to grow and change. Doublebinding is seen as a major cause of pain and confusion, and the therapeutic paradox is a major tool in breaking through the impasses of a self-reinforcing, homeostatic system.

Modern family therapists tend to be quite eclectic, recognizing that each of the major approaches to families captures a part of the truth and that each offers useful guidelines. In general, the therapist will begin with a fairly direct approach, taking the problem at face value and helping the family to come up with a solution. The child who acts younger than his age will be encouraged to grow up, and his parents will be helped to provide the kind of environment in which growing up is best accomplished. The parent who acts more like one of the siblings will be empowered so that he or she can function in a more role-appropriate way. Parents who are confused about whether it is right to insist that their children behave well (and who thus have misbehaving children) will be encouraged to set and enforce clear limits and, if necessary, will be taught how to do so.

If the family does not respond to a straightforward approach, it is assumed that more is going on than the obvious presenting problem: the underlying system is out of kilter and has acquired homeostatic properties. In other words the family now is reinforcing itself so that the problems are self-sustaining. In families that have acquired this kind of stable dysfunction, efforts to change tend to further intensify and entrench the problem. In fact, by the time the family reaches the therapist's office, the major ongoing problems often are caused by the ways in which the family is trying to solve their original problems. The therapist will go about unbalancing and/or rebalancing the system by means of shifting subsystems, opening or closing communication channels, redefining behaviors, or doing whatever else is needed to allow the family to change its perspective, its way of experiencing itself. Family members must be maneuvered so as to step out of their old patterns— patterns that they did not even know they were in. In order to ease them into this sort of change, the therapist will use language which matches the family's beliefs and assumptions, while simultaneously inviting them to consider other perspectives. Using language that coincides with the family's belief system, but doing so in such a way as to change that belief system, is the essence of the family therapist's art.

TOOLS AND TECHNIQUES

Family therapy has a history even shorter than individual therapy, and that history is quite fragmented. It has not developed in an organized way, one step leading to another, but rather out of bits and pieces contributed by many theorists and practitioners working relatively independently. One result of this helter-skelter growth is that the literature is full of techniques, "chunks" that can be used to accomplish this or that effect, but the techniques do not fall into a neat pattern. The tool box has many tools, but they are in a disorderly heap. To order and organize the heap would be a theoretical task of no small magnitude, one which is well beyond the scope of this chapter. Yet the tools and techniques are valuable and, taken together, help us to get a sense of what actually goes on in working with families. Let's take a few pages to examine some of these tools, these ways of conceptualizing and moving in and upsetting the pain-producing balance of a dysfunctional family.

LEVEL SHIFTING

Families in which the solution to an old problem has become a new (and more serious) problem have worked hard to make things better. They probably have tried everything they could think of to deal with their situation, or at least everything that seemed to have any possibility of working. In the process they probably also have tried everything the therapist could think of, as well. Or, they have compelling reasons why the things they haven't tried won't work. As long as the therapist stays at the same level of problem solving, accepting the family's view of what is wrong and attempting to right it, nothing much is likely to get better.

The experienced family therapist is very interested in the family's view, very interested in what each family member thinks is wrong and what should be done. Her interest, however, goes well beyond the content of the problem. In fact, talking about the actual problem (as seen by the family) is often just a vehicle for exploring the family's process. How do they go about *thinking* about what's happening to them? What are they *not* talking about or dealing with? What are the unspoken rules that guide their interactions? In setting up a level-shifting intervention, the family therapist doesn't voice these questions out loud; she asks them of herself and uses the answers to formulate a question or a suggestion that redirects the family's attention. The family that has been wrestling with son Roger's poor school performance may, for instance, find the therapist suddenly interested in the ways in which secrets are kept, or the possibility that Dad is afraid of hurting Mom's feelings, or who in the family is most like Grandpa.

While these interests are based on real hypotheses about the way in which the family system operates, they also have major value in refocusing the family's concern—on helping the family to stop trying to solve the "problem" in whatever way they have been doing so that the pathological balance that has been established can right itself. If Mom and Dad stop being so interested in Roger's schoolwork, Roger may discover that he no longer is able to distract them from their own fundamental communication difficulties. Once Roger is relieved of his job as family lightning rod, he may find that he really doesn't enjoy doing poor schoolwork.

People are surprised when they expect a certain message and receive instead a message at a totally different level. The message that they receive is often not a verbal one; changing the subject in an unexpected way sends a subtle signal that the family's preoccupation with the "problem" may be leading them in the wrong direction, that the therapist sees something that they may have missed. Such a maneuver not only can cut through the unproductive stuckness that the family is mired in, but it also gets the family's attention. It startles them and takes them off guard. In so doing, it can get past the habitual defenses and thus prepare the ground for change.

REFRAMING

Language is a powerful influence, both for making changes and for maintaining the status quo. Families often find themselves prisoners of their own language.

Because of the words they use to describe and understand what is happening, they create a situation that they cannot change. By changing the definition of the family's behavior, new possibilities for change can emerge. Shifting the description of a behavior so that the behavior becomes positive rather than negative (or, rarely, negative rather than positive) is known as reframing.

There are many ways of reframing a given situation. One can shift the role of "patient" onto another person, redefine misbehavior as "helpfulness," or insist that a "helpless" person is really quite powerful. In fact, any adjective describing a family member can be turned into its opposite. Amazingly, such reframing nearly always can be defended as a logical and reasonable way of understanding the family dynamic. The most effective reframes will involve each of the family members, defining the way they are interacting as positively intended and as very different from how the family has been presenting itself. "The family system is comprised of interdependent members and...by strengthening and supporting the family unit and not just the child the chances of making a significant positive impact upon ALL family members are enhanced considerably" (Dunst, Trivette, & Deal 1988, p. 6). The reframe that describes as well as surprises each family member will have the best chances of success.

Consider a family consisting of Mom, Dad, and three kids as an example. The two older children are Mom's from a prior marriage, and the third is a product of the present marriage. The second-oldest child, eight-year-old Ellie, is school-phobic, **and** it is her problem that brings the family to treatment. Ellie cries frantically if forced to go to school, and if the parents persist in taking her she invariably throws up before she has been there an hour. Needless to say, her behavior is disrupting not only the family but the school as well, and the parents are at their wits' end. One way of reframing the family is to talk about the power that Ellie has: she is able to command the attention and concern of so many people whenever she chooses to do so. Going on, this reframe would describe the behaviors of the other family members as they respond to Ellie's power. Ellie could be framed as a highly generous and loyal person, willing to sacrifice herself in order to keep Mom from having to be alone during the day. Gordon and Marlene, the other children, could be made the patients: the therapist could be very concerned that they are too conforming and have not learned to express their individuality or to say no to their parents (as Ellie obviously has learned to do). The possibilities go on and on; the therapist's choice is determined by the actual dynamics of the family and by her own creative ingenuity.

Many students, when first introduced to this sort of approach, experience a kind of indignation: How could a therapist say such things to a family? Isn't it lying? Disrespectful? Would any family be taken in by it? What good could it possibly do, anyhow? Dallos's answer to these criticisms is fairly typical of the position of systemic family therapists. He asks, "Which is less ethically justifiable, to 'trick' a family into...therapy or to leave them in distress out of a principle of 'honesty'?" (1987, p. 141). My own response is somewhat different. I believe that if the reframe *is* a lie then it should not be used. Reframes which cannot be logically justified are indeed disrespectful. Most families won't accept a reframe that the therapist, at some level, cannot herself believe. But if the reframe is valid, if it is *both* "true" and "not true," then it can have tremendous power. To check this out imagine yourself in turn to be each family member in Ellie's family. Think about how you would feel and react if a believable, knowledgeable therapist, whom you had learned to trust, described your family in these ways.

POSITIVE CONNOTATION

The most effective reframing techniques nearly always involve describing in positive terms a behavior that the family has considered to be negative. As we have said, the most powerful reframes are able to positively connote each family member's part in the problem. Sometimes, however, only one behavior is focused on, or an interaction between two members will be defined positively.

Positive connotation tends to weaken or bypass resistance. It allows family members to change without losing face. L'Abate points out:

> It is important for therapists to achieve control so that, and to the extent that, they can help others learn to control themselves. The family is not going to carry out instructions that are contrary to its world view....However, when symptomatic behavior is positively connoted, it is easier for the family to accept control over the symptom and to carry out assignments. [1984, p. 13]

It is somehow less difficult to stop being a nag or an autocrat or insensitive or lazy if you are invited to believe that you have really been "over concerned" or "too generous with your time" or "protecting yourself from pain" or "expressing your playfulness." And it is easier for all other family members to assist you in changing, in a way that feels good to you, if they too believe in the benign intent of your behavior.

Positive connotation of a problem behavior allows the therapist to define *any* change as positive. No matter what the family does differently, it's good—either it continues in the direction of the positively connoted behavior or interaction, or it lessens the problem as originally presented. "In our work with families," say Carpenter and Treacher, "we should be concerned not with what is keeping things the same but with what is changing. The emphasis should be not on how clients resist change but on how they cooperate with the therapist" (1989, p. 14). As soon as some positive change occurs (in whatever direction), the family has indeed cooperated, by proving that change is possible—the first step toward success.

GIVING DIRECTIVES

Reframing and positive connotation help to catch the family's attention and to shift their perspective so that they can see other options for themselves. But talk and insight are cheap; actual behavior change is the ultimate goal for family therapy. Effective therapy moves the family from concerns to needs to actions, and does so as rapidly as possible. To lever the family into trying out changes, the family therapist will use directives: she will tell family members what they are to do outside the therapy session. These directives are generally described as "experiments" rather than "this is how your family ought to operate," and they are set up so that no matter what the family does with them, the result can be framed as a success.

Ideally, the family will listen to the directive and then go home and carry it out, thus learning whatever the therapist intended for them to learn. Mom will praise Dad rather than criticize him, or Dad will cook dinner while Mom goes bowling, or son will take ten minutes a day to brag about his schoolwork, or daughter will clean her room in exchange for driving lessons. If it is a well-constructed directive, however, it will provide useful information even when one or more members sabotage it. There are, in fact, whole groups of paradoxical interventions that can be given with the expectation that someone *will* sabotage them and the family will end up not following the directive—and *not* following it is exactly what the therapist really wanted. These interventions are designed to break families out of the self-reinforcing, stuck-in-a-rut patterns that result when dysfunction has been present over a relatively long period of time.

Paradoxical strategies, however, definitely fall into the category of advanced techniques—not to be attempted without specific training and to be used only under the supervision of an experienced family therapist.

FAMILY TASKS

One of the most common tasks assigned to families is that of "writing it down." Family members can be instructed to write down what happened, with whom, when, what led up to it, what happened next, what one wishes would happen instead—the possibilities are nearly endless. One family member can be the reporter or can act as scribe and write what another family member tells him to write. Each can describe an incident from his own point of view—or each can describe it from someone else's point of view. Writing it down is doable; it takes very little time, can be fitted into a busy schedule, and costs virtually nothing. Therefore, it is ideal as a check on whether the family will be compliant. If carried out, it has significant benefits: not only does it provide the therapist with information about how the family functions, but it gives the family information as well. It also creates a sense of competence, a feeling of we-are-doing-something-about-it. "It is very important for families to keep running accounts of contracts, of conferences, of when they are depressed, of sibling rivalry, of temper tantrums, and so forth. By putting it in writing the family learns to be in charge of itself" (Williams & Weeks 1984, p. 20).

Another frequently used instruction is that of the family ritual. The family members are given a very specific set of behaviors to follow, in a ritualized pattern. The ritual may be straightforward or paradoxical; it may involve the sharing of information; it may (much later in treatment) be a forum for apologies and forgiveness. Sometimes a diagnosis/description of the family's behavior is written in a letter to the family, and a ritual may be prescribed in which one member of the family reads the letter to the others. Or a playful or fantasy ritual may be devised which acts out, symbolically, either some aspect of the family deviant behavior or the underlying purpose of that deviant behavior (Madanes 1984). The ritual, like writing, serves a joint function: it is easily doable and thus is a test of the family's compliance; it also is a therapeutic intervention in its own right.

A third kind of directive is the family contract. Family contracts take the form of "if she/he does this, then you do that." If Junior gets himself up before 7:10 on school days, Dad will cook breakfast for everyone. If Dad carries out the garbage, Mom will watch the baseball game with him and the boys. Or, they can deal with what happens when a family member does *not* do something: for every five minutes that Junior is late getting up, he will do fifteen minutes' worth of hard labor for Mom; and for every morning that Mom forgets and reminds him to get up, he gets to stay up fifteen minutes past his regular bedtime.

All of these directives have one thing in common: they assume that the family members are competent to do what needs to be done. A directive that in any way furthers the definition of one or more members of the family as unable to change, unable to function in the family, is a harmful directive. It is this kind of subtle labeling that often gets families in trouble in the first place: person A assumes that person B can't or won't do something, so A does it (resentfully); B no longer has to do it so doesn't even try; A's worst fears are thereby confirmed, and so it goes. It is not helpful to do things for someone who can do them for himself. "If [our] help does not require the recipient to acquire effective behavior and thus renders the person helpless or dependent, the immediate needs of the person may be met, but the ability to teach and foster effective behavior are diminished" (Dunst, Trivette, & Deal 1988, p. 37).

CHOOSING A STRATEGY

There are so many strategies available to the family therapist that one may be tempted to throw up one's hands and choose randomly what to do with a particular family. The literature often doesn't help here. An intervention may be described in detail, together with the results of that intervention, but seldom do the authors discuss their thinking in choosing that strategy. There are, however, some guidelines for what to do and when to do it.

When the therapist is in a position of power, when she is clearly seen as the expert and is trusted by the family (or at least by the family member toward whom the intervention is directed), then a direct, compliance-based strategy is indicated. Straightforward, rather than paradoxical, interventions should be used when possible; there's no need to get fancy when the family is ready and willing to work cooperatively. Families in an acute crisis generally fall into this category. Such families likely will comply with a therapist's directive since they usually are frightened and looking for something that will give them immediate relief. Moreover, the crisis is new, fresh; the family hasn't had time to settle into the kind of homeostatic pattern that the paradoxical intervention is designed to break up.

Even when cooperation is unlikely or reluctant, though, there still are some families for which paradoxical interventions are inappropriate. One such family is the childlike family, in which "all members, including adults, tend to function on an immature level seeking parenting from the therapist. Such systems are...too loose and lack sufficient cohesiveness and unity of purpose for a paradoxical ploy to be effective" (Fisher, Anderson, & Jones 1981, p. 33). Fisher also recommends that paradoxical strategies not be used in chaotic or poorly organized families. The intervention that depends for its effectiveness on noncompliance tends to break up collusions and alliances within the family, and families that are poorly organized don't have enough such alliances in the first place.

The general rule of thumb, then, is first to assess how the family patterns—the process—are getting in the way or creating problems. More often than not, this process will have developed out of an attempt to solve some earlier problem situation; the solution will have become the problem. When the assessment has been made, assign the family some task that will require a change in the process, something they must do that will be incompatible with their current way of operating. In other words, redirect their behaviors into more constructive channels. If they follow through, well and good. If they don't, the way in which they undermine or sabotage or defeat the instructions will give you a clue as to the kind of strategic approach which is likely to be most effective with them. Reframing, which is probably the gentlest of the strategic armamentarium, is most useful with families who exhibit moderate resistance, who are able to reflect on and think about what they are doing, who can handle frustration and uncertainty, who aren't actively hostile and are not involved in severe impulsive or acting-out behaviors, and who aren't in the middle of an acute crisis (Weeks & L'Abate 1982). Restraining (warning them not to change too fast or too much) and symptom prescription (directing them to do, in one way or another, the very thing they came to treatment in order to stop doing) are more powerful tools and are more appropriate with families in which resistance is firmly entrenched. For families in which one or more members are cooperative but others are highly resistant, combinations of strategic interventions may be required. Again, remember that such interventions are complicated and can backfire badly if misused. They should not be lightly or casually undertaken.

One characteristic of the strategic approach, though, is applicable to nearly all family therapy, and that is the quality of indirection. Indirection is the art of seeing where you are not looking, of talking to one person by addressing someone else, of acting upon one process by intervening in another. It is a slippery sort of concentration—it's hard not to get caught up in what is happening on the surface and lose track of the underlying structure, finding yourself focusing on a particular person or interaction and ignoring everything else.

Because this sort of lapse is so easy to fall into, perhaps the best way of dealing with it is to expect it to happen. Recognize it, forgive yourself for it, and go back to what you need to be doing with this family. Perhaps even learn from it—it probably is no accident that you chose to lose your perspective just at this moment rather than at some other—so what is there about what the family as a whole is doing right now that invited you to tune it out? Here, then, is your very own paradox: the times when you do badly with a family can be welcomed as the best of all opportunities to learn about yourself as well as about them.

At some point in this discussion, we need to say a word about the ethics of indirect and strategic interventions, and this is probably as good a place as any. When first introduced to these approaches to family work, students will almost invariably ask, "But isn't this manipulative?" My answer is that of course it is—so what's the problem? People come to therapy in order to be changed. If they could change themselves, therapists would be out of business. Manipulation or nonmanipulation isn't the issue. The issue is who is to benefit from the manipulation being carried out, and whether it is being done with respect and with skill. Watzlawick puts it well:

> One cannot *not* influence. It is, therefore, absurd to ask how influence and manipulation can be avoided, and we are left with the inescapable responsibility of deciding for ourselves how this basic law of human communication may be obeyed in the most humane, ethical, and effective manner. [1978, p. 11]

Part of being humane, ethical, and effective is not to experiment with paradoxical (or any other) methodology until one has been trained in its use; another part is to ensure that one has available *and uses* consultation whenever a family is being dealt with paradoxically. Using consultation and supervision is the best preventative I know for becoming too impressed with our own cleverness—an occupational hazard which seems particularly virulent among some paradoxically oriented therapists.

PITFALLS AND HOOKS

Being too impressed with one's own cleverness is but one of the hidden pitfalls that lay in wait for the unwary family therapist. On the assumption that to know one's enemy is to be prepared to do battle, let's take a look at some of the others. Do recognize, by the way, that these dangers are by no means unique to working with families. We need to be on guard against them in any kind of therapy we do, but it does seem that they may lurk more insidiously in the family arena than in one-to-one therapy.

We talked at the beginning of this chapter about the need to think circularly in terms of interaction patterns and processes rather than in a more simplistic cause-and-effect way. Yet, because we have been taught all our lives to look for causes and effects and to expect that A leads to B leads to C in an orderly way, it's easy for us to slip back into that kind of thinking. Jackson, one of the pioneers of modern family therapy, comments: "Despite our best intentions, clear observations of interactional process fade into the old, individual vocabulary, there to be lost, indistinguishable and heuristically useless" (1965, p. 4). In families there almost never is a single "cause" of a problem, a single starting point, a single culprit or innocent victim. All members interact to create a pattern, and it is the pattern—the interacting system—that is at once the problem, the solution, the villain, and the victim. The family therapist who forgets this will soon be lured into a quest for a mythical starting point or focal person—a quest which, should the family join it, is almost sure to harm rather than help them.

Therapists are, by and large, a well-intentioned lot. We really do want to help people; we feel good when our clients improve and feel bad when they don't. This need to be "helpful" is both a blessing and a curse to our clients. It's a blessing because, when controlled and used in their benefit, it helps us to do our best work. It's a curse because, when not controlled, it lures us into being overconcerned, into "helping" too much. Family members are not likely to learn to take care of themselves when their therapist provides them with ready-made answers, patches up their quarrels for them, pours oil on their troubled waters and sends them on their way. Any time we find ourselves working harder than our clients are working, we need to stop and reexamine what is happening; any time we do more than 50 percent of the work in a session, we are not doing good therapy.

Being overconcerned is first cousin to being overly responsible. The overly responsible therapist really believes that she can "cure" a dysfunctional family system and that it is her job to do so. As Haley and Hoffman warned in one of the earliest books on the systemic approach, "if you accept the sole responsibility, even implicitly, for treating them, in the sense of curing them, then they are going to foist it off on you at every opportunity, in ways that can be highly unpleasant because you won't know what to do" (1967, p. 18). The family therapist's job is to provide a structure within which the family can cure itself; it is up to the family to decide whether or not to use that structure, just as it is up to the would-be body builder to decide whether or not to use the weight training equipment. To suggest otherwise is to invite the family to lean back and wait for you rather than engage themselves in the hard work of making things different—and if you *believe* that you can or should or ought to be able to do it for them, you will indeed suggest it whether you intend to or not.

All of the above pitfalls—searching for the "cause," working too hard, feeling too responsible—are forms of therapist induction. Induction occurs when a therapist loses her objectivity and begins to think like a member of the family she is treating rather than like a therapist. It is most likely to occur when the family you are working with is similar, in some important way, to your own family. Satir warns that this correspondence between a client family and the therapist's own family is bound to occur, sooner or later. "When this happens and the therapist has not yet worked out the difficulties with his or her own family, the client may be stranded or misled because the therapist also is lost"(1987 p. 21). She may be inducted into taking sides with one member or faction against another, or with (or against) the whole family in a battle with some outsider. She may be inducted into believing a family mythology: that Dad is unable to deal with feelings, or that Barbara's physical appearance makes all the other kids pick on her, or that Mom just can't help being high-strung and nervous. Worst of all, she may be inducted into thinking of the family as helpless and of herself as their only hope for salvation and health. Pity the poor therapist in that trap, and pity the poor family with whom she works.

What are the antidotes? How can we family therapists avoid the pitfalls and hooks? One of the best ways is to let our client family remind us of what they are trying to accomplish. "When therapy is stuck because the therapist is 'at sea' and unable to state her clients' goals, she should invite the clients to review progress and to define their respective goals more precisely. It is worth recalling that a clearly defined goal is always framed positively and specifies observable behavior" (Carpenter & Treacher 1989, p. 158). Over and over again, I have rediscovered that my sense of stuckness with a family melts away as I force myself to listen more carefully to what each of them thinks is happening, and how that matches what they would like to have happen.

In order to turn to your client family for direction, you must believe that they can give it to you. This implies that you must maintain a position of firm respect for them. No matter what sort of nonsense they are involved in or how unhealthy their behavior, they are at bottom human beings doing the best they can to survive. I have yet to meet a person who gets up in the morning and tries to figure out how much damage he can do during that day. We might argue the theology of evil, or whether there are people who are truly "bad"; as a therapist, whoever, you will do best to believe that people would rather be good. This will allow you to function as an advocate for rather than an adversary of the families with whom you work. It also, by the way, helps to inoculate you against that "too clever" problem that I mentioned earlier: for who would want to cleverly outwit people who are working with you, striving for the best outcome of which they can conceive?

Consultation, of course, is another means for getting unstuck. Meet regularly with colleagues and make a point of talking more about the families you are stuck with and the times when you really aren't sure of what you are doing than about your triumphs. If you use your consultation or supervision well, you often will find yourself wondering if the others in your group think you are quite incompetent, because you will spend so much of your time describing your worst, rather than your best, work. But that's all right, because you will be able to sound so very brilliant when discussing *their* mistakes and uncertainties!

They—we all—will make mistakes and have uncertainties. With families, things are often other than they seem, and it is very easy to be misled. As Madanes says:

In human relations, nothing is ever all black or all white; where there is love there is hate, power is always associated with dependence, behavior is never totally voluntary or involuntary. As soon as one seems to have defined the situation and understood it without ambiguities, the opposite definition comes to mind and appears equally feasible. It may be that what is characteristic of a good therapist's thought processes is a particular tolerance for ambiguity. [1984, p. 140]

As we learn to tolerate not knowing, we free ourselves from the responsibility of having to know. Simplistic, right? But ever so important in the list of anti-dotes to those toxic family therapy errors. Being willing to work with what presents itself in the family process, not knowing its cause or its result or even if it will continue long enough to find out much more about it; being willing to be seen by the family as fallible and only partly (rather than all-) knowing; keeping firmly in mind that what will *work* for this family is much more important than what is really going on, and that you may never find out much about the latter—all of these seem alien at first to our scientifically trained minds, but all are enormously important in our kit of family therapy tools.

Along with tolerance of ambiguity comes a kind of therapeutic detachment, a willingness to play with ideas and possibilities rather than to hang on to them with grim seriousness. It's not that the family therapist loses sight of the very real distress of the family, but rather that she refuses to let herself get sucked into that distress. She must insulate herself from it or she won't be able to work with it—just as linemen must insulate themselves from the current that flows along the wires on their towers and poles. Thus insulated, she is free to imagine options and alternatives that are not available to the family members themselves. Moreover, she can leave the family behind at the end of a session and return to the healing pleasures of her own private life.

What might on the surface seem a cavalier position (don't take too much responsibility, stay detached and playful, make the family do the work) is balanced in the good family therapist by a commitment to learn from each family with whom she works. Everything the family does is important; moreover, everything they do can be considered as (partially) an output of the therapist's own behavior. The family, then, can never respond "wrong"; it is the therapist's intervention that was ill-chosen or ill-timed for that family. It's a paradox, right? The family is responsible for their behavior, their cure; and the therapist is responsible for their responsibility. X and not-X are both equally true and must be believed.

When it doesn't work—when the family remains stubbornly stuck or terminates treatment in the same or worse shape than when they arrived—what then? Then at least we can review and use our errors for the benefit of our next clients: Did I use the family's language rather than expecting them to learn mine? Did I base my interventions on what actually happened in the sessions rather than on my fantasies about what happened outside of sessions? Did I attend to everyone present rather than focus prematurely on one or two? Did I frame the assignment of new behaviors as permissions rather than as punishments? Did I consistently respect and give credit to the family's motivation and hard work rather than my own cleverness? Finally, one last line of self-questioning that often leads to surprising insights: had I deliberately set out to keep this family stuck/sick/unchanging, what would I have done and how is that similar to what actually happened?

END POINTS

Beavers and Hampson tell us: "The hope for families and family members resides in this bit of magic—get two people close *enough without losing the awareness of separateness* and the hunger of each is the food of the other" (1990, p. 129). That kind of closeness, in which all support each other, yet each experiences his individual autonomy, really is the overriding goal of all family therapies. It is the ideal, a model against which we can measure our overall success with each client family.

There are, within that ideal, some specific rules of thumb for healthy family functioning. While not invariable (all the rules I can think of have exceptions) they are nearly always useful in assessing how far a family has come and what may need to be done next. One of the first of these is that whichever person has been the first to show a change or shift in behavior needs to be helped to maintain that new behavior until the rest of the family catch up. People don't grow at the same rate, and someone will have to lead the way. If we aren't careful to support and nurture the change, that leader may give up in despair because it "isn't working"— i.e., the others haven't done their share.

A second rule or goal is that, in a healthy family, children are *not* equal to their parents. Parents make family decisions, sometimes after consulting with their children; the children live with these decisions. Healthy parents don't let their children make decisions for them. A major function of family therapy is to reinstate the parents to a position of leadership and decision making and to dethrone a rebellious or power-drunk sibling or sibling subsystem.

If children are not responsible for family decisions, neither are they in charge of the well-being of their parents. As they grow and mature, children need to move from positions of dependence on parents into positions of autonomy; parents can be respected and cared about but are not determinants of life style or happiness. Selvini-Palazzoli et al., commenting on the myth that a child must have healthy parents in order to be healthy him- or herself, say that the therapist must

> behave in a manner as to destroy this false belief that the parents must be changed before the child can grow....This message must succeed in stating that it is not the task of the children to improve the relationship between their parents or to substitute for them in their functions, that an adolescent can successfully grow up and become mature regardless of the type of relationship between his parents. [1978, p. 111]

While children can do well even when parents are doing badly, it is nevertheless much easier for them if the parents are doing well. Reinstating the parents as parents means helping them to continue to do the things they are doing right, giving them permission to change the things they are doing badly (and always assuming that the parents will of course want to change these things since they are invested in being good parents), and giving them credit for everything. When the family improves, it is primarily due to the efforts of the parents and secondarily due to the efforts of the children; the therapist is a pleased or surprised or confused coach and cheering section. Criticizing the parents will only reinforce their sense of helplessness and inadequacy, which will in turn render the therapist helpless and inadequate. Taking credit for the family's changes will likewise undermine the parents' authority and competence. Believing that the family as a whole can and does make positive changes will allow that belief to be true.

As the belief does begin to become true—when you work with a family and the family begins to change—many things will begin to happen all at once. Not infrequently, one or more members will complain that the situation is getting worse, not better. Nearly always, some members will respond (usually without conscious awareness) to changes by behaving so as to bring back the old, stuck symptoms. Each time one person in the system makes a shift, the others also must shift to accommodate the new behavior; not all of these shifts will be comfortable for them or for the other family members. Lasting change in one person often requires a shakedown cruise during which everyone else adjusts to the new patterns of communication, the new subsystem alliances, and the new reward and punishment patterns.

When this is accomplished and the family is well and truly launched into a new way of being and growing, what then? Be prepared to hear that nobody did anything different, that change "just happened," or that although the original problem no longer exists there are new ones that are equally troubling. If the family does understand and enjoy its changes, be prepared to get no credit yourself for what has been accomplished. It is not that the family is ungrateful but rather that they literally cannot see what you have done—especially if your work is elegant. Being parts of a system, the individual members cannot stand back and be objective about their overall process; changes at the system level are likely to seem somewhat mysterious and inexplicable. That is okay; the important thing is that change has happened, that the family is different now, and that each person must willy-nilly be a part of that difference.

CARE AND FEEDING OF THERAPISTS 11

In all these many pages we have discussed various topics having to do with the welfare of clients, how to do what is most helpful to the client in managing his growth and happiness. Now, in this last chapter, we change our focus. Instead of looking at what the client needs, we will look at what the therapist needs. The two are not so very different, for one of the most basic needs of any client is to have a therapist who is competent, confident, and handling her own life well. Only when she is in this kind of personal space can the therapist be fully present and available to her clients.

But how difficult it is for therapists to maintain that kind of personal serenity! The peculiar demands of our profession seem almost designed to keep us off balance and uncertain. Stress is our daily fare; we spend our hours dealing with pain and anxiety. Says Kramer: "It is difficult to practice in a field in which it seems anything is permitted and in which simultaneously, because of patients' need, much of what is permitted is in fact demanded. It provokes anxiety—and hope and excitement and titillation and shame and a number of other emotions—to practice in a profession where needs are so great and our ability to define limits is so weak" (1989, p. 196).

Our work demands much of us, and it can give much back. There is, in the practice of psychotherapy, an enormous possibility of reward, challenge, and joy. This chapter is all about ways to maximize the joy, excitement, and satisfaction while minimizing the frustration and pain. I must say at the outset that it will be a very personal chapter. I shall speak of issues that are and have been real for me; I may neglect issues that are equally important to others. Each of us has our own tender spots, our areas of special vulnerability, just as each of us develops our own unique ways of coping with these problems. Still, underlying the individuality of each particular therapist with each particular client, there is a common base: the strengths and limitations of psychotherapy as a tool for change and the accumulated wisdom of colleagues and predecessors who have weathered their own storms and have been willing to share what they have learned. It is upon this wisdom, as well as my own experience, that I shall base the following pages.

Proper care and feeding of a therapist, as of any other living creature, involves much more than providing for basic physical needs. It includes maintaining a safe environment, education for growth and expansion, and loving support and encouragement. "As a group," says Kantor, "mental health professionals can be too permissive with their patients, too unpermissive with themselves" (1990, p. 9). How sad, and how true! Therapists need to learn to help themselves and to get help from others. We need to know what to do to avoid painful situations before they occur, as well as how to deal with them when they happen. We need to learn to recognize and correct our errors, lovingly, when they are correctable, and to let go of them when no correction is possible. In fact, we need to do for ourselves the very things we try to teach our clients to do.

In order to give some structure to this mass of need-to's, I have arbitrarily divided the whole into three sections: professionalism, legal and ethical issues, and therapist self-care. In the first section, we will discuss what it means to be a professional, the attitudes and behaviors that are appropriate and useful in maintaining one's professional role. The second section, dealing with legal and ethical issues, is a logical extension of the first; as professionals, we are bound by somewhat different and more stringent rules of conduct than a friendly neighborhood helper. The third section, which focuses on overall health, explores some of the particular stresses and demands placed on therapists and suggests a number of strategies for coping with such demands. Finally, we shall talk about how to keep ourselves alive, growing, and excited about our work and ourselves.

PROFESSIONALISM

If you, the reader, are newly arrived to the field of therapy, you are probably still turning the corner between amateur and professional. Throughout your student years, you were only too eager and grateful for people willing to share their concerns with you, willing for you to practice your skills with them. You took practicum courses, did volunteer work or completed internships in which you were paid meagerly if at all (and often you did the paying) for working with clients. You may have found yourself playing therapist with friends, family members, and colleagues. Most of us did that when we were learning, and many of us still occasionally do—usually to our sorrow. "In daily life one can strive to live the theory of therapy; but to attempt to live its practice is a disaster. Witness the suffering of spouses condemned to live with beginning counselors who go about 'treating' everyone in sight" (Combs 1989, p. 135). The attitude of a therapist is hard enough to maintain for an hour; it is virtually impossible to do so consistently with the people we live or work with.

All in all, you have had a long and intensive training period in which you learned through hard experience that your services were worth very little in terms of hard cash. You also learned to accept whatever working conditions were set up for you: you saw clients in uncomfortable offices, at hours that fit someone else's convenience. You took the clients who were assigned (or available) to you. You made relatively few decisions on your own, and those were subject to revision should a supervisor insist.

Now all that has quite suddenly changed. You are expected to charge money for your work ("All that? Just for talking to someone for an hour!" I heard one newly licensed therapist remark in an unguarded moment). You may be maintaining your own office and setting your own hours. You can decide what kinds of clients you will and will not work with. You may be faced with the necessity of marketing your skills, and that means actually telling people that you are highly competent and that they can benefit from your services. You set your own therapeutic course, and you are responsible for everything you do. It is an extraordinary transition, and one that most new therapists are ill-equipped to make, mainly because nobody has prepared them for it.

Old hands, too, may have some trouble with maintaining an appropriate professional stance, but for different reasons. Here, the "I've always done it this way and always will" syndrome may creep into our attitudes and behaviors. No matter how long we have been practicing our art (and being paid to do so), it is a good idea to pause now and then to reexamine the rules and guidelines that we normally take for granted. Just as the best-organized closet needs an occasional cleaning, so the clearest guidelines can stand inspection and possible revision at regular intervals.

THE SETTING

The first real introduction between a client and therapist often comes not through words but through visual impressions of the therapeutic setting. The client usually arrives in a state of anxious expectation: What will this experience be like? What kind of person will my therapist be? How am I supposed to behave? Consciously or unconsciously, he uses all sorts of information to begin to answer these questions. He notices the location of the office, the kind of furniture, the color scheme, the activity level, the sounds and the smells. He experiences this place as comfortable or uncomfortable, scary or reassuring. Before you say a word to him, he has usually formed some sort of expectation about how helpful or difficult or demanding the therapy experience is likely to be for him.

By creating a setting that matches our own personal style, that is comfortable and congruent for us, we can minimize false expectations in our clients. This certainly makes our job easier, and we do not have to wait for the client to figure out that we really are not the formal/sloppy/stiff/hurried/careless sort of person that some settings suggest. Even beyond the effect of the setting on the client, our physical surroundings have an effect on us. More than twenty years ago, Chessick pointed out that "through his personality and office setting and routines the therapist demonstrates to the patient his integrity, sincere therapeutic intent, willingness to work hard and seriously for the patient's benefit, and perhaps above all his genuine respect for the patient as a human being" (1969, p. 79). It is still a valid observation. We also remind *ourselves* of these qualities. Our physical surroundings can help us in maintaining our professionalism, simply through reminding us of who we are and what we are about.

The place where I work should fit me, my beliefs, attitudes, and esthetics. It should, first and foremost, be a place where I can be comfortable. The colors, the furniture, the pictures on the walls should not jar or distract me from the work I am doing. It should be neither stark and sterile nor cluttered. It should be reasonably soundproof, so that I and my client may trust that our conversation will be private. I put a few books and objects in my office that have special meaning to me; they help me to remember ideas and experiences that have been markers on my personal journey into competence, or remind me of people who have given me important gifts along the way. My office becomes, for both me and my clients, an extension of myself. All of the elements—the people, the work, and the setting—are coordinate parts of this whole that we call therapy.

One's dress, too, contributes to the therapeutic whole. Again, the clothing I wear should fit who I am, while reflecting and reminding me of my professional role. I am seeing clients now, not going to the opera or mowing the yard.

"The therapist's mode of dress indirectly conveys the dignity and respect with which the client is received....It can only be cautioned that the therapist's mode of professional dress should not be determined exclusively by considerations of his or her comfort or personal style" (Schofield 1988, p. 125). No matter how right you may feel in tennis shoes, cutoffs, and an old T-shirt, a forty-year-old business executive is unlikely to be favorably impressed by such a costume. On the other hand, a suit and tie or high heels and a tailored dress may feel constricting and artificial. If so, do not wear them. Clothing that is comfortable, clean, and appropriate to your setting and life style is another important part of your therapeutic self.

THE EXCHANGE

The essence of professionalism is that the practitioner receives tangible rewards for what she does. This means, for the great majority of therapists, that we expect to be paid money for our work with clients. If we are salaried employees of an agency or some other institution or corporation, the transition from unpaid student to paid staff member is not particularly difficult. We do not have to take money directly from the client; there is an intervening structure which disguises the exchange.

When we move into private practice, the disguise disappears. Suddenly we are asking that the client pay us for what we do. We even have to decide how much and whether or not to make exceptions! There is a great temptation for beginners in private practice to see people for little or no money, to be overflexible about being paid on time, and to be apologetic about fees. The sooner you can get past this stage, the better. If you convey to the client that you are not worth what he is pay-ing you, he is likely to believe it, and the work will suffer.

"The therapist who resents treating a patient at a fee lower than he or she believes is deserved is not playing fair with the patient; the resentment will come through in some form, if only in disinterest, boredom, and relief when the patient does not show up for an appointment" (Wolberg 1988, p. 559). This situation is one of the first way stations on the road to professional burnout. Not only will the client come to value me less, but I may also come to value myself less. Or I may value the client less and do poorer work with him than with another who pays me more. It is important to make a clear and straightforward statement of your charges and your expectations about how they will be met at the outset of treatment, com-ing to an agreement about money before proceeding with therapy.

Many therapists use a sliding fee scale in which clients who have few resources are charged less than others. Each practitioner must, of course, make her own decisions about fees. I have found that discussion about sliding my fees gener-ally results in an arrangement that is unsatisfactory to both myself and my client; the decision of how much can/should he pay is difficult for me to be objective about, and it seems unrealistic to expect more objectivity from him than from myself.

When you have decided what to charge for an hour of work, stick with it. Except in unusual situations, fees should not change once they have been set. The idea of accelerating treatment by charging a fee that increases with each session, or of allowing a client to continue long-term work by lowering the fee, is not a good one. Once the charge is seen as variable, this becomes another therapeutic issue and can muddy up the professional relationship between therapist and client, to the great detriment of the overall process. A client whose insurance coverage runs out, or who finds himself in a financial crisis, may be allowed to put his charges "on the cuff" for a while and pay his bill off over time; this arrangement lets the client continue his work while still assuming that he can and will behave responsibly with regard to payment.

Similarly, a clear agreement should be reached and held to with regard to missed sessions. My clients are informed at the beginning of treatment that missed sessions, or sessions canceled less than twenty-four hours ahead of time, will be charged to their account. I may use the first such missed session as a warning, par-ticularly if the client is ill or there is some other unexpected emergency. After that, he will be charged for his appointment whether he is there or not. Again, the princi-ple is one of a professional exchange: the client has contracted for an hour of my time, and I have reserved that time for him and should be reimbursed for it. To do otherwise is to discount both my own value and his ability to respect a commitment.

Before we leave the subject of payment, one other issue should be touched on: gifts from client to therapist. What should be done about the client who brings you a potted plant, a hand-knit sweater, a book that "I know you'd enjoy reading"? There is no hard-and-fast rule here; depending on the particular client, it may be therapeutically important either to refuse the gift or to accept it. It is essential, though, that the therapist be clear about the reasons for her decision. She needs to ask herself why this client is choosing to bring a gift at this point, and what will be the implication of her accepting or refusing it. Is the client making a subtle bid for specialness, for friendship beyond the therapist-client relationship? Is this the first of a series of manipulative moves? Is the client genuinely appreciative and simply wanting to demonstrate that appreciation? Has the therapist conveyed in some way that she needs or wants reassurance from this client? Whether or not you accept the gift, these are the questions that need to be addressed, directly or indirectly, in your thinking about the client and in subsequent sessions with him.

The principle of the exchange is simple. The therapist offers a unit of time and skills; the client pays a set amount for each unit. Even though the two parties agree to involve themselves in a close relationship in which intangible and emotional factors play an important part, this simple structure must be maintained. Indeed, it is precisely because of the nonmeasurables on both sides of the relationship that a clear understanding of and adherence to the principle is so important; it provides structure and protection within a climate of intimacy and change.

THE ATTITUDE OF A PROFESSIONAL

A central aspect of my professionalism is my attitude toward my client and toward myself. Do I see my clients as somehow inferior to myself, as potential payers-of-the-rent, as critics whom I must manage to please, as children, students, threats to my sense of competence? Yes, sometimes I will respond to them in these ways but, hopefully, not often. Do I see myself as a purveyor of wisdom, a scared kid pretending confidence, a healer, a magician, responsible for solving each client's problems? Again, I may feel all of these ways at times, and again I must not do so often.

The single most important aspect of the professional's attitude toward self and toward clients is that of seeing both as autonomous individuals. They are working together to accomplish certain goals, but each has the right to decide, at every step of the way, what they will or will not do, believe, strive for. "Abuse of client autonomy occurs," says Thompson, "whenever [the] process of diagnosis and communication results in the IMPOSITION of the therapist's values, moral outlook, or point of view upon the client, as opposed to their EXPOSITION, in which the therapist freely allows the client to make an informed, selective acceptance among useful perspectives" (1990, p. 18). What this amounts to is *respect*— respect for myself and my needs, as well as for those of my client.

In order to maintain this kind of respect, I have found it helpful to think in terms of two components of my internal behavior: caring and curiosity. I must genuinely care for my clients, care for them as fellow humans, as people whose joy and pain is important to me. I must be curious, interested in what they say and how they say it, in how they came to be who they are, in how the strands of their lives weave together to create this exact way of being at this precise moment. My caring makes me real for them, makes the relationship work as a curative factor. My curiosity allows me to pull back, to be involved without being too vulnerable, to formulate and hypothesize and plan. The balance of the two provides genuine respect for them and for me.

As I try to create this balance, I find that what I am feeling toward a particular client from moment to moment gives me important feedback. Am I feeling bored, wondering why the time is passing so slowly? I am probably not giving free rein to my curiosity. Am I annoyed or indifferent? Perhaps I need to allow myself to care more for this person. Am I impatient with a rambling account of day-to-day happenings or working hard to get answers to my questions? Then I am being too involved in my own agenda and not curious enough about the client's. Or am I feeling overburdened, responsible for solving the unsolvable, stuck in the mire of my client's despair? Then there is too much caring; pull back and let curiosity have its way.

Of course, to see all therapeutic attitudes as based on just these two concerns is an oversimplification. There are many other possibilities, many ways of being with self and clients. Some are helpful, some are not. Some are more familiar than others, depending on our own personal style. We can learn much about what to avoid in relating to clients simply by noticing how we are with people in our personal lives: the patterns we play out with parents, spouse, friends, and children will tend to be repeated with our clients.

One particularly dangerous attitude that the unwitting therapist may fall prey to is the love of power. It can feel wonderful to be influential in someone's life, to be privy to their innermost secrets, to have an important part in their decisions and choices. The client's wish to be cured by a magician may be equalled by the therapist's wish to *be* a magician. "There is in every healing profession the temptation to play God, and an all-wise, all-powerful-acting therapist may soon run into unpleasant difficulties, just as new-found powers proved heady for the sorcerer's apprentice. A psychotherapist is really not God, nor even a close relative of his" (Colby 1951, p. 21).

I have often found it useful to remind myself and my clients that I am really a tool for their use. I put my skills at their disposal, but they must decide what to do with those skills. Just like a computer that needs to be programmed in order to solve problems, or an exercise machine that will only help you lose weight if you work with it, the therapist makes herself available. We do not really cure or heal people any more than we grow them. People cure and heal themselves, with our help and encouragement, using our knowledge and expertise, benefiting from our curiosity and caring. We can and must be responsible *to* our clients, but we are not (and should not try to be) responsible for them. For me, this is the essence of respect.

LEGAL AND ETHICAL ISSUES

As a therapist, you are bound not only by the laws of the state in which you practice but also by a professional code of ethics. Most of the time, the legal and ethical guidelines form a comfortable and consistent framework within which to work. Occasionally, they may conflict or appear to conflict. Ultimately, each individual therapist must decide what she will and will not do in a given situation. "We cannot avoid moral decisions," says McKechnie, "even if we had infinite knowledge. What is essential is that we make our moral decisions explicit and ensure that they are consistent" (1987, p. 169). The guidelines are just that: guiding principles. They cannot provide specific directions for dealing with individual clients.

The first step in making legal and ethical decisions is to know the laws governing practice in your own state or area. Although all states have similar laws, the details will differ. It is the responsibility of each of us to know what is required and what is forbidden: When, for instance, must we report dangerous or criminal behavior to the appropriate authorities? Under what conditions can a client be hospitalized against his will? What are the rules governing treatment of minors or other people who cannot give informed consent for their therapy? For what client behaviors can therapists be held liable? What are your legal responsibilities to your client in terms of availability, recordkeeping, contracting for services? Some state governments will provide, on request, a compendium of the laws pertaining to therapy; in other states these laws have not been gathered together but must be pulled out of general codes and statutes. It is unfortunate that the education of many therapists does not include an introduction to the laws governing the practice of therapy, how they have been interpreted in the courts, and how they can be used to help both client and practitioner. If you are among those who have not received such formal training, you should find a good lawyer, one experienced in the area of psychological practice, and arrange for ongoing consultation and updating.

In recent years, the number of malpractice suits against psychotherapists has increased enormously. Some of this increase is beneficial; it has put therapists on notice that they must behave responsibly toward their clients and that they will be called to account if they default on their responsibilities. In other ways, the need for a growing concern about malpractice has hurt us badly: we have learned that we must avoid even the appearance of wrongful behavior—even if a client may receive less than our best as a result. Because our society is growing more litigious all the time, it is reasonable to expect that—no matter how ethically you operate your practice—you may some day be sued for malpractice. "Your initial reaction is likely to be shock. 'How could someone I have tried to help do this to me?' More often than not, this will be followed by anger. It is best to remember not to do something you may later regret" (Austin, Moline, & Williams 1990, p. 19). Consult your professional insurance carrier and your lawyer, and do what they tell you to do. Being sued is not the end of your professional career (even though it may feel that way); as long as you have behaved according to the standards of the profession, you will weather the storm.

But that "as long as" clause is important! Knowing and adhering to the bare legal requirements is not enough to protect you, either legally or emotionally. The ethical guidelines for each of the professional groups involved in therapy and/or counseling go beyond legal technicalities; they attempt to define good practice as it is understood by therapists, counselors, social workers, and psychiatric nurses. One of the most complete sets of guidelines is provided by the American Psychological Association. Their *Standards for Providers of Psychological Services*, together with the more generic *Ethical Principles of Psychologists*, are reviewed and updated regularly and supplemented by casebooks that illustrate how the *Standards* have been applied in specific cases.

You are not the only one who needs to know about the code of ethics that guides your professional behavior: your clients also have a right to that information. Knowing what they can and cannot expect from you will help them to use their therapy wisely and to avoid asking either too much or too little of you. Brenner suggests:

> The best way to let people know of these protections is to have available in quantity in your office or reception area copies of your ethical code. Be sure each client receives a copy by the first visit and is encouraged to read it and ask questions about it. Undoubtedly the code will answer questions that the client may be reluctant to ask or may not have time to ask, [e.g.] questions regarding confidentiality, sexual involvement, your area of expertise. Do not overlook the relevance of the fact that you are part of a profession that has been developing for generations and has been struggling to answer these questions in ways most beneficial to the client. [1982, p. 17]

What exists beyond formal codes of ethics? We move inevitably into the area of personal values and decisions. Even such a simple and obvious principle as that of putting the client's best interests first can become cloudy and uncertain in the face of questions such as, "When does the welfare of society become more important than the welfare of the individual client?" or "To what degree am I obliged to sacrifice my own needs (for time, money, personal freedom) in the interest of meeting the needs of a client?" Kramer states the dilemma well:

> The truth about this business is that we are often at an impasse: we know perfectly well what conventional treatment is and also we have a strong opinion that it will not work. So we are obliged to face the boundaries we have set for ourselves and decide whether to challenge them. We must ask whether we can flout individual rules and still remain within some broader professional strictures, ethical and technical.[1989, p. 199]

Ultimately, each of us must decide what we believe, what we stand for, what we will and will not do regardless of consequences. Knowing the law and the standards of our profession is essential, but such knowledge cannot substitute for a clear examination and understanding of our own values and commitments.

Legal requirements, ethical standards, personal behavior. Let us examine a few of the major areas of concern, areas on which legal and ethical issues have traditionally focused. As we do so, I invite you to continue to question: Do I, myself, agree with this? Am I willing to be bound by it? Are there any circumstances under which I would feel morally obliged to act otherwise? For here, as in every other aspect of our profession, knowing myself is as important as knowing the rules.

RESPONSIBILITY TO THE CLIENT

The therapist's first duty toward her client is that she be professionally competent and exercise that competence for the benefit of that client. Competence is, of course, hard to define in any broad or general way. The following is a typical legal description of what is required: the therapist must "(1) possess the degree of learning, skill, and ability that others similarly situated ordinarily possess; (2) exercise reasonable care and diligence in the application of his knowledge and skill to the patient's case; and (3) use his best judgment in the treatment and care of his patient" (*Stone v. Procter* 1963; quoted in Furrow 1980, p. 23). A responsible therapist will only accept a client when she believes that she has the training and skill necessary to help that particular person with that particular problem. And do note that "accepting a client" may occur in a variety of ways: "Occasionally a concerned person...will call for advice concerning someone's suicidal talk or behavior. Offering advice constitutes accepting clinical responsibility" (Doyle 1990, p. 400). Just because *you* don't consider a person your client does not mean that he (or the law) will see it that way. No matter how tempting it may be to discuss someone's situation with him, either casually or by formally taking on his case, we must do so only if we are qualified to deal with the kind of problem he presents. Clients seek therapy in order to get help for themselves, not to entertain or to educate their therapists. If I feel unsure of my ability to work with someone, I am legally and ethically obligated to send that person elsewhere.

Having decided that I am willing to treat a client, I must next help that client to decide whether or not to accept my treatment. Clients must agree to be treated, and it is the responsibility of the therapist to ensure that the client knows what he is agreeing to. The principle of informed consent is one of the cornerstones of therapeutic ethics. However, how can someone know what psychotherapy will be like before he has actually experienced it? How can he give informed consent if he cannot really be informed of what he is getting into? The only answer is the common-sense one: we do the best we can. We tell the client as clearly as possible what sorts of things he can expect during treatment, how long we think it may take, how much it may cost. We tell him in language he can understand; we do not throw jargon or technical language at him, and we give him a chance to ask questions and get answers. When we do not know, we tell him that.

Many clients will not know what sorts of questions to ask or, if they do know, may be reluctant or embarrassed to ask. Again, the responsibility is ours: they must be informed, and we must inform them. They should be told what we think is going on for them and what we propose to do about it. They should be told what we think will happen to them as a result of treatment, about how long it may be expected to take, and what risks may be involved.

Notice that you are not required to guarantee the results of treatment. Buying psychotherapy is not like buying a toaster or a clothes dryer. It is more like buying a textbook; a satisfactory outcome depends both on the book being adequate and on the user doing his job. If you guarantee that a client will be cured, you may be held legally responsible for his failure to improve, even though such a failure may be due to his refusal to cooperate. You owe it to him to tell him the likelihood of success, given his full participation in the program; but he also needs to know that improvement depends as much on his own input as it does on yours, and that even with both of you doing your best there is still no 100 percent guarantee that he will emerge from therapy feeling exactly as he would like to feel.

Once informed consent has been given and treatment begun, the therapist enters into a new kind of responsibility relationship with her client. She must not only provide appropriate treatment and protection during the therapy hour but must also be reasonably available should the client need her between sessions. Of course, "reasonably available" is an elastic term. What does it really mean? For most non-crisis clients, returning a call within twenty-four hours is generally sufficient availability. The crisis client may need closer monitoring; and many clients will neither need nor request between-session contact at all. The key here is to make clear to the client exactly what you are willing to provide: Will you accept between-session phone calls? How often, and of what duration? Will you charge for such calls? If you have an answering service or machine, how often do you check for messages? Spelling all this out for your client, and notifying him explicitly should the situation change, lets both you and him know what to expect of each other.

Therapists need time off, just like everyone else. But sometimes clients do not want their therapists to take time off, or indeed may actually need the therapist during a vacation period. Part of the therapist's responsibility is to provide backup for her clients when she herself is unavailable. Give your client the names of one or two colleagues whose work you respect and who have agreed to serve on standby during your absence, or contract with one of these colleagues to check your messages and handle any emergencies that might arise. This should be done whenever you will be unavailable for more than twenty-four hours at a time.

For absences that will involve missing scheduled appointments with a client, your responsibility extends beyond providing a backup option. You must let the client know ahead of time that you will be gone and help him to decide how he will handle your absence. If you will be away for some time, and if the client has developed a dependency relationship with you, then your leaving will be a therapeutic as well as a practical issue, and you should provide plenty of advance warning so that the client will have time to work this issue through. A good rule of thumb is to let the lead time equal the time you will actually be gone: for a single missed weekly session, a week's warning is sufficient; if you plan to be gone a month, let your clients know at least a month ahead of time.

Speaking of dependency leads me to another aspect of therapist responsibility, one that is not generally spelled out in formal codes of ethics but which is of fundamental importance. Therapists differ in the degree to which they allow or encourage clients to become dependent upon them. Some deny that any dependency is necessary or even desirable. A strict behavior therapist, for instance, or an Adlerian or Dreikursian might well see dependency on the part of the client as impeding rather than furthering progress. Others, more psychoanalytically oriented, view dependence (transference) as an essential ingredient of therapy. Most, I suspect, fall between these two extremes, seeing dependency as common but not inevitable, more useful for some clients and less so for others. Whatever your theoretical stance on this issue, however, your ethical responsibility is clear: client dependency should never be encouraged beyond the point of therapeutic usefulness, and the client should be helped in recovering his independence and autonomy as soon as it is therapeutically advisable to do so. This is not to deny that we do, inevitably, influence our clients, sometimes in ways that they cannot understand or anticipate. Sometimes even the therapist is unaware of the degree of influence he wields. Says Beitman, "Whether aware of it or not, therapists are teaching their patients to be like them or to assume roles of which they approve" (1987, p. 223). Under no circumstances, though, may we use our influence or encourage dependency in order to meet our own needs for ego gratification or professional status, or prolong such dependency or influence for similar reasons. Our job as therapists must be eventually to become unnecessary, rather than necessary, to each client.

CONFIDENTIALITY

In order to deal openly and honestly with all of his issues, the client needs to know that his privacy will be respected, that the therapist will keep to herself whatever the client tells her. This principle of confidentiality has long been an explicit requirement in all medical treatment. It is a part of the Hippocratic oath: "Whatsoever I shall see or hear in the course of my profession in my intercourse with men, if it be what should not be noised abroad, I will never divulge, holding such things to be holy secrets." Traditionally, only a few professions have had the legal right to claim privileged communication. Lawyers, physicians, ministers, and psychotherapists are among those few. The doctrine of privilege, however, is not the same in every state. It is applied differently to different specialties within the mental health field (psychiatrists, psychologists, counselors, social workers, psychiatric nurses) and does not always cover every possible communication a client may make. In a few states, for example, most but not all mental health providers are required to report instances of child abuse to the appropriate authorities. You may be required to report other instances of known or potentially illegal behavior, or of behavior which threatens the right of safety for the client or his associates. Again, the place to start in determining your own personal guidelines is the law. Once you know what is legally required of you, you can then decide how you will apply those requirements to your practice.

Unfortunately, it is in the area of confidentiality that the laws governing clinical practice are perhaps at their murkiest. Actual statutes are less likely to be relevant than case law—that is, courtroom decisions that set precedents on which future decisions will be made. The best known of such recent cases is that of *Tarasoff vs. Regents of the University of California*. A client told his therapist, who worked at the university, that he intended to kill Tatiana Tarasoff, a woman with whom he had been in love. The therapist, taking the threat seriously, informed the police as a first step in having the client legally committed. The police, however, believed that the client was lucid, accepted his promise to leave Ms. Tarasoff alone, and took no further action. The client was enraged at what he experienced as his therapist's betrayal and did not return for further treatment. Two months later, he killed Tatiana Tarasoff. Her parents thereupon sued the therapist (and also the police and the University of California) because nobody had warned them that their daughter was in danger; the California Supreme Court, reversing a lower court decision, upheld their suit.

In the state of New Jersey, a court handed down a similar decision to that of the Tarasoff case (*McIntosh vs. Milano* 1979). However, a Maryland court came to an opposite conclusion (*Shaw vs. Glickman* 1980), holding that a therapist should respect the client's confidences except when the law expressly and explicitly prohibits maintaining confidentiality. Case law, it is apparent, is not always consistent. Moreover, until a precedent-setting case has been decided in a given state, there is no way of knowing which of the other states' decisions would be most influential in making a ruling there.

Tarasoff and subsequent cases have thrown the whole question of privileged communication and appropriate protection into a kind of legal no man's land. The therapist in the Tarasoff case was held liable for not warning Tarasoff's parents about the client's intentions. Had he taken the opposite course and warned the parents (and Tarasoff herself), the client conceivably could have sued him for breach of confidentiality. In either case, the therapist's decision could have been wrong and could have placed him in jeopardy.

So how can we, as ethical therapists, protect ourselves? I would suggest a number of steps to take when you suspect that a client may pose a threat to someone. I list them in consider-this-first order:

1. Discuss your concerns with your client. Tell him that you are obliged to warn the potential victim, if you think that person is in danger; and that, because you believe in your client's sincerity, you do think so. Ask your client how he would like you to handle the situation. If possible, work out with him a way to either defuse the violence or warn the victim.

2. If this can't be done to your satisfaction, tell your client that you intend to talk to the potential victim, and do so. Get the client's consent, written if possible, to contact the victim. If it is feasible, let the client know what you have told the victim: let him hear the phone conversation or give him a copy of the letter you send.

3. If you are still not reasonably sure that the danger has been averted, consider hospitalizing the client. Again, if possible, get his cooperation; a voluntary hospitalization will be less disrupting of the course of therapy. When considering hospitalization, make use of the client's social resources: bring in family members, pastor, or close friends if you think this will help the client to make a wise choice.

4. If the threat of violence is immediate, notify the police; ask them to get back to you and let you know the disposition of the matter.

Wexler (1981) cites literature on victimology to support his position that the therapist should work with both the client and his threatened victim. Not only are most victims part of an interpersonal system which includes the client, but they may also be behaving (either consciously or unconsciously) in ways that tend to trigger violence. Intervention at a system level may help both client and victim to change their behaviors and thus avert a tragedy.

Whatever course you take, whichever one or combination of possible interventions seem appropriate, there are two additional steps that should be taken as early in the sequence of events as possible. These are consultation with colleagues and getting legal advice. The first is protective of client, victim, and therapist; the second is primarily for your own benefit. Your own safety and protection are important and appropriate considerations in determining what you will do in this— or any other—emergency situation.

The Tarasoff case not only illustrates the ambiguity of the law in dealing with cases where the rights of the client may conflict with the rights of other individuals but also introduces the question of involuntary commitment. It is your absolute obligation as a professional care provider to know the laws regarding such commitment in the state in which you practice. Moreover, you must know the specific procedures for such commitment in your particular area: Whom do you call? What evidence do you need? What exactly will be done, how soon, and for how long? Many states have several kinds of involuntary restraint, from twenty-four hour holds (usually for the purpose of psychiatric evaluation) to full commitment procedures. Know what they are; know what options are available.

Be aware that any such restraint necessarily involves violating your client's confidentiality. Even though you will be careful to divulge as little detail as possible, consistent with the client getting the help he needs, you can still expect that your client will be angry with you. He may feel abandoned, betrayed, or even vindicated ("See, you proved it; I knew you couldn't be trusted!"). Should he continue in treatment, these will be issues which must be discussed; they will almost certainly take precedence over whatever else he has been dealing with.

Another area of confusion with regard to confidentiality has to do with minor clients, or clients who are otherwise considered legally incompetent. Again, the right of privileged communication varies from state to state, among professionals and among settings. A psychologist working for a school district, for example, may have different legal constraints than the same psychologist in private practice. Confidentiality is also dependent on the topic or issue; you may not be required to answer parents' questions about their daughter's pregnancy and subsequent abortion, for instance, but you might be absolutely required to answer questions about her use of marijuana or her school truancy.

The bottom line, of course, is that no one can compel you to talk if you are determined to keep silent. Would you go to jail rather than break what you consider to be an ethical or moral commitment to a client? Would you destroy records rather than allow them to be subpoenaed? Our legal system is the best we have been able to devise so far, but it is far from perfect—how far would you go in breaking a law that you considered to be wrong, unjust, not protective of your client? Laws are subject to revision, Schofield points out, as they are tested in the courts. "Historically, this has meant some professionals, risking contempt of court charges, have held to their ethical principles; improved laws have sometimes resulted" (1988, pp. 123–124). Are you willing to be one of these pioneers? The question may never arise for you, but it is one you should think about very clearly and carefully. Having thought through your own personal stance, your own values and commitment to them, at a time when you are not under pressure, will make it easier to make good decisions if and when a pressure situation does arise.

Another threat to confidentiality is the set of demands for information made by third-party payers. Insurance companies, in an effort to stem the tide of increasing costs, are paying closer and closer attention to the kinds of problems that their mental health monies are being applied to. This means that therapists are being asked to report in greater and greater detail just what is going on with clients. Almost twenty five years ago, Goldberg noted that "already third-party payment has had marked effect on the type of treatment offered, created problems of confidentiality and diagnosis, influenced the nature of the transference relationship, and raised complex issues for client resistance" (1977, p. 5). The problem has been growing every year; many clients now face the prospect of intimate details of their lives (drug and alcohol abuse, sexual problems, incest, child abuse) being placed in insurance company records, with little or no guarantee that they will be kept secret. The alternatives: either the therapist perjures herself or the client has no insurance coverage. Again, no one can tell you what to do, what the ethical course of action is, in such situations. You will have to decide for yourself and live with the consequences. What *is* demanded of you is that you learn, to the best of your ability, what will be done with insurance reports, that you inform your client, and that you consider your client's wishes as you make your decisions.

Most breaches of confidentiality do not occur in the drama of an involuntary commitment or the formal submission of an insurance report. They come through carelessness, through a memo left where it can be seen by others, through an off-hand comment, through coffee-break conversation. Brenner relates:

> I remember vividly a particular first meeting that went very well. I later learned that, when this person was leaving the office, she noticed (although she had to tilt her head upside down to do so) a note being typed that had another individual's name on it. Almost a year later, at another setting, the client told me that she never returned for a second visit because she assumed that if I was that "careless" about the identity of one person, I might not treat information about her carefully. [1982, p. 18]

Therapists should make it a rule to be scrupulous in guarding the identity of a client, or the details of that client's work, from anyone who has no compelling need for the information.

One final word about confidentiality: do not promise it to a client unless you are sure you can follow through. Do not tell a client that you will never reveal what is said in a therapy hour; tell him that there may be circumstances under which you would have to break confidentiality and what those circumstances might be. Make sure that members of a therapy group agree to respect confidentiality, but make equally sure that each member understands that such an agreement, while it may be morally binding, has no legal status. Never offer to your client more than you are prepared to deliver; in the great majority of cases, he will respect your honesty, and the therapeutic relationship will be strengthened rather than weakened by your candor.

EXTRA-THERAPEUTIC RELATIONSHIPS

"Deep down in his mind, no patient wants a nonprofessional relationship with his therapist, regardless of the fact that he may express himself to the contrary" (Fromm-Reichmann 1950, p. 46). Clients will often ask for or maneuver to set up contacts with the therapist outside the therapeutic setting. Experts are divided as to the advisability of such contact; some see it as harmless or even beneficial, while others believe that it can interfere seriously with the course of treatment.

There is no question but that multiple relationships with a client do complicate the therapy situation. They are difficult to manage well and can easily get out of hand. It seems sensible, then, to avoid such relationships if possible, unless there is some compelling reason for behaving otherwise. This rule is particularly valid for relative beginners, who may not yet be aware of all the tangles into which multiple roles can lead.

What is true for relationships during therapy is also true immediately following therapy. We have discussed this issue at some length in Chapter 6, so it need only be mentioned briefly here: the therapeutic relationship does not automatically end at official termination; the emotional attitudes of both client and therapist toward each other may linger for months or even years. There is no way that friendship with a former client can fail to be affected by the client-therapist relationship, any more than therapy with a friend as client can be immune from the attitudes and attachments of the friendship.

While the rule of "no extra-therapeutic relationships" can sometimes be broken—and, in small communities, sometimes will be broken in spite of all your efforts to the contrary—romantic relationships between therapist and client, or ex-client, are *never* acceptable. Because the relationship between therapist and client is inherently unequal in terms of power and authority, a sexual relationship between them simply cannot be healthy. No matter how much either therapist or client may want such a relationship, no matter how sincerely either or both may believe that they are somehow different and can make it work, it will not. The therapist, says Storr, "must accept declarations of love with tenderness and understanding, but he must also make it clear...that there is no hope of the patient's desire being fulfilled" (1989, p. 100). As for romantic advances on the part of the therapist, there are no circumstances under which such behavior is acceptable. Not only is it morally reprehensible to use one's therapeutic influence in this way, but it also constitutes legal malpractice.

THERAPIST SELF-CARE

Therapists are people, not machines. It may seem silly for me to emphasize that we need to take care of our physical and emotional needs. After all, anybody knows that. However, therapists, like physicians, tend to be notorious for neglecting to care for themselves. One interesting set of statistics may suffice to underline my point: in the United States, while male physicians commit suicide at the same rate as other males, female physicians do so at four times the rate of other females. And psychiatrists, of either sex, commit suicide at double the rate of other doctors (Simon 1989). While the figures may not be as startling for other mental health practitioners, it is still true that we tend to treat ourselves much worse than we would allow our clients to treat themselves. We neglect our bodies and ride roughshod over our feelings. We can take it; we can be strong. Later, when there is time and we are not so busy, then we will take care of ourselves. How foolish! Cooks and carpenters know enough to keep their working tools well oiled and sharpened; surely we mental health workers should have the sense to do the same.

PHYSICAL WELL-BEING

A good therapist, who intends to continue to be effective in her work, must keep herself in good physical and emotional health, seeing to it that her life provides her with adequate satisfaction, making sure that her personal and social needs are being met outside her therapy office. Obviously, if your physical energies are depleted, you will have less to offer to your client. The task of the therapist is difficult and requires a great deal of energy and concentration. Although most of us recognize the mental/emotional effort needed to do good therapeutic work, it is easy to over-look the physical demands. After all, the therapist just sits and listens, doesn't she? No, she does not. The kind of focused concentration demanded of a therapist creates a physical energy drain as well as a mental one. Colby said it well: "To remain serene in the face of transference aggressions and to treat patients with a gentle benevolence requires that the therapist himself be in good physical and emotional condition. If you have a pain or feel sleepy or 'hung over,' then you should not see patients until your malaise has cleared....Like an athlete, the psychotherapist has to keep himself in an efficient working state" (1951, p. 24). The wise therapist is care-ful to get enough rest, to maintain a healthful diet, to exercise regularly, and to see her doctor and dentist for regular checkups as well as when anything goes wrong.

Taking good physical care of yourself also involves taking reasonable pre-cautions to protect yourself physically. There is nothing noble about exposing yourself to unnecessary danger from a potentially violent client. Clients can and do become violent with therapists, although perhaps not as often as we fear. A 1981 survey of 453 therapists showed that while 60 percent feared being attacked, only 14 percent had actually been assaulted by a client (Bernstein 1981). Fourteen percent, though, is a lot; approximately one in seven of us, according to these data, can expect violence at the hands of a client.

The best defense against violence is preparedness: knowing your own limits, letting your client know that violence is unacceptable, and knowing what you would do to take care of yourself should it occur. Some standard and common-sense precautions include making sure that help is available, if needed, when meeting with a potentially violent client; refusing to give clients your home address or phone number; refusing to allow clients to bring weapons into the session; refusing to see a client who is under the influence of drugs or alcohol. Failing to take such elementary precautions not only is a discount of your own right to safety but also fails to provide the client with adequate protection from his destructive impulses.

EMOTIONAL WELL-BEING

Carl Rogers, whom many hail as the father of modern-day psychotherapy, commented in an interview with Michele Baldwin, "I think it is important to realize that one has a need and a right to preserve and protect oneself. A therapist has a right to give, but not to get worn-out trying to be giving" (1987, p. 46). Sensible advice, but oddly difficult to follow! It is all too easy for therapists to become so caught up in our work that we cannot really leave it, cannot love or play or work fully at anything else. That is sad for us and for our clients. Of course, we should enjoy our work, should take pleasure in doing it well; but it must not be our only or even our primary source of gratification. If the therapist comes to depend on her clients for emotional support and satisfaction, she will soon be taking from them rather than giving to them. The best way to void this state of affairs is to find and experience plenty of emotional closeness in our personal lives, to have interests and hobbies beyond our work as therapists, to care about people and things other than our clients.

Even if a therapist does a good job of balancing her interests and attachments, she will still find herself experiencing a great deal of emotional stress at times. Dealing with client issues, being a frequent spectator to and a participant in emotionally charged interactions, will inevitably bring to the fore whatever unresolved problems the therapist herself has. Therapists do not have to be better or more stable than the average person, but they should certainly be more aware of their own issues. If I am not aware of my psychological games, I will inevitably play them out with my client—with unfortunate consequences for us both. My issues are likely to be stirred up in my interactions with clients; his problems remind me of my own. Rollo May, the great existentialist therapist, has commented on this phenomenon: "To speak frankly, I have never dealt with a counselee in whose difficulty I did not see myself, at least potentially. Every counselor, at least theoretically, will have this same experience" (1934, p. 39).

I know of only one way to deal with this problem, and that is to see to it that my own therapeutic needs are attended to. I believe that all therapists need to have experienced therapy as a client, not only to "know how it feels," but also because we simply cannot deal effectively with a client's problems until we have resolved or at least recognized our own. I also believe that therapists need to return to therapy more than once during their career. It is more than preventive mental health for us; it is a matter of making sure that our tools are sharp, our vision clear. As a therapist, I offer myself to my client as an instrument for change. I am professionally obligated to maintain that self in as clear, uncluttered, and effective a state as possible.

A final word on emotional well-being has to do with burnout. While burnout is probably the last thing a beginning therapist is likely to be worried about, you would be surprised at how quickly and insidiously it can creep up on you, particularly if you are not attending carefully to your own physical and emotional needs. The best protection here is awareness: knowing the early warning signs and being committed to doing something about it should you find yourself in the danger zone. Gambrill provides us with a list of these early warning signs: "sleepiness during sessions; drifting attention; being late for therapy sessions with increasing frequency; annoyance with patients; overzealous relief at the end of the work day; feelings of relief when a client cancels; sardonic or humorous references to patients; psychophysiological responses; increased irritability with staff, family and clients; and disillusionment with the work of psychotherapy" (1990, p. 327). If you are experiencing three or more of these symptoms with any regularity, it is time for a long and hard look at how you are taking care of yourself.

SPECIAL CONCERNS

There are a number of situations that can create particular emotional strain for the therapist, things that arise so frequently that they need specific mention here. One of the foremost is lack of confidence. We fear that we will be mistaken or inadequate, that the client will not find us helpful, that we will say the wrong thing or at least fail to say the right thing. Wachtel warns: "Psychotherapy is no profession for the individual who likes certainty, predictability, or a fairly constant sense that one knows what one is doing. There are few professions in which feeling stupid or stymied is as likely to be a part of one's ordinary professional duty" (1982, p. xiii).

There really is no way that we can avoid making mistakes; even when we have not been mistaken, we will often believe we were. "Thus conscience doth make cowards of us all," as Hamlet said. In our own anxiety and our need to conceal that anxiety from our clients, we close down and cover up, withholding what is often most needed. The therapist's anxiety makes the likelihood of error even greater, as we protect ourselves and, in so doing, pull back from making good therapeutic contact with our clients. The last act in this sad little antitherapeutic drama comes when the client must switch roles and reassure the therapist, thus changing from care-receiver to care-giver, which is most assuredly not why he came for treatment. Again, either personal therapy or collegial consultation is the best way to deal with the problem of therapist anxiety. Talking it out with someone who has herself been there, discovering that you are not alone, and working on your underlying issues will help you to meet your own needs outside of the session with your client.

Another common therapist pitfall is countertransference: experiencing feelings toward the client that are more appropriately directed toward someone else in your past or present life. Countertransference is not always a problem. It becomes a problem only when the therapist is not aware of it or when she begins acting on the basis of it rather than on the here-and-now reality of her interaction with her client. There will always be some countertransference in a therapeutic relationship; the trick is to recognize it when it arises. Corey lists a number of signs that you may be unwittingly involved in a transference reaction:

- You become easily irritated by certain clients.
- You feel intense anger toward a person you hardly know.
- With some clients you continually run overtime.
- You find yourself wanting to lend money to some unfortunate clients.
- You feel like adopting an abused child.
- You quickly take away pain from a grieving client.
- You regularly feel depressed after seeing a particular client.
- You feel excited knowing that a certain client is soon to arrive.
- You tend to become very bored with a certain client.
- You are aware of typically working much harder than your client.
- You get highly emotional and get lost in the client's world.
- You become aware of giving a great deal of advice and wanting to have clients do what you think they should do.
- You are quick not to accept a certain type of client, or you suggest a referral with little data.
- You find yourself lecturing certain kinds of clients. [1990, p. 95]

Attending these danger signals allows the therapist to maintain neutrality, by guarding against the possibility of unaware countertransference reactions to her clients. Knowing what she feels, and why she feels it, is the first and best deterrent of improper behavior.

A third kind of stressful situation occurs when one's client begins to act in a potentially dangerous or damaging way. Even after having taken all the legally required steps, doing everything we can think of to safeguard the client (and/or others), we are still prone to feel anxious and responsible for his behavior. Consultation helps, both emotionally and practically. Consultants are often able, because of their greater objectivity, to come up with options that the primary therapist has overlooked. But, as Schutz points out, "no amount of group collaboration can completely remove the therapist from his lonely position on the firing line when a client threatens suicide or some other form of destructive behavior. He simply has to learn to 'sweat it out,' recognizing that he may be impotent to effect any beneficial change" (1982, p. 47). And if your client does decompensate, become violent, commit suicide, you are almost certain to second-guess yourself. Therapists whose clients commit suicide are haunted by feelings of guilt; they wonder what they should have done differently, and often seriously question their adequacy as professionals. If one of your clients gets himself into serious trouble, you are likely to be in emotional trouble yourself—don't try to deal with it by yourself. Talk with colleagues, or find a trustworthy therapist to help you work it through.

If at all possible, do not allow yourself to be treating more than two suicidal or violent or otherwise unusually needy clients at any given time. Two is enough; a therapist can handle only a finite amount of that kind of ongoing demand and drain.

In one sense, the therapist is in an emotional no-win situation. On the one hand, she must attempt to understand the client's world and experience from that client's point of view; she must enter into that subjective world in order to help the client to change it. On the other hand, she must maintain enough emotional detachment to keep herself healthy and in balance. Taking on the client's problems, becoming infected by his feelings and issues, is another pitfall for the unwary therapist. Too much empathy becomes confluence, in which the therapist is no longer able to differentiate between her own feelings and those of the client. Again, there is no substitute for working with a professional colleague, becoming a client yourself, and sorting out your feelings. The alternative is ineffectiveness and therapeutic error, as well as needless personal discomfort.

Of course, no amount of personal work can make you immune to error. You will make mistakes, and sometimes your clients will suffer for them. Mistakes come with the territory. They cannot be avoided, but they can be recognized. The real mistake lies not in committing an error but in failing to learn from it. Every mistake can be the signal for a new step toward therapeutic competence, if it is recognized, analyzed, and used for growth. Do not be complacent about your mistakes. They are not good, and nobody likes to make them. However, do not magnify them out of proportion, either. Like rocks in a stream, they can be used to trip and fall over or as a bridge to a new and better place.

GROWTH AND DEVELOPMENT

Most of what I shall say in this last section is a repeat and reemphasis of what I have said earlier. It revolves about a single theme: your competence as a therapist cannot exceed your competence as a human being. If you are an enthusiastic, growing, open person, you may be an enthusiastic, growing, open therapist. If you lose your personal awareness, your zest for life, your curiosity, your sense of humor, you will lose those qualities as a therapist as well.

I have already made my position clear regarding the need for therapists to tend to their own personal therapeutic needs. I shall content myself here with one last comment, this one from Aponte and Winter: "Engaging in therapeutic work with clients is a social context which, for a therapist, jostles his own personal issues in ways that few other encounters do. Repeatedly, such a process moves a therapist to seek to resolve his own life issues, especially as his dilemmas are inevitably brought to the foreground by the people he is seeing" (1987, p. 94). Their logic speaks for itself.

Beyond personal therapy, the therapist stays alive and open through ongoing consultation, supervision, and education. We can never know everything; we will never know enough. There is always something around the corner—some new insight, some new way of listening to a client, some new theoretical perspective that will help us work more effectively. Unless we are flexible and courageous enough to try new things—things we didn't learn in our formal training—our profession will never change or develop. And we will never grow as therapists. We have to be willing to try things that will seem strange, forced, even downright wrong, because new things seldom feel right the first time we do them. Like most other professionals, therapists believe that ongoing education is an essential commitment. It is not only necessary but fun! When it stops being fun, when you lose your capacity to be excited and intrigued by new ideas, then you are ready for a vacation from your clients; and they are in need of a vacation from you.

Above all, then, the professional therapist must be committed to growth: to personal and emotional growth, to professional growth, to constantly learning and experiencing and becoming. The only static thing about our profession is that we must never become static; the one thing we can expect is the unexpected. If you want a predictable, settle-down-and-be-comfortable job, do not become a therapist! At best, you will be run-of-the-mill and bored, and at worst you will make yourself and your clients miserable. Says Singer:

> The question then is never how many or how much of life's problems the therapist has solved already but much more how much he continuously strives toward increased understanding and subtle solutions of issues in his life, how much he cherishes his own struggle for freedom and active involvement; or conversely, how much he has given up this effort, how defeated and resigned he is, how much he despairs about his own life and rejects the value of growth. [1965, p. 118]

The choice is clear: grow or give up, learn or decay, expand or stagnate. No other profession that I know of offers quite the same challenge. We know little that is certain, and we risk much that is unknown. We share the highest peaks and the lowest ebbs of our fellow humans' existences. We climb, stumble, fall, and climb again. We get tired and have to rest; but we cannot stay away for long. The excitement of discovery, of exploring the ever-intricate patterns of human experience, calls us back. To you who would join this band or would renew your membership—welcome! May we support each other on our journeying, sharing the excitement and bearing the burden together.

REFERENCES

Ables, B. S. *Therapy for Couples.* San Francisco: Jossey-Bass, 1977

Ackerman, E. H. *Short History of Psychiatry.* New York: Hafner, 1968

Amantea, C. *The Lourdes of Arizona.* San Diego: Mho & Mho Works, 1989

American Psychiatric Association. *Diagnostic and Statistical Manual of Mental Disorders* (3rd ed., rev.). Washington, D. C.: American Psychiatric Association, 1987

Aponte, H. J. & Winter, J. E. "The Person and Practice of the Therapist: Treatment and Training." In M. Baldwin & V. Satir (eds.) *The Use of Self in Therapy.* New York: Haworth Press, 1987, pp. 85–96

Ard, B. N. "Introduction." In B. Ard (ed.), *Counseling and Psychotherapy: Classics on Theories and Issues.* Palo Alto: Science & Behavior Books, 1975

Austin, K., Moline, M. & Williams, G. *Confronting Malpractice.* Newbury Park, Calif.: Sage Publications, 1990

Aveline, M. "The Process of Being Known and the Initiation of Change." In W. Dryden (ed.), *Key Cases in Psychotherapy.* New York: New York University Press, 1987, pp. 21–47

Baldwin, D. C. Jr. "Some Philosophical and Psychological Contributions to the Use of Self in Therapy." In M. Baldwin and V. Satir (eds.), *The Use of Self in Therapy.* New York: Haworth Press, 1987, pp. 27–36

Baldwin, M. & Rogers, C. "Interview with Carl Rogers on the Use of the Self in Therapy." In M. Baldwin and V. Satir (eds.), *The Use of Self in Therapy.* New York: Haworth Press, 1987, pp. 45–52

Balsam, A. & Balsam, R. *Becoming a Psychotherapist.* Boston: Little, Brown, 1974

Basch, M. F. *Understanding Psychotherapy.* New York: Basic Books, 1988

Beavers, W. R. & Hampson, R. *Successful Families.* New York: W. W. Norton, 1990

Beck, A. *Love Is Never Enough.* New York: Harper & Row, 1988

Beitman, B. D. *The Structure of Individual Psychotherapy.* New York: Guilford Press, 1987

Bergin, A. E. & Lambert, M. J. "The Evaluation of Therapeutic Outcomes." In A. E. Bergin & S. L. Garfield (eds.), *Handbook of Psychotherapy and Behavior Change* (2nd ed.). New York: John Wiley, 1978

Berman, A. *Suicide Prevention.* New York: Springer, 1990

Berne, E. *Games People Play*. New York: Oxford University Press, 1964

Bernstein, H. A. "Survey of Threats and Assaults Directed towards Psychotherapists." *American Journal of Psychotherapy*, vol. 35 (1981), pp. 542–549

Boldt, M. "Defining Suicide." In R. Diekstra, R. Maris, S. Platt, A. Schmidtke, & G. Sonneck eds.), *Suicide and its Prevention*. New York: Basic Books, 1989, pp. 5–13

Borriello, J. "The Group as a Whole." In I. Kutash & A. Wolf (eds.), *The Group Psychotherapist's Handbook*. New York: Columbia University Press, 1990, pp 78–96

Bowen, M. *Family Therapy in Clinical Practice*. New York: Jason Aronsen, 1978

Brammer, L. & Shostrun, E. *Therapeutic Psychology*. Englewood Cliffs, N.J.: Prentice-Hall, 1968

Brenner, D. *The Effective Psychotherapist*. New York: Pergamon Press, 1982

Bugental, J. F. T. *The Art of the Psychotherapist*. New York: Norton, 1987

Carkhuff, R. R. & Berenson, B. G. *Beyond Counseling and Therapy* (2nd ed.). New York: Holt, Rinehart & Winston, 1977

Carpenter, J. & Treacher, A. *Problems and Solutions in Marital and Family Therapy*. Oxford, England: Basil Blackwell, 1989

Chessick, R. D. *How Psychotherapy Heals*. New York: Science House, 1969

Colby, K. *A Primer for Psychotherapists*. New York: Roland Press, 1951

Combs, A. W. *A Theory of Therapy*. Newbury Park, Calif.: Sage, 1989

Confer, W. N. *Intuitive Psychotherapy*. New York: Human Sciences Press, Inc., 1987

Corey, G. *Theory and Practice of Group Counseling* (3rd ed.). Belmont, Calif.: Brooks/Cole, 1990

Cornier, L. S. & Hackney, H. *The Professional Counselor*. Englewood Cliffs, N.J.: Prentice-Hall, 1987

Corsini, R. "Adlerian Groups." In S. Long (ed.), *Six Group Therapies*. New York: Plenum Press, 1988, pp. 1–47

Crown, S. "Contraindications for Intensive, Dynamically-Oriented, Insight Psychotherapy: A Sequential Approach." In F. Flach (ed.), *Psychotherapy*. New York: W. W. Norton & Company, 1989, pp. 148–169

Dallos, R. "Ethics and Family Therapy." In S. Fairbairn & G. Fairbairn (eds.), *Psychology, Ethics and Change*. London: Routledge & Kegan Paul, 1987, pp. 136–160

Dixon, D. N. & Glover, J. A. *Counseling*. New York: John Wiley, 1984

Doyle, B. "Crisis Management of the Suicidal Patient." In S. Blumenthal & D. Kupfer (eds.), *Suicide Over the Life Cycle*. New York: American Psychiatric Press, 1990, pp. 381–423

Dryden, W. "The Therapeutic Alliance as an Integrating Framework." In W. Dryden (ed.), *Key Issues for Counselling in Action*. London: Sage Publications, 1989, pp. 1–15

Dunst, C. , Trivette, C. , & Deal, A. *Enabling and Empowering Families*. Cambridge, Mass. : Brookline Books, 1988

Egan, G. *The Skilled Helper*. Monterey, Calif.: Brooks/Cole, 1975

Ewing, C. P. *Crisis Intervention as Psychotherapy*. New York: Oxford University Press, 1978

Eysenck, H. J. "The Effects of Psychotherapy: An Evaluation." *Journal of Consulting Psychology*, vol. 16 (1952), pp. 319–324

Fisher, L., Anderson, A., & Jones, J. "Types of Paradoxical Intervention and Indications/Contraindications for Use in Clinical Practice." *Family Process*, (1981), p. 33

Flach, R. *Psychotherapy*. New York: W. W. Norton, 1989

Fong, M. L. & Gresbach, B. C. "Trust as an Underlying Dynamic in the Counseling Process." In W. Dryden (ed.), *Key Issues for Counselling in Action.* London: Sage Publications, 1989, pp. 26–36

Foxman, J. *A Practical Guide to Emergency and Protective Crisis Intervention.* New York: Charles C. Thomas, 1990

France, A. *Consuming Psychotherapy.* London: Free Association Books, 1988

Frank, J., Hoehn-Sark, R., Imber, S., Liberman, B., & Stone, A. *Effective Ingredients of Successful Psychotherapy.* New York: Brunner/Mazel, 1978

Freeman, D. R. *Marital Crisis and Short-Term Counseling.* New York: The Free Press, 1982

Fromm-Reichmann, F. *Principles of Intensive Psychotherapy.* Chicago: University of Chicago Press, 1950

Furrow, B. R. *Malpractice in Psychotherapy.* Lexington, Mass. : Lexington Books, 1980

Gambrill, E. *Critical Thinking in Clinical Practice.* New York: Jossey-Bass, 1990

Garfield, S. L. "Psychotherapy: A 40-Year Appraisal." *American Psychologist,* vol. 36 (1981), pp. 174–183

Gelcer, E., McCabe, A., & Smith-Resnick, C. *Milan Family Therapy: Variant and Invariant Methods.* New York: Jason Aronson, 1990

Gibson, R. L. & Mitchell, M. H. *Introduction to Counseling and Guidance.* New York: Macmillan, 1986

Golan, N. *Treatment in Crisis Situations.* New York: The Free Press, 1978

Goldberg, C. *Therapeutic Partnership.* New York: Springer Publishing Company, 1977

Greenberg, L. S. & Safran, J. D. "Emotional-Change Processes in Psychotherapy." In R. Plutchik & J. Kellerman (eds.), *Emotion Theory, Research, and Experience,* vol. 5. San Diego: Academic Press, Inc., 1990, pp. 59–84

Groome, E. "Goal Setting and Marital Therapy." In G. Weeks (ed.), *Treating Couples.* New York: Brunner/Mazel, 1989, pp. 22–37

Grove, D. *Metaphors to Heal By.* Edwardsvill, Ill.: David Grove Seminars, 1989

Hatton, C. L. & Valente, S. M. *Suicide: Assessment and Intervention* (4th ed.). Englewood Cliffs, N.J.: Prentice Hall, 1984, pp. 57–58

Haley, J. & Hoffman, L. *Techniques of Family Therapy.* New York: Basic books, 1967

Havens, L. *Making Contact.* Cambridge, Mass.: Harvard University Press, 1986

Hendren, R. "Assessment and Interviewing Strategies for Suicidal Patients Over the Life Cycle." In S. Blumenthal & D. Kupfer (eds.), *Suicide Over the Life Cycle.* New York: American Psychiatric Press, 1990, pp. 235–252

Hof, L. & Treat, S. "Marital Assessment." In G. Weeks (ed.), *Treating Couples.* New York: Brunner/Mazel, 1989, pp. 3–21

Hollander-Goldfein, B. "Basic Principles: Process Elements of the Intersystem Approach." In G. Weeks (ed.), *Treating Couples.* New York: Brunner/Mazel, 1989, pp. 85–118

Holmes, T. H. & Rahe, R. H. "The Social Readjustment Rating Scale." *Journal of Psychosomatic Research,* vol. 11 (1967), pp. 213–218

Howard, G. S., Nance, D. W., & Myers, P. *Adaptive Counseling and Therapy.* San Francisco: Jossey-Bass, 1987

Hutchins, D. E. & Cole, C. G. *Helping Relationships and Strategies.* Belmont, Calif.: Brooks/Cole, 1986

Jackson, D. "The Study of the Family." *Family Process,* vol. 4 (1965), pp. 1–20

James, M. *Techniques in Transactional Analysis.* Reading, Mass. : Addison-Wesley, 1977

Kantor, M. *Problems and Solutions.* New York: Praeger, 1990

Kenny,V. & Browne, I. "How Does Psychotherapy Work? Part II: A Systems Approach to Psychotherapy Practice." In F. Flach (ed.), *Psychotherapy*. New York: W. W. Norton & Company, 1989, pp. 16–29

Keutzer, C. "Synchronicity Awareness in Psychotherapy." In F. Flach (ed.), *Psychotherapy*. New York: W. W. Norton & Company, 1989, pp. 159–169

Kopp, S. *Back To One*. Palo Alto: Science & Behavior Books, 1977

Kramer, P. D. *Moments of Engagement*. New York: W. W. Norton & Company, 1989

Kupers, T. A. *Ending Therapy*. New York: New York University Press, 1988

L'Abate, L. "Beyond Paradox: Issues of Control." *American Journal of Family Therapy*, vol. 14 (1984), pp. 12–20

Luborsky, L., Singer, B., & Luborsky, L. "Comparative Studies of Psychotherapy." *Archives of General Psychiatry*, vol. 32 (1975)

Madanes, C. *Behind the One-Way Mirror*. San Francisco: Jossey-Bass, 1984

Mahoney, M. *Human Change Processes*. New York: Basic Books, 1991

May, R. *The Art of Counseling*. Nashville: Cokesbury Press, 1934

McKechnie, R. "The Moral Context of Therapy." In S. Fairbairn & G. Fairbairn (eds.), *Psychology, Ethics and Change*. London: Routledge & Kegan Paul, 1987, pp. 161–172

McKenzie, K. R. "The Changing Role of Emotion in Group Psychotherapy." In R. Plutchik & J. Kellerman (eds.), *Emotion Theory, Research, and Experience*, vol. 5. San Diego: Academic Press, Inc., 1990, pp. 147–173

Mead, M. *Male and Female: A Study of the Sexes in a Changing World*. New York: William Morrow, 1949

Metzloff, J. & Kornreich, M. *Research in Psychotherapy*. New York: Atherton Press, 1970

Minuchin, S. *Families and Family Therapy*. Cambridge, Mass.: Harvard University Press, 1974

Morrison, J. K. "A Psychotherapist at the Crossroads: A Personal and Professional Turning Point." In W. Dryden (ed.), *Key Cases in Psychotherapy*. New York: New York University Press, 1987, pp. 5–20

Ohlsen, M., Horne, A., & Lawe, C. *Group Counseling* (3rd ed.). New York: Holt, Rinehart & Winston, 1988

Ottens, A. & Fisher-McCanne, L. "Crisis Intervention at the College Counseling Center." In A. R. Roberts(ed.), *Crisis Intervention Handbook*. Belmont, Calif.: Wadsworth, 1990, pp. 78–103

Parry, G. *Coping with Crisis: Problems in Practice Series*. New York: Routledge, 1990

Patterson, W. M. et al. "Evaluation of Suicidal Patients: the SAD PERSONS Scale." *Psychosomatics*, vol. 24 (1983), pp. 343–349

Peterson, L. & Bongar, B. "The Suicidal Patient." In A. Lazare (ed.), *Outpatient Psychiatry* (2nd ed.). New York: Williams & Wilkins, 1989, pp. 569–584

Petretic-Jackson, P. & Jackson, T. "Assessment and Crisis Intervention with Rape and Incest Victims." In A. R. Roberts (ed.), *Crisis Intervention Handbook*. Belmont, Calif.: Wadsworth, 1990, pp. 124–152

Pittman, F. S. *Turning Points*. New York: Norton, 1987

Plutchik, R. "Emotions and Psychotherapy: A Psychoevolutionary Perspective." In R. Plutchik & J. Kellerman (eds.), *Emotion Theory, Research, and Experience*, vol. 5. San Diego: Academic Press, Inc., 1990, pp. 3–38

Rice, D. "Marital Therapy and the Divorcing Family." In M. Textor (ed.), *Divorce and Divorce Therapy Handbook*. New York: Jason Aronson, 1989, pp. 151–195

Rigby, D. N. & Sophie, J. "Ethical Issues and Client Sexual Preference." In H. Lerman & N. Porter (eds.), *Feminist Ethics in Psychotherapy*. New York: Springer, 1990, pp. 165–175

Roberts, A. R. "An Overview of Crisis Theory and Crisis Intervention." In A. Roberts (ed.), *Crisis Intervention Handbook*. Belmont, Calif.: Wadsworth, 1990, pp. 3–16.

Rosenbaum, D. P. & Beebe, J. E. *Psychiatric Treatment: Crisis, Clinic, Consultation*. New York: McGraw-Hill, 1975

Rowan, J. *The Reality Game*. London: Routledge & Kegan Paul, 1983

Rowan, J. "Siding with the Client." In W. Dryden (ed.), *Key Cases in Psychotherapy*. New York: New York University Press, 1987, pp. 103–126

Roy, A. "Suicide." In H. Kaplan & B. Sadock (eds.), *Comprehensive Textbook of Psychiatry*, vol. 5. New York: Williams & Wilkins, 1989, pp. 1414–1427

Ryder, R. G. *The Realistic Therapist*. Newbury Park, Calif.: Sage Publications, 1987

Sager, C. *Marriage Contracts and Couple Therapy*. New York: Brunner/Mazel, 1976

Salzman, L. "Terminating Psychotherapy." In F. Flach (ed.), *Psychotherapy*. New York: W. W. Norton & Company, 1989, pp. 223–230

Satir, V. "The Therapist Story." In M. Baldwin & V. Satir, *The Use of Self in Therapy*. New York: Haworth Press, 1987, pp. 17–26

Schneidman, E. "Approaches and Commonalities of Suicide." In R. Diekstra, R. Maris, S. Platt, A. Schmidtke, & G. Sonneck (eds.), *Suicide and Its Prevention*. New York: Basic Books, 1989, pp. 14–36

Schofield, W. *Pragmatics of Psychotherapy*. New Brunswick: Transaction Books, 1988

Schutz, B. *Legal Liability in Psychotherapy*. San Francisco: Jossey-Bass, 1982

Seligman, L. *Diagnosis and Treatment Planning in Counseling*. New York: Human Sciences Press, 1986

Selvini-Palazzoli, M., Boscolo, L., Cecchin, G., & Prata, G. *Paradox and Counterparadox*. New York: Jason Aronson, 1978

Shack, J. *Couples Counseling*. New York: Continuum, 1989

Shea, S. C. *Psychiatric Interviewing*. Philadelphia: W. B. Saunders Company, 1988

Shulman, N. "Crisis Intervention in a High School." In A. R. Roberts (ed.), *Crisis Intervention Handbook*. Belmont, Calif.: Wadsworth, 1990, pp. 63–77

Simon, W. "Suicide among Physicians." In R. Diekstra, R. Maris, S. Platt, A. Schmidtke, & G. Sonneck (eds.), *Suicide and its Prevention*. New York: Basic Books, 1989, pp. 187–198

Singer, E. *Key Concepts in Psychotherapy*. New York: Random House, 1965

Slaby, E. "Other Psychiatric Emergencies." In H. Kaplan & B. Sadock (eds.), *Comprehensive Textbook of Psychiatry*, vol. 5. New York: Williams & Wilkins, 1989, pp. 1427–1441

Smail, D. "Psychotherapy and 'Change': Some Ethical Considerations." In S. Fairbairn & G. Fairbairn (eds.), *Psychology, Ethics and Change*. London: Routledge & Kegan Paul, 1987, pp. 31–43

Smith, M. L. & Glass, G. V. "Meta-Analysis of Psychotherapy Outcome Studies." *American Psychologist*, vol. 32 (1977), pp. 752–760

Steinzor, B. *The Healing Partnership*. New York: Harper & Row, 1967

Stewart, N., Winborn, B., Johnson, R., Burks, H., & Engelkes, J. *Systemic Counseling*. Englewood Cliffs, N. J.: Prentice-Hall, 1978

Storr, A. "Transference." In F. Flach (ed.), *Psychotherapy*. New York: W. W. Norton & Company, 1989, pp. 93–103

Stuart, R. *Helping Couples Change.* New York: Guilford Press, 1980

Teyber, E. *Interpersonal Process in Psychotherapy.* Chicago: Dorsey Press, 1988

Thompson, A. *Guide to Ethical Practice in Psychotherapy.* New York: John Wiley & Sons, 1990

Thorne, B. "Beyond the Core Conditions." In W. Dryden (ed.), *Key Cases in Psychotherapy.* New York: New York University Press, 1987, pp. 48–77

Tracey, T. J. "The Stages of Influence in Counseling." In W. Dryden (ed.), *Key Issues for Counselling in Action.* London: Sage Publications, 1989, pp. 63–72

Turner, N. W. & Strine, S. "Separation and Divorce: Clinical Implications for Parents and Children." In D. Goldberg (ed.), *Contemporary Marriage.* Homewood, Ill. : Dorsey Press, 1985, pp. 484–500

Wachtel, P. *Resistance.* New York: Plenum Press, 1982

Ward, D. E. "Termination of Individual Counseling." In W. Dryden (ed.), *Key Issues for Counselling in Action.* London: Sage Publications, 1989, pp. 97–109

Watkins, C. E. "Transference Phenomena in the Counseling Situation." In W. Dryden (ed.), *Key Issues for Counselling in Action.* London: Sage Publications, 1989, pp. 73–84

Watts, F. "Listening Processes in Psychotherapy." In F. Flach (ed.), *Psychotherapy.* New York: W. W. Norton & Company, 1989, pp. 114–124

Watzlawick, P. *The Language of Change.* New York: Basic Books, 1978

Weeks, G. R. & L'Abate, L. *Paradoxical Psychotherapy.* New York: Brunner/Mazel, 1982

Wessler, R. L. & Hankin-Wessler, S. "Emotion and Rules of Living." In R. Plutchik & J. Kellerman (eds.), *Emotion Theory, Research, and Experience*, vol. 5. San Diego: Academic Press, Inc., 1990, pp. 231–252

Westfall, A. "Extramarital Sex: The Treatment of the Couple." In G. Weeks (ed.), *Treating Couples.* New York: Brunner/Mazel, 1989, pp. 163–190

Wexler, D. *Mental Health Law.* New York: Plenum Press, 1981

Whitaker, L. "Suicide and Other Crises." In P. Grayson & K. Cauley (eds.), *College Psychotherapy.* New York: Guilford, 1989, pp. 48–70

Wile, D. "An Even More Offensive Theory." In W. Dryden (ed.), *Key Cases in Psychotherapy.* New York: New York University Press, 1987, pp. 78–102

Williams, J. M. & Weeks, G. R. "Use of Paradoxical Techniques in a School Setting." *American Journal of Family Therapy*, vol. 12 (1984), pp. 47–51

Wiseman, J. *Mediation Therapy.* Lexington, Mass.: Lexington Books, 1990

Wolberg, L. R. *The Technique of Psychotherapy*(4th ed., part 1). Orlando, Fla.: Grune & Stratton, 1988

Yalom, I. *Existential Psychotherapy.* New York: Basic Books, 1980

Yalom, I. *The Theory and Practice of Group Psychotherapy.* New York: Basic Books, 1970, 1975, 1985

INDEX